Demon

or

Doll

Demon or Doll

Images of the Child in Contemporary Writing and Culture

Ellen Pifer

University Press of Virginia

Charlottesville and London

The University Press of Virginia
© 2000 by the Rector and Visitors of the University of Virginia
All rights reserved
Printed in the United States of America

First published in 2000

⊗The paper used in this publication meets the minimum requirements of the
American National Standard for Information Sciences—Permanence of Paper for
Printed Library Materials, ANSI Z39.48-1984.

Library of Congress Cataloging-in-Publication Data

Pifer, Ellen.
    Demon or doll : images of the child in contemporary writing and culture / Ellen Pifer.
       p. cm.
    Includes bibliographical references (p.) and index.
    ISBN 0-8139-1963-0 (cloth : alk. paper) — ISBN 0-8139-1964-9 (paper : alk. paper)
    1. American fiction—20th century—History and criticism. 2. Children in literature.
   3. English fiction—20th century—History and criticism. I. Title

PS374.C45 P54 2000
823'.9109352054—dc21   99-462125

For *Drury, and for Rebecca,*
Glenn, and Gabriel

Contents

Acknowledgments

I am grateful to the following agencies and institutions for their generous support of this project: the Delaware Arts Council, for an Individual Artists Fellowship that allowed me to begin research; the National Endowment for the Humanities, for a Summer Stipend for Research that afforded me time to continue; and the University of Delaware, for a Center for Advanced Studies Fellowship that enabled me to complete the bulk of a first draft. Under the auspices of a Fulbright Award to France, and with the additional support of travel grants awarded by the University of Delaware, I was able to present the results of my research at various stages of its development to audiences at home and abroad.

Professors Robert Alter and Carl Dawson tirelessly wrote in support of this project whenever I asked, and I am grateful to them both for their patience and generosity. Thanks are also due to a number of colleagues whose kind invitations to lecture, contribute essays, and present papers on topics relevant to this project gave me a marvelous opportunity to test out my ideas on a wide variety of audiences. They include Professors Vladimir E. Alexandrov, Yale University; Géraldine Chouard, University of Paris IX; Julian W. Connolly, University of Virginia; Maurice Couturier, University of Nice-Sophia Antipolis; Susan Goodman, University of Delaware; Christine Raguet-Bouvart, University of Bordeaux III; Daniel Royot, University of Paris III; Pekka Tammi, University of Tampere, Finland; and Hubert Teyssandier, University of Paris III (Sorbonne Nouvelle).

My friends and colleagues in the International Vladimir Nabokov Society were a wonderfully patient and attentive audience for my early forays on the subject of Nabokov's literary children. The initial tryout, as I recall, took place during the memorable First International Symposium on Vladimir Nabokov, held in Moscow and Saint Petersburg. As the project took shape, I presented new and exploratory versions at numerous conferences and meetings, from the Modern Language Association and the American Literature Association in the United States to several delightful colloquiums in the south of France. Numerous other colleagues, students, and friends at the University of Delaware and elsewhere have kindly alerted me to materials related to this study; I thank them all. Special mention goes to James Kincaid, who generously allowed me—a mere stranger—to read his fascinating study *Erotic Innocence* while it was still in page proofs. For endurance beyond the call of duty, Drury Pifer once again has my heartfelt gratitude. As always, his support was unflagging, his criticism true.

Demon *or Doll* contains a generous sampling, in portions great and small, of essays and articles I composed while this project was taking shape. I am grateful to those who kindly granted me permission to reprint, often in distinctly altered form, parts of my original publications. Chapter 4 incorporates material from the following works: "Her Monster, His Nymphet: Nabokov and Mary Shelley," in *Nabokov and His Fiction: New Perspectives,* ed. Julian W. Connolly (Cambridge: Cambridge Univ. Press, 1999), 158–76; *"Lolita,"* in *The Garland Companion to Vladimir Nabokov,* ed. Vladimir E. Alexandrov (New York: Garland, 1995), 305–21; "*Lolita* and Her Kin," *Q/W/E/R/T/Y* 5 (Oct. 1995): 349–58; "Innocence and Experience Replayed: From *Speak, Memory* to *Ada,*" *Cycnos* 10, no. 1 (1993): 19–25. Chapters 4 and 5 draw on major portions of my article "Birds of a Feather: Nabokov's *Lolita* and Kosinski's *Boy,*" *Cycnos* 12 no. 2 (1995): 165–71. Chapter 7 borrows elements of two previous essays: "*The Book of Laughter and Forgetting:* Kundera's Narration against Narration," *Journal of Narrative Technique* 22, no. 2 (spring 1992): 84–96; and "*The Fifth Child:* Lessing's Subversion of Pastoral," in *The Celebration of the Fantastic,* ed. Donald E. Morse et al. (Westport, Conn.: Greenwood Press, 1992), 121–32. Chapter 9 incorporates a revised version of my essay "The River and Its Current: Literary and Collective Memory in Toni Morrison's *Beloved,*" which originally appeared in *Sounding the Depths: Water as Metaphor in North American Literature,* ed. Gayle Wurst and Christine Raguet-Bouvart (Liège, Belgium: L3, Liège Language and Literature, 1998), 45–59.

Demon
or
Doll

Introduction

"The way in which a society cares, or does not care, for its young," a contemporary social scientist observes, "is indicative of its own vitality and social fabric." A culture's literary treatment of the child, I would add, informs its literal conduct. In this study I investigate the ways in which past and present formulations of childhood both shape and are reflected in figures of the child in recent fiction. Seeking insight about rather than answers to the many questions surrounding the image and idea of childhood in contemporary writing and culture, I examine some of the most provocative novels of the latter half of the twentieth century. "A culture, while it is being lived," Raymond Williams comments in *Culture and Society,* "is always in part unknown, unrealized."[1] Where, if not in the novel, do we find a medium for exploring our cultural terra incognita? Or, to put it another way, where else do we find a language daring, supple, and precise enough to plumb the formidable complexities and contradictions of late-twentieth-century experience?

As I point out in chapter 1, the image of childhood is a cultural construction that changes over time and within societies. For novelists this image has undergone radical transformation since the nineteenth century, when Charles Dickens and his contemporaries translated the Romantic idyll of natural innocence into touching versions of "poor children" set adrift in a harsh and inhumane world. At the end of that century the fiction of Henry James marked a crucial turning point in the development of both the novel and the image of childhood. In recognition of James's lasting influence, and its interesting parallels with Sigmund Freud's legacy, I launch my examination by considering two pivotal turn-of-the-century fictions by James, *What Maisie Knew* and *The Turn of the Screw*. The ambiguous light that these works shed on the nature of childhood innocence establishes the basis for subsequent developments in the image of childhood in contemporary fiction.

In each succeeding chapter I discuss a postwar novel or cluster of related novels from the vantage of the child's created image. In each case, albeit in different ways and to dramatically different effect, the figure of the child serves as a nexus between details of narrative structure and the wide-ranging cultural issues that each text calls into question. The focal role of the child in these novels undermines Reinhard Kuhn's contention, in a 1982 study subtitled *The Child in Western Literature,* that children have virtually disappeared from recent fiction. "With the modern novel," Kuhn asserts, "a door has indeed been closed on children, and the *voci puerili* seem, for the time being at least, to have been silenced."[2] Perhaps expecting to find childhood rendered in familiar form, Kuhn may be confusing authorial silencing with the dramatic changes that twentieth-century writers have rung on this traditional theme.

The "child's relation to the family," as Lionel Trilling says in *Sincerity and Authenticity,* has always been the novel's province. "Traditionally the family has been a narrative institution: it was the past and it had a tale to tell of how things began, including the child himself." The relatively "low status of narration" in an increasingly technological culture caught up in the flux of daily events and largely indifferent to "narrative history" may even be connected, Trilling speculates, with the breakdown of family life and "revisions in the child's relation to [it]."[3] By the same token, I would suggest, the breakdown of family life and the child's relation to it, which intensified during the twentieth century, has given rise to new and often devastating images of childhood in contemporary fiction.

Evincing the theme of social and familial breakdown, many of the novels I discuss—including works by William Golding, Jerzy Kosinski, Doris Lessing, Milan Kundera, Toni Morrison, and Salman Rushdie— bring readers face-to-face with shattered, even grotesque images of the child. At the same time, however, major works by other authors—from Vladimir Nabokov to Ian McEwan and Don DeLillo—demonstrate the amazing resilience of the Wordsworthian child in diverse quarters of contemporary writing. As I will demonstrate, the latter three writers register a persistent faith in childhood innocence—even though their fiction signals a radical departure from the style, structure, and epistemology of traditional novels. Readers may be surprised, for example, at the degree to which such celebrated works as Dickens's *Bleak House* and Mary Shelley's *Frankenstein* illuminate Nabokov's homage to childhood in *Lolita*—a novel whose infamous subject, devious narrator, and self-reflexive structure tend to obscure its profound debt to the Romantic idyll of natural innocence. On the other hand, Lessing's modern-day fable of monsterhood, *The Fifth Child,* recalls *Frankenstein* only to subvert its central themes. Through the birth of the novel's eponymous, and monstrous, fifth child, nature takes revenge on the protagonists' romantic faith in nature.

Whether the image of childhood in recent fiction appears intact or in pieces, wholesome or horrifying, its many facets constitute a kind of mirror in which we seek reflections of our naked, or original, selves: what we once presumably were but now can only faintly recall or reconstruct. Even when the notion of a primal self is regarded as illusory—betraying a "nostalgia for origins . . . and natural innocence," as Jacques Derrida puts it—a novelist's refracted image of childhood can formulate, by giving form to, doubt and disbelief.[4] The boy who aimlessly wanders through the landscape of Kosinski's *The Painted Bird,* for example, never finds his way back to that primal state of nature happily embraced by his literary precursor Huckleberry Finn as he drifts, stretched naked on a raft, down the Mississippi. For Kosinski's boy, unlike Mark Twain's, such origins remain illusory.

In a radically different key, Morrison's *Beloved* also provides a variation on Twain's celebrated idyll of childhood. Here the fractured and fantastic child dramatically embodies the psychic and physical dismemberment of a people stripped not only of family and community but of their deepest memories and feelings. Morrison's Czech contemporary Kundera, on the other hand, constructs the child's image to suggest the forces of oblivion overtaking mass society and a progressively infantile culture. In *The Book of Laughter and Forgetting* the once potent future signaled by the child's hopeful image looms as a terrifying void: an oblivion that threatens to turn all citizens into slaves—powerless, inarticulate, disfranchised objects of history. The obliteration of self and memory is also a theme in Rushdie's *Midnight's Children,* where the crushing forces of history both dwarf and threaten to destroy the child. That these three internationally renowned writers—Morrison, Kundera, and Rushdie—construct images of childhood radically cut off from the myth of original innocence is hardly coincidental. Whether they confront the history of African Americans sold into slavery, the Czech people held in thrall under Soviet communist rule, or the colonization of the Indian subcontinent by the occupying forces of the British empire, these novelists construct images of childhood that reflect the experience of a subjugated people or nation. Each of their literary children, in other words, proves "handcuffed to history" at birth (*Midnight's Children* 3).

Registering a bewildering array of attitudes and images of childhood, images that often contradict and even clash with one another, the novels I discuss expose the deep-seated ambivalence of contemporary culture toward its young. These accomplished fictions, however disturbing, also provide one of art's oldest consolations: the power to render insoluble dilemmas with such clarity, force, and eloquence that the most bitter ironies, the most irreconcilable conflicts are made wonderful to behold. Clarity and eloquence do not, of course, come free for the writer or the reader. Critics, most particularly, must probe the difficulties, question the ambiguities, articulate the doubts that attend any serious attempt to interpret a literary text. A novel's cultural resonances derive, at least in part, from the fact that literary characters—in this case, literary children—are cultural constructions: images organized and rendered sensible by humanly created language, ideas, and assumptions. Fictional characters are, in other words, images of human beings implicitly or explicitly existing as ideas or inventions. They are the product not only of a writer's talent, voice, and vision but of the social forces influencing both writer and reader.

By contrast, real human beings have an immediacy that impedes our speculation about the way that culture acts on or constructs them or the way that we read and understand them. I do not mean to imply that people exist only as cultural inventions or fabrications (although that has been one of the more radical implications of some recent fiction and criticism). The point is, rather, that we know ourselves and those around us through our thoughts and perceptions—which are culturally derived, influenced, organized. To examine the images of childhood reflected in a novel, a patently constructed world of words, is to become more conscious of the cultural and epistemological implications of those images for us and our culture.

Readers of novels stand a good chance, therefore, of developing the kind of dual awareness that Valerie Suransky identifies with true "anthropologists of childhood," who recognize that they "are both embedded in, and yet distanced from," the "very culture" and characters they study. Novels, Patricia Meyer Spacks points out, are both products and catalysts of such dual awareness. The "collective imagination of a culture," she observes in *The Adolescent Idea,* inevitably and "simultaneously contains opposing ideas." Novels, more than any other literary genre, engage with a culture's "latent" as well as "manifest content, with meanings a writer never consciously intended, although he or she would not necessarily disavow them." Novels have the power, therefore, to inform us about our own "fantasies" and "social mythology."[5]

Registering the tensions produced by opposing ideas and allegiances, the novel is grounded in rich contradictions. Thus, Spacks notes, the novel springs from "the subversive energies of the imagination" while flourishing "in the garden of the taken-for-granted. It reflects social values while proclaiming its iconoclasm." In her recent study of the genre, *The True Story of the Novel,* Margaret Doody makes a similar observation: the novel announces itself as "a product of its own era" even while it reaches with "long roots" into the past. Both structurally and thematically, Doody maintains, the novel rehearses ancient patterns and "ritual." Because of its paradoxical allegiance to both the present moment and the distant past, the novel proves a "marvelous means of incorporating and interpreting current culture."[6] Critics like Spacks and Doody help to explain why—in a culture deluged with visual images and dominated by electronic media—the novel may yet offer the most supple and precise, ambitious and wide-ranging kind of imaginative inquiry into the competing claims of public and private experience.

To demonstrate the novel's resources for subverting as well as reflecting the cultural habits and conditions from which it arises, I open chapter 1 with a discussion of current issues about and images of childhood—drawing on both the popular media and the work of cultural critics and historians. Then, after a brief overview of the development, or invention, of childhood in the past few centuries, I shift the focus to the text and context of each work of fiction. Matching, or contrasting, specific texts with the far-reaching cultural contexts I address, readers should gain fresh appreciation of the novel's capacity to incorporate and interpret a variety of twentieth-century images of childhood: images that speak to readers, subliminally as well as rhetorically, of the conflicting forces at work in themselves and their cultures.

In "the cultural particularities of people," says Clifford Geertz in *The Interpretation of Cultures,* "some of the most instructive revelations of what it is to be generically human are to be found." What holds for this cultural anthropologist also applies to the approach taken here. Any generic observations on the contemporary image of childhood are drawn from the wealth of particularities that differentiate one literary image from another, one author and cultural context from another. The insights gleaned from this study are meant, as Geertz says of his own, to grow "out of the delicacy of its distinctions, not the sweep of its abstractions."[7] In keeping with the diversity of contemporary writing and culture, not to speak of the diversity of images of childhood, I seek out rather than suppress literary and cultural differences among works of fiction.

This study differs markedly from others that it might seem, at first glance, to resemble. In contrast to Kuhn, in his *Corruption in Paradise: The Child in Western Literature,* for example, I do not attempt to achieve, in Kuhn's words, "a better comprehension of the real child by proposing a phenomenological description of his fictional counterpart." Kuhn is undoubtedly correct when he says that "the child is more than an aesthetic invention leaping *ex nihilo* into a fictive existence." Instead of emphasizing the cultural context from which the child's image leaps onto the pages of fiction, however, he endeavors to plumb the "enigma" of the child's "essential nature" and its "transformative power."[8] By contrast, I neither assume the child's essential nature nor seek to uncover the naked truth about real children allegedly reflected in their fictional counterparts.

Of the relatively few studies on the child theme in twentieth-century fiction, most tend to concentrate on a particular author or branch of literature—as indicated by the titles of Muriel Shine's *The Fictional Children of Henry James,* Naomi Sokoloff's *Imagining the Child in Modern Jewish Fiction,* and Andrew Wachtel's *The Battle for Childhood: Creation of a Russian Myth.* The most narrowly focused, Virginia Blum's *Hide and Seek: The Child between Psychoanalysis and Fiction,* singles out four novels to demonstrate their "function as extensions and interpretations of psychoanalytic theories of the child." The scope of this study is wider, acknowledging the global conditions of contemporary writing and culture. The novel has been shaped and influenced by a cross-cultural exchange of social, political, and aesthetic ideas that has only intensified with the acceleration of communication and commerce. Thus Malcolm Bradbury, in his account of the development of the modern American novel, acknowledges the impossibility of confining his subject to a single continent. The modern novel, he points out, is "an international form": "it is also the product of a larger history of fiction in a changing international world."[9]

To stress the international identity of the modern novel is not to dismiss the differences in gender, race, and ethnicity that distinguish writers and their works. But as the backgrounds and experiences of novelists from the Russian American Nabokov, to the African American Morrison, to the Anglo-Indian Rushdie suggest, the cultural and historical forces at work in a world linked by electronic media and a global economy do not halt at national borders. As Rushdie points out in *Imaginary Homelands,* we live "at a time when the novel has never been a more international form." Just as Jorge Luis Borges claims "the influence of Robert Louis Stevenson" and Heinrich Böll that "of Irish literature," Rushdie claims for his "polyglot family tree" such writers as "Gogol, Cervantes, Kafka, Melville, [and] Machado de Assis." Borrowing elements of the fantastic from both Hindu and Islamic myth, Rushdie fuses these features in *Midnight's Children* with a parody of British and continental European literary traditions. Addressing not only Indians, Anglo-Indians, or Indo-Anglians, he says that he writes "for everyone else whom I can reach"—an audience of readers, in other words, as "inescapably international" as the writers they read (*Imaginary Homelands* 20–21).

Of the novelists I discuss, a good number belong to the category of "literary migrant" in which Rushdie places himself and other foreign-born or minority writers: they include not only Kundera, Nabokov, and Kosinski but Lessing and Morrison as well. Lessing immigrated to England from colonial Rhodesia as a budding novelist of thirty; Morrison writes out of the wrenching cultural displacement imposed on all African Americans by the history of slavery. Yet Rushdie's discussion of the displaced writer has still wider implications for the novels I treat. "America, a nation of immigrants," he says, "has created great literature out of the phenomenon of cultural transplantation, out of examining ways in which people cope with a new world" (*Imaginary Homelands* 20). Here he touches on the increasingly uprooted, or transplanted, conditions of contemporary life for more and more people.

Among today's novelists and their readers one would be hard-pressed to find many who are *not* coping with the new world that advanced technology and mass media have opened up. Who in our

globally connected (and atomically threatened) universe does not participate, to some extent, in that sense of displacement Rushdie locates
in the "post-diaspora community" of writers? "Our identity is at once
plural and partial," he declares. "Sometimes we feel that we straddle
two cultures; at other times, that we fall between two stools. But however ambiguous and shifting this ground may be, it is not an infertile
territory for the writer to occupy" (*Imaginary Homelands* 15). Displaced
writers, I might point out, are not the only ones trying to negotiate
this "ambiguous and shifting" territory. Among these writers' readers,
how many can ignore the shifting cultural sands beneath their feet?
Who does not sense the chasm separating past and present social
structures? Is not this ambiguous and shifting territory an apt description of the new world in which so many find themselves?

Writing out of several markedly different but interacting (and
conflicting) cultures, Rushdie—by an awful irony—lived for a decade
under an Islamic death threat that, although recently revoked, still
denies him freedom of contact with these cultural worlds. Since the
mid-1970s Kundera has endured a more comfortable version of exile
in Paris. Whether contemporary novelists have been forcibly uprooted
by political revolution and strife, as were Nabokov and Kosinski, or,
like Lessing and Golding, they have simply borne witness to the forces
of deracination unleashed by two world wars—each writer's vision is
best studied and appreciated, I believe, in a context that acknowledges
the international scope of the novelistic enterprise today. Like other
aspects of contemporary culture, the social constructions of childhood
are ambiguous and shifting. What remains clear, however, is that diverse
images of the child—particularly those reflected in major works of
fiction—are shaped, influenced, and shared by readers around the
world.

In this study I have not sought to offer an encyclopedic overview of
the child theme in recent fiction. The intention, rather, is to develop an
incisive, engaging, and provocative account of its most telling features
and cultural ramifications. I should like to encourage readers to recon-
sider the images of childhood in their favorite works of fiction. The
questions raised will, I hope, spark discussion in the classroom and the
café as well as in professional journals. Such questions begin and end
with the texts themselves: the verbal and structural forms that constitute their articulate power. The theories and observations of social

historians, psychologists, and cultural critics—from Philippe Ariès to Raymond Williams, from Freud to Foucault—should help further to clarify the possible meanings and significance of the literary phenomena I examine. Together, novelists, critics, and commentators should help readers to develop an informed appreciation of both contemporary fiction in all its fascinating diversity and—no less fascinating and diverse—our culture's collective values, fantasies, and fears.

CHAPTER

1

The Image of Childhood, Present and Past

Contemporary Issues and Images

Hardly a day passes when we do not hear from newspapers and magazines, on radio and television, about the current "crisis" of children in today's society. The Sunday paper features an article on the difficulties of child rearing in an age of divorce and single-parent families. In the dentist's office a table of magazines broadcasts the latest news about the widespread use of drugs and handguns by preadolescents. On television CNN broadcasts a special program titled "My Child, My Fear" that addresses the increasing violence done to and by children.[1] ABC's *Prime Time* features a story demonstrating how, in a mere thirty seconds, an adult stranger pretending to have lost his dog can entice a child away from the playground where her parents think they are keeping safe watch. An anxious parent stares at news footage of smooth-faced convicts interviewed in jail cells and group-therapy sessions who confess their rapture at molesting and murdering their tiny victims. Social awareness of the "monsters among us," as one television documentary puts it, has grown so acute that many adults have been falsely arrested and imprisoned for molesting children. Not only individuals but history itself has proved vulnerable to our current obsession. A recent documentary on Hitler Youth defines the Nazi youth-indoctrination program as "a massive case of child abuse."[2]

The vast array of publications on the subject of children offers every manner of treatment, from the confessional to the therapeutic, from the scholarly to the sentimental. Treatises by doctors, psychologists, sociologists, anthropologists, and criminologists cover virtually every

aspect of the child question, occupying rows of shelves in libraries and
bookstores. (They are also turning up in lecture form at video stores.)
Meanwhile, the boundary separating our collective fears *for* children
from those we harbor *of* them has become increasingly blurred. The
1993 trial and conviction of two ten-year-old boys who abducted, tortured, and murdered a two-year-old neatly—and horrifically—signal
the difficulty of distinguishing between our fears for and of the child.[3]

As one newspaper commentator observed during the heat of the
1996 electoral campaign, "special efforts" were made by both political
parties to capitalize on widespread "citizen fear" of youth. Such fear is
fed, he pointed out, by prominent researchers who forecast a future as
violent as the one depicted in Anthony Burgess's 1962 novel *A Clockwork
Orange*. Burgess's dystopian vision of a society held hostage by gangs of
raping and pillaging teenagers is alarmingly projected, for example, by
one Princeton University professor who predicted in a recent study
that by the year 2010 the number of "juvenile superpredators" roam-
ing the streets of America will have increased by approximately
270,000. Whether or not the future will confirm such dire forecasts,
few would argue the point made by a prominent French historian,
Philippe Ariès, more than three decades ago in his groundbreaking
study, *Centuries of Childhood:* "Our world is obsessed by the physical,
moral and sexual problems of childhood."[4]

Since the publication of Ariès's seminal work, the problem, and problematic nature, of childhood has been analyzed not only by sociologists,
psychologists, and other experts concerned with child development
but by literary scholars and social historians. Suggesting a possible reason for this attention, Leah Marcus contends in *Childhood and Cultural
Despair* that concern for children increases during times of cultural
crisis. In *The Disappearance of Childhood* Neil Postman identifies one
major crisis as that of childhood itself, currently under siege by a technological society rapidly dismantling this "fragile" institution. Not
only individual children, Postman argues, but a centuries-old institution of Western culture is at risk. Children, he warns, are no longer
given the kind of attention, education, and protection they require.
Pointing to the plethora of studies on childhood, his own included,
as evidence of the current crisis, Postman tells us: "As if to confirm
Marshall McLuhan's observation that when a social artifact becomes
obsolete, it is turned into an object of nostalgia and contemplation,
historians and social critics have produced, within the past two decades,

scores of major works on childhood's history, whereas very few were written between, say, 1800 and 1960," when childhood flourished.[5]

The reasons for the intensification of interest in childhood will undoubtedly remain a subject of debate among scholars and social critics. Virtually all agree on one point, however: that, as Ray Hiner and Joseph Hawes say, "childhood as an experience and social category is part of the historical process and subject to change over time." Beyond question as well is the sheer number of recent studies of childhood and the family to which Postman refers. Much of this research is cited in the five-volume series *A History of Private Life* published in France during the 1980s and recently issued in English. As Roger Shattuck has noted, this mammoth study of private life in Western culture, from ancient Roman times to the present, was "willed, conceived, and prepared" by Ariès, who died in 1984, when the series was half completed. Following Ariès's lead, scholars have tended to view childhood as a relatively modern invention or discovery in the West—a discovery that, in Ariès's view, began to take root in the seventeenth century, was firmly established by the middle of the eighteenth, and flowered in the nineteenth.[6]

Not all historians, of course, agree with Ariès's time scheme or his underlying premise: that the modern concept of childhood, while increasing the cultural value placed on children, often worked against them—restricting their spontaneity and freedom and subjecting them to greater institutional control and punishment. Some recent studies, for example, emphasize a different aspect of this paradox, pointing to the disparity between the sentimental value our culture ascribes to children and their economic or social uselessness. Viviana Zelizer regards this inverse relationship as "an essential condition of contemporary childhood." Even the child's allowance, she points out, is dispensed not as payment for work or chores but as a way to train children to handle money. In a rapidly changing society, she notes, this condition may also disappear. The "sacred, economically useless child may," she warns, "become a luxury or an indulgence that the contemporary family no longer . . . can afford."[7]

In *Hide and Seek* Virginia Blum locates the source of the inverse relationship "between the sentimental and material value of children" in the unconscious mechanisms of collective repression and "masculinist fantasy." Adopting a feminist and revisionist approach to psychoanalytic theory, she argues that modern Western culture, as exemplified in both "psychoanalytic and literary fictions" of the nineteenth and twentieth centuries, "invests [in] fictive children while treating living children with comparative indifference." Unable to realize the powers invested in them by "the communal fantasies of an entire culture," actual "children cannot help but prove the inadequacy of the child to the projective grandiosity of adult expectations."[8] As different as Blum's theoretical approach is from the social scientist's and the historian's—or, for that matter, from my own—she also notes the profound ambivalence toward children evinced in contemporary attitudes and images.

Our culture's obsession with children, as suggested earlier, may well betray as much fear as sympathy, as much dread as love. The conflict between anxiety and sympathy—our fears both *of* and *for* the child—manifests itself not only in the polarized images broadcast by the mass media but in the disagreements dividing academic and professional opinion. On the one hand, revisionist studies by feminists and other scholars increasingly challenge the Freudian assumption that a patient's accounts of childhood sexual abuse are merely psychological projections or fantasies stemming from oedipal conflict. On the other hand, there is growing suspicion among many trained experts, faced with the volume of belated charges leveled at parents by their grown-up children, that patients allegedly suffering from repressed memory syndrome are being manipulated by therapists to recover dubious memories of abuse.[9] Society's concern for the welfare and safety of children is real, but so is anxiety about adults' safety and welfare—to which, unless a great many observers are mistaken, children pose a threat.

Since the 1960s increased emphasis on equality and freedom (sexual freedom in particular) has been reflected in relaxed modes of child rearing that, in turn, have generated new tensions between generations. The frustration that many parents, teachers, and other adults experience at their inability to control society's offspring is sharpened by the fact that youthful rebellion mirrors the previous generation's insistence on liberation and self-fulfillment. Anger at their children and at themselves may fuel, in Marie Winn's words, "the widespread fear among today's parents that manageable children will turn overnight into dope fiends, school dropouts, or voracious sexual voluptuaries." There may even be "an element of wish fulfillment," she suggests, in "the appetite of today's adult audience for television documentaries about child abuse, child prostitution, child molestation."[10] As James Kincaid argues in *Erotic Innocence: The Culture of Child Molesting,* adult anxiety over the welfare of children often masks buried resentment, or suppressed desire, played out in the media's myriad reports and reenactments of child abuse.

Latent conflicts and polarized attitudes also emerge when we compare the reverence for children expressed by child experts and advocates with the frequently ominous images of children projected in the media. In recent years the Romantics' worship of the child's divine or transcendent origins has revealed a shadowy underside. The cult of sacred childhood has turned satanic, supplanting angelic children with demonic ones who serve the powers of darkness. Viewed with regularity on late-night television movies, these predatory creatures, ready to beat and bludgeon helpless animals or unsuspecting adults, contrast bizarrely with the round-cheeked youngsters who, with gurgles of advertised pleasure, sip name-brand soup and sodas on the commercials that interrupt the movie's gory story. The prevalence of these satanic child-monsters sounds an antiphonal note to the chorus of concern raised on behalf of the child's welfare.

Noting signs of increasing hostility to youth during the last several decades, Winn traces "the changing image of children in the movies":

> In the sixties a new sort of child appeared in motion pictures; from a sweet, idealized Shirley Temple or Margaret O'Brien poppet, the movie child grew into a monster. First came ... a prepubescent killer in *The Bad Seed* in 1956. Then, in *Village of the Damned* (1962), sweet-faced children turned out to be malevolent beings from outer space. The trend accelerated in the late sixties and early seventies, culminating in the appearance of a spate of satanic juveniles on movie screens. *Rosemary's Baby* was the first, a mild exercise in horror compared to *The Exorcist,* which featured the first true teenage werewolf, a darling little girl transformed, just at puberty, into a ravening, sexually rapacious, and murderous creature.[11]

Now, one might argue, for every satanic child projected in the popular media, there are many lovable ones, such as the kids in Steven Spielberg's *E. T.* who befriend a visitor from outer space. On the other hand, widespread polarization of the child's image into a demonic or angelic figure may help to prove the point concerning adults' deep-seated ambivalence. What makes the child so powerful an image of human creativity and potential—that sacred soul or self worshiped by the Romantics and still evoked in various guises today—is exactly what

makes our darker visions of the child's mysterious nature and origins
so terrifying. In both cases the child represents the other side—original
or shameful, beautiful or monstrous, forgotten or repressed—of the
adult self. The child's image is always bound up in "Otherness," Naomi
Sokoloff points out, because the "sensations and perception of childhood are to some extent always irretrievable to [adult] memory and
articulation."[12]

The ambivalence of contemporary attitudes toward children is
manifested, as Postman points out, in the language we use to describe
them. That idealizing language "still carries within it many of the assumptions about childhood that were established in the eighteenth
and nineteenth centuries"; but it "does not match our present social
reality." Implicit in Postman's reference to our present social reality is
his awareness of the rising crime rate among children. "Between 1950
and 1979," he states, "the rate of serious crimes committed by children
increased 11,000 percent." It is an understatement to say that Alice
Miller's Wordsworthian celebration of the child does not match, linguistically or experientially, the current social facts: that, for example, an
increasing number of ten-year-olds peddle dope, pack handguns, and
are found guilty of kidnapping and murder. Between our current,
much-touted reverence for children and the violence they both suffer
and enact lies a schism as deep as the one that divided nineteenth-
century culture. As numerous scholars have explained, the proliferation of idealized images of childhood in Victorian England was
matched only by the era's flourishing trade in child pornography and
child prostitution.[13] If, as I have been suggesting, the image of childhood mirrors the social and historical circumstances of both children
and adults, that mirror works both ways: it reflects on those who gaze
into its recesses. As one American father, interviewed about "the problem with children today," said, "Is there a problem with children?
I don't think so. I think there's a problem with us. . . . We need to look
at ourselves."[14] To study the image of childhood is to study ourselves,
not only because we all were once children but also because the child's
changing image is inscribed by the force of our feelings and fears—
our beliefs, prejudices, anxieties, and conflicts. The fate of the fictional
or literary child, in particular, says much about the way we view our
own nature and destiny and even, as many works of contemporary
fiction attest, our chances for succeeding as a species on this planet.

Cultural Constructions of Childhood: A Brief Overview

In contrast to children, childhood as we know it, or have constructed it, has not existed since the beginning of time. Parental concern for the welfare of children, many experts point out, is embedded in biology. As Postman persuasively argues, however, the institution of childhood, like language learning, "has a biological basis [that] cannot be realized unless a social environment triggers and nurtures it." Underscoring the symbiosis of culture and biology, anthropologists have observed that culture, not human physiology, establishes the dietary laws to which a community adheres. "The moment of weaning," Mary Douglas points out, "often proves fatal to infants in traditional societies."[15] This transition signals a crucial stage in the process by which nature's offspring becomes culture's child; but no one can pinpoint the exact moment at which acculturation begins.

"The nakedness of human nature is clothed so soon by every culture," Guy Davenport observes, "that we are at a wide variance, within and among cultures, as to what human nature might be."[16] The little boy in the fable who declares that the emperor has no clothes could not have done so, one might say, unless he and the emperor were, culturally speaking, already clothed. Whether his body is dressed or naked, the emperor's perceived nature is by definition already decked out— constituted, constructed, formed, and formulated by the culture that clothes him. Knowing that the emperor *is* the emperor, the child testifies to the fact that, no matter how unself-conscious and outspoken, he, too, is already clothed: the creature of his culture.

Approaching the subject from a different vantage, Michel Foucault also suggests that human nature cannot be seen or known in its nakedness, but only when clothed in "historical reality." This is what Foucault apparently means when, in *Discipline and Punish,* he satirically reverses Judeo-Christian formulations to proclaim "the soul is the prison of the body." The human soul, he adds, is not, as Christian theology would have it, "born in sin and subject to punishment." Rather, the "noncorporal soul" is an element produced "around, on, within the body by the functioning of a power that is exercised on those punished—and, in a more general way, on those one supervises, trains, and corrects; over madmen, children at home and at school, the colonized." The soul is not an innate "substance" but what the body wears: the

clothing that culture produces around, on, and within the conjectured
(but inaccessible, unknowable) "nakedness" of primal human nature.
Culture thus "brings [the individual] into existence," subjecting the
primal body to the pressures of a specific time, place, and history.[17]

For Foucault the process of cultural formation, or subjection, can
be understood as the operation of external forces, or "power," on the
individual. In "The Subject and Power" he describes the goal of his
own writing: "to create a history of the different modes by which, in
our culture, human beings are made subjects." The soul, he points out
in another essay, is an "instrument and vector of power," to which each
individual is subjected at birth. Born to nature, the child comes into
existence as subject, or prisoner, of culture—whose technology, the
"technology of the 'soul,'" has been increasingly wielded in our own
time by "educationalists, psychologists, and psychiatrists." Increasing
too since the eighteenth century, Foucault contends, is the power
wielded by the family. He finds, like Ariès before him, that the family
in Western culture gradually ceased to be a mere "system of relations"
or "mechanism for the transmission of property." With its ever-
tightening relations, the modern family became, says Foucault, "a
dense, saturated, permanent, continuous physical environment which
envelops, maintains, and develops the child's body."[18]

One does not have to share Foucault's overriding assumption—
that, to simplify his point, culture is tyranny—to recognize, as Clifford
Geertz says, that "there is no such thing as human nature independent
of culture." Geertz suggests, however, that to view this relationship as
one of mere power is to miss the point. "Culture," those "interworked
systems of construable signs," is "not a power"—not "something to
which social events, behaviors, institutions, or processes can be causally
attributed"—but "a context, something within which they can be in-
telligibly described." He adds, "The apparent fact that the final stages
of the biological evolution of man occurred after the initial stages of
the growth of culture implies that 'basic,' 'pure,' or 'unconditioned'
human nature, in the sense of the innate constitution of man, is so
functionally incomplete as to be unworkable. Tools, hunting, family
organization, and, later, art, religion, and 'science' molded man somat-
ically; and they are, therefore, necessary not merely to his survival but
to his existential realization."[19] What Foucault ironically calls the soul
is not, in Geertz's view, a set of mental, psychological, and emotional
trappings that bind and finally imprison the body in a deterministic

environment. The soul is, rather, the context or setting for the human being's psychic and somatic realization; without that cultural clothing the human species would not and could not exist.

Geertz's influential study also points, albeit indirectly, to the crucial role of the child in debates about human nature. Citing his anthropological research in Java, Geertz quotes the popular Javanese saying "To be human is to be Javanese," which to him demonstrates this people's recognition of the symbiotic relationship of nature and culture. Culture, in this case Javanese culture, is the context that completes human beings both "as a single species" and "as separate individuals." Thus, Geertz adds, "small children, boors, simpletons, the insane, the flagrantly immoral are said to be *ndurung djawa*, 'not yet Javanese.'"[20] Those who are culturally rather than physically deficient are not fully human—whether they are boors who have chosen this condition or simpletons who cannot help it. Children are included in this category not because they are not yet fully grown physically but because they are not yet culturally finished or complete: they are "not yet Javanese," that is, not yet altogether human.

Unlike the mentally or morally impaired, children can claim strength in incompleteness. From an adult's point of view their vulnerability is an aspect of their power. Children are weak, socially as well as physically, because they contain so much potential. Not yet complete, they are not yet fully clothed, or formed, by culture. Our society's fascination with children may well be fueled by this paradoxical condition. That children, moreover, are not yet fully acculturated undoubtedly contributes to their significance as literary images. As human beings partially formed—half dressed, if you will—by culture, they hold out the tantalizing if illusory promise of exposing human nature in its nakedness. How that nakedness is revealed, of course, depends on the way it is culturally configured, or clothed. The paradox remains: the only image of human nature accessible to us cannot be divested of the observer's cultural cloth. Still, as Geertz suggests, it is not necessary to see or "know everything in order to understand something."[21]

The Romantic Legacy

In ancient Athens the "monument to a dead little girl put up by her sorrowing family" reveals, says Margaret Doody, "the extent to which a mere little girl child could be loved, cherished, and lamented." Still, as the earlier discussion of Ariès and his successors makes clear, the nature and role of children have been differently construed and constructed throughout history. Since the Middle Ages, at least, children have been alternately regarded as innocent or depraved, the most vulnerable or the most vital representatives of humankind. In seventeenth-century England, when, as Robert Pattison points out, "the child figure began to appear with more frequency," these polarized concepts were equally distributed between those taking sides in the controversy. In Leah Marcus's view the tension in seventeenth-century thought derived from opposing religious outlooks: "Puritan emphasis on original sin" and "conservative Anglican emphasis on original innocence."[22]

With the Romantic discovery of original innocence in the eighteenth century, the child acquired a new and glorious significance as the embodiment of natural goodness in a fallen world. In mid-eighteenth-century France, Mark Spilka points out, Jean-Jacques Rousseau developed his "seminal views" of the "uncorrupted child of Nature, born in a state of innocence and threatened by the corruption of the adult social world." Associating "Nature with innate human qualities like Feeling, Sensibility, and Imagination," Rousseau challenged the "Christian doctrine of Original Sin, the fallen state of natural vice from which children were [according to pre-eighteenth-century formulations] to be rescued by rational virtue." Rousseau "replaced this older view, surviving from the Middle Ages, with another Christian doctrine, that of Original Innocence, or natural virtue, as evinced in the attitude of Christ himself toward little children." The "enormous secular influence of the new doctrine of childhood innocence" was quickly registered in England: "English Romantic poets, notably Blake, Wordsworth, and Coleridge, transposed this doctrine into poetry . . . and, in the process, gave the childhood theme its first important literary utterance."[23]

Existing close to the source of human existence, the child occupies a privileged, even sacred, position in the visionary landscape of the English Romantics. In his "Ode: Intimations of Immortality from Recollections of Early Childhood" William Wordsworth celebrates a Neoplatonic vision of the child, who arrives in this world "trailing clouds of glory" from a transcendent realm that is his true "home" (ll. 64–65). Hard-pressed though one might be to find a contemporary poet echoing Wordsworth's sentiments, his legacy is evident in a wide variety of studies by child specialists and advocates. In a well-known series of books, for example, the psychoanalyst Alice Miller expresses her reverence for the child's original innocence in terms that echo Wordsworth's and William Blake's. Like them, Miller warns of the "destruction of vitality" that neglect of "the child within" spells for human life and culture. Although she is Swiss and writes in German, a passage of her translated prose can sound remarkably like a paraphrase of Wordsworth's verse: "someday," she avows, "we will regard our children not as creatures to manipulate or to change but rather as messengers from a world we once deeply knew, but which we have long since forgotten."[24]

At the same time that the Romantics idealized the child's origins—postulating a transcendent realm inaccessible to mortal memory and adult experience—they also saw the image of childhood as embodying a sense of hope for the future. "In talking about childhood," says Peter Coveney in his seminal study *The Image of Childhood,* "the great Romantics were . . . talking of the whole condition of Man." For them "the child was an active image, an expression of human potency in the face of human experience. Innocence for them was valuable for what it might become, if it could survive the power of corrupting experience." Wordsworth's immortality ode thus became the central reference "for the whole nineteenth century in its attitudes to the child." Having read their Wordsworth and Blake, the Victorians "knew that the child," says Morton Cohen, "had recently come from God and . . . still possessed a modicum of divine knowledge." Of all the prominent nineteenth-century novelists espousing this theme, "it was Dickens," Spilka asserts, "who made the child the emotional, the *affective* center of fiction and used him or her as his validating touchstone for human worth." None of the other early Victorians treating this theme—not "Disraeli, Mrs. Gaskell, [or] Kingsley"—could "command the emotional and attitudinal range which Dickens brought to his subject." As Raymond Williams puts it, the "innocence" of Dickens's literary children, maltreated by a harsh and heartless society, "shames the adult world."[25]

For most of the nineteenth century, novelists writing in English—including the Brontës and George Eliot as well as Mark Twain—paid tribute to the idyll of childhood innocence. In France, Geoffrey Carter observes, Victor Hugo, although considered "more or less dangerous or immoral in England at that time," enthusiastically shared the Victorians' idealizing attitude toward children. In his collection of poems titled *L'art d'être grand-père* (1877), Hugo depicts himself as "Victor, *sed victus*," the heroic writer "vanquished by a small child." Humbled by this tiny being's original innocence, Hugo finds in the child's image "a profound peace made entirely of stars." As Patricia Meyer Spacks points out, however, with the century drawing to a close, "the Victorian propensity for glorifying childhood" became more difficult to sustain. Increasingly cut off from nature and the past, the later Victorians drifted away from the "social and moral assumptions" that inspired Romantic faith. Nineteenth-century thinkers—"valuing innocence over experience, yet understanding the distortions implicit in efforts to preserve innocence"—finally "reached a logical impasse."[26]

Freud, James, and Their Literary Offspring

By the turn of the twentieth century Sigmund Freud was drastically rewriting the child's role. If, as James Kincaid asserts in *Child-Loving,* the Victorian image of the child had become a blank—pure "nothingness" emptied of substance by society's insistence on original innocence —Freud was busily plowing that fallow field, sowing the seeds of a radically new conception of childhood. At the conclusion of that explosive document, *Three Essays on the Theory of Sexuality,* he appears well aware of the damage he is doing to the Romantic myth of natural innocence. "We found it a regrettable thing," Freud says, "that the existence of the sexual instinct in childhood has been denied. . . . It seemed to us on the contrary that children bring germs of sexual activity with them into the world, [and] that they already enjoy sexual satisfaction when they begin to take nourishment."[27] Here Freud's language takes a figurative turn as it strategically invests, or infects, the Wordsworthian child with the "germs of sexual activity." Instead of "trailing clouds of glory" into this world from their lofty "home," Freud's children arrive carrying the "germs," or seeds, of corruption.

The implications of this secular version of the fall have not been lost on Freud's critics. Even Spilka, whose commentary bears a decidedly Freudian stamp, draws an analogy between Freud's "appearance at the end of the last century" and "the return of a doctrine rather like that of Original Sin: the doctrine, that is, of the sexual nature of childhood experience in its unconscious aspects, and of the neurotic nature of family experience in its rivalries and tensions and regressive romances. . . . It was a doctrine, moreover, toward which novelists themselves were clearly working even before it was formulated, as Freud himself acknowledged."

Coveney, on the other hand, disagrees with those who detect a resemblance between Freud's image of the child "as the heir of libidinal impulses and the father of adult neurosis" and "the religious idea of the child's 'corrupt' nature." Such comparisons, he says, "ignore, of course, the whole attitude from which Freud made his investigation of mental structure and organization. Concepts of 'corruption,' 'innocence' and 'sin' were wholly alien to his scientific approach." In the light of recent revisionist studies of Freud, which challenge his allegedly scientific methodology and approach, Coveney's premise—that Freud aspired to deal only in the "facts" of "human consciousness"—is not wholly convincing.[28]

Coveney agrees, however, that Freud's theories of infantile sexuality rendered a deathblow to the nineteenth-century myth of childhood innocence, based as it was on the rigid philosophical equation of innocence with asexual purity. By the time Freud delivered this fatal blow, the once-resonant theme of original innocence had already begun to decay, sickened as it was by nostalgia and blind sentiment. Announcing the onset of literary rigor mortis, a number of Dickens's epigones had lapsed into sheer morbidity. "In the latter decades of the century," Coveney observes, the image of the child had become "a means of escape from the pressures of adult adjustment. . . . The children of Mrs. Henry Wood and Marie Corelli, for whom it was better not to grow up, but die, were the commercial expression of something detectably sick in the sensitive roots of English child fiction at the end of the century."[29]

Just when the literary child was, so to speak, crying out for a cure, enter Henry James, the father of Anglo-American modernism. Within two short years, in *What Maisie Knew* (1897) and *The Turn of the Screw* (1898), he laid the sickly Victorian child to rest—breathing new life and vitality into the offspring of English and American fiction. After a decade of writing short stories and plays, he had turned his attention back to the novel. With the publication of *What Maisie Knew* James added, says Malcolm Bradbury, "a whole new concept of reality to the art of fiction" and initiated "the change in his later work [that] clearly points it towards modernism."[30] That James launched the modern novel in English and simultaneously transformed the literary image of the child hardly seems coincidental. Both processes led to the artistic creation of new and vital representations of the nascent human self. Tellingly, James's problematic image of the child, particularly in *The Turn of the Screw*, reflects some of the same ambivalence toward childhood innocence that Freud evinced in the late 1890s, when he was formulating his theories of infantile sexuality.

In his introduction to Freud's *Three Essays on the Theory of Sexuality* James Strachey documents Freud's ambivalence. "Many elements of Freud's theory of sexuality were already present in his mind by 1896," he observes, and Freud's "realization that sexual impulses operated normally in the youngest children" is stated in his letters to his colleague Wilhelm Fliess, written during the summer of 1897. Strachey adds:

> It took some years, however, for him to become entirely reconciled to his own discovery. In a passage, for instance, in his paper on "Sexuality in the Aetiology of the Neurosis" [1898] he blows hot and cold on it. On the one hand he says that "children are capable of every psychical sexual function and of many somatic ones" and that it is wrong to suppose that their sexual life begins only at puberty. But on the other hand he declares that "the organization and evolution of the human species seek to avoid any considerable sexual activity in childhood."

Freud's ambivalence extends, Strachey notes, even to the first edition of *The Interpretation of Dreams* (1900), where there occurs "a curious passage towards the end of Chapter III . . . , in which Freud remarks that 'we think highly of the happiness of childhood because it is still innocent of sexual desires.'" Noting that "a corrective footnote was added to this passage in 1911," Strachey says that the passage "was no doubt a relic from an early draft of the book, for elsewhere . . . [Freud] writes quite unambiguously of the existence of sexual wishes even in normal children."[31] Freud appears to have forgotten, or wished to discount, his earlier ambivalence by the time *Three Essays on the Theory of Sexuality* was published in 1905. Here he says, "As long ago as in the year 1896 I insisted on the significance of the years of childhood in the origin of certain important phenomena connected with sexual life, and since then I have never ceased to emphasize the part played in sexuality by the infantile factor."[32]

In the year to which Freud alludes, 1896, James began writing *What Maisie Knew*, after which he produced a series of novels and tales that, in his biographer Leon Edel's words, carry out a "conscious intellectual exploration of states of childhood." In "a striking historical parallel," James and Freud—albeit in "two different cities of the Old World"—returned "to the stuff of childhood." James, Edel adds, "rendered in fictional form—and in complete independence—those very subtleties of the human personality and of the unconscious which Freud systematically studied" in Vienna. Even if one does not draw a direct parallel between the two men, it is clear that James participated in the same intellectual ferment that led Freud, along with Charles Darwin, Karl Marx, and others, to dismantle the edifice of nineteenth-century thought. According to Malcolm Bradbury, James, "engaged with questions of consciousness and unconsciousness," led the movement in "American fiction of the 1890s" toward a "whole new body of themes and energies." Although James had by this time taken up residence in England, the novels of his "late phase" give "a fresh account of the deep-seated processes—genetic, biological, sexual, social, and scientific—that lay beneath modernizing American life." The "curve of James's career," Bradbury concludes, traces the turning point "from nineteenth-century to new twentieth-century practices in fiction."[33]

Half a century after James—and registering the impact of two world wars, global genocide, nuclear disaster, and inner-city violence—writers have tended to emphasize the darker, more violent elements of human nature and childhood. By the same token, some prominent twentieth-century writers look back with nostalgia at the nineteenth-century image of childhood—much as Twain, in the waning years of the nineteenth century, gazed back at his boyhood, the American past, and European Romanticism's vision of the child's Edenic innocence. Drawing on "sentimental stereotypes of the child as Noble Savage and the child as victim of society," Twain, says Leslie Fiedler in *Love and Death in the American Novel,* "represents a belated and provincial blossoming of a literary movement already outmoded on the continent."[34] Just as J. D. Salinger's midcentury best-seller, *The Catcher in the Rye,* echoes Twain's celebration of the child's innate morality in *The Adventures of Huckleberry Finn,* Kurt Vonnegut, for all his postmodernist experimentation, announces the longing for innocence in the subtitle of his most searching novel, *Slaughterhouse-Five; or, The Children's Crusade.*

Like William Golding's *Lord of the Flies,* Muriel Spark's *The Prime of Miss Jean Brodie* signals a radical departure from the attempt to recapture the idyll of youthful innocence. Blurring the border between public and private spheres, Spark uncovers the political nature of personal conduct and experience. Without relying on the schematic or allegorical features of Golding's wartime fable, *The Prime of Miss Jean Brodie* exposes the fascist forces at work in an out-of-the-way school for girls in Edinburgh, Scotland, during the early 1930s, linking their lives and relationships—both with their teacher Miss Brodie and with one another—to the catastrophic events that Mussolini and Hitler were about to stage for the world at large. Since the decade immediately following World War II, as popular culture has grown more escapist and upbeat, the most interesting writers continue to probe the darker dimensions of reality—exposing the unspoken depths beneath the bright surface of a world filled to bursting with consumer goods. Still, the diversity and sheer inventiveness of contemporary fiction do not allow for overschematization. As suggested earlier, the discovery of unexpected reversals and affinities awaits those who explore the imaginative constructions of childhood by some of this era's most innovative novelists.

Sentimental or satiric, fractured or foreboding, the image of childhood still offers contemporary writers "a focal point of contact," as Coveney puts it, between "human consciousness and the 'experience' of an alien world." In an earlier time that point of contact appeared more fixed and stable, defined by tradition and a coherent sense of history and society. It was a society that—however cruel, unjust, hypocritical—espoused (if it did not always live up to) a more sanguine vision of human nature and its creative potential. Its members still hoped that the innocence embodied in the child could regenerate a world sullied by experience. Perhaps because the child theme was so positive an element of fiction in the nineteenth century, few studies of the subject have ventured beyond that century's border. When scholars of earlier periods turn their attention to the twentieth century, they do so only briefly, to suggest, as Coveney does, that further study would require "another volume." In his epilogue to *The Image of Childhood* Coveney expresses the hope that his project "will have at least suggested some of the criteria upon which the immense proliferation of literature concerned with children in more recent times may be assessed."[35]

Certainly the criteria established by Coveney have proved helpful to those examining more recent fiction, as my references to his work throughout this book indicate. At the end of *The Image of Childhood* Coveney offers some cursory, yet suggestive remarks on novels by James

Joyce, D. H. Lawrence, and Virginia Woolf. He notes, for example, the way the modernist fascination with creative consciousness inevitably drew on Romantic reverence for the child but in doing so radically changed its emphasis. In Joyce's *A Portrait of the Artist as a Young Man,* for example, the "vivid re-creation of Stephen's childhood merely serves as prologue to the central conflict."[36] The formative stage of childhood is not a focal point or resonant theme for Joyce but a necessary introduction to his central preoccupation: the growth of the artist's awareness and his conflict with his environment.

Coveney's comments on Joyce and other modernists, albeit brief, are almost always convincing. At times, however, his championing of the Romantic legacy of natural innocence works against his appreciation of post-Romantic writers—most particularly, as I note in the following chapter, of James. Coveney's adamant condemnation of *The Turn of the Screw* contrasts oddly with his forceful critique of late-Victorian nostalgia and the "falsification of the myth" of childhood innocence. Despite his trenchant observations on late-Victorian sentimentality, Coveney does not entertain the possibility, for example, that the ambiguities in *The Turn of the Screw*—rather than expressing James's "disordered sensibility"—constitute a healthy imaginative reaction to the more sickly tendencies of Victorian child worship.[37]

Other critics who focus on the child theme in nineteenth-century literature evince similar limitations when they turn their attention to twentieth-century fiction and culture. In a study subtitled *Parents and Children in Nineteenth-Century Literature* David Grylls claims that children are at the present time (his book was published in 1978) more integrated into family life than ever before: "Their integration with their families has not diminished but grown; and the nature of the bond, once mainly economic, is now mainly emotional."[38] As I hope to make clear, many twentieth-century writers offer far more telling constructions of contemporary childhood. Readers may gauge for themselves the great distance (*chasm* might be the more accurate term) between Grylls's reading of the conditions in which today's children exist and those imaginatively rendered by some of the finest contemporary novelists.

Innocence on the Brink

James's *What Maisie Knew*

At the end of a decade "devoted to writing about young people," Henry James produced two of his most celebrated works on the theme and image of childhood: the novel *What Maisie Knew* (1897) and the novella *The Turn of the Screw* (1898).[1] So crucial are these narratives to explorations of the child theme in twentieth-century fiction that I have chosen to devote a chapter to each. In his preface to the New York edition of *What Maisie Knew,* published a decade after the novel first appeared, James hints at the way this work both complicates and transforms the Victorian image of childhood. Defining his theme as "the misfortune of [a] little victim" and employing a vocabulary familiar to readers of Dickens, James refers to his tiny heroine as a "luckless child," "wretched infant," and "small creature." When, therefore, he announces the "security and ease" to which she can look forward at the end of the novel, first-time readers are likely to envision Maisie's reward in Dickensian terms. Surely the child will assume her rightful place at the hearth of a loving family (*Art of the Novel* 140–41).

Readers acquainted with *What Maisie Knew* can better appreciate James's bold variation on the Dickensian theme of childhood. In contrast to Maisie, many (though by no means all) of Dickens's children are passive creatures. Oliver Twist, Paul Dombey, Little Nell, and a host of other unfortunates must wait for innocence to work its magic on the frozen hearts and minds of adults, on whom the children's fate depends. Sometimes, as in Paul Dombey's case, the revelation arrives too late; the boy is on his deathbed before his father succumbs to paternal affection. The circle of adults orbiting James's luckless child, on the other hand—Maisie's parents, stepparents, and their numerous acquaintances and companions—seem incapable of Christian regeneration. Alone among them, Maisie's stepfather, Sir Claude, is inspired by the child's innate goodness; but he is too weak, too vulnerable to temptation, to pursue the light.

Largely indifferent to the child's nature and plight are Sir Claude's wife and Maisie's mother, Ida Farange; Ida's ex-husband and Maisie's father, Beale Farange; and Beale's current wife and Maisie's stepmother, Mrs. Beale—who eventually becomes Sir Claude's mistress. All are caught up in a cycle of marital squabbles, sexual liaisons, and domestic rearrangements that, with the advent of the new century, become a virtual hallmark of modern life. In keeping with the new era, these adults are no closer to achieving marital harmony at the end of *What Maisie Knew* than they are at the tumultuous beginning. The Dickensian idyll of a tender family clustered around the hearth, secure in the warmth of love's regenerative flame, lies beyond the pale of Maisie's turn-of-the-century universe. At this late date secular laws hold sway over moral and religious ones not only in the courts but in the minds and hearts of James's characters.

Unlike Oliver Twist, Maisie Farange cannot afford to wait patiently for rescue. Nor does she continue for long to play the passive role of little victim. If the adults responsible for uprooting her life can be regarded as quintessentially modern, so can Maisie herself. Her precocity is a sign both of her extraordinary intelligence and sensibility and of her parents' disruptive domestic relationships. As Marie Winn observes of a later period of American culture, the "disappearance of marriage as a dependable, permanent structure within which children can live out their childhood" makes inevitable inroads on their innocence. Exposed to "new knowledge" about their parents' "formerly secret sexual and emotional involvements," contemporary children "find themselves pushed out of childhood and into a precociously adult awareness of life."[2] A century before the divorce rate in Anglo-American society reached today's prodigious heights, James created—as the central character, or "web of consciousness," in his novel—a fictional child actively engaged in acquiring that "precociously adult awareness of life" that signals, in Western culture at least, contemporary childhood.

As James says in his preface, Maisie becomes the "little wonderworking agent" who, "without design" but with instinctive resourcefulness, introduces "fresh elements" into the unsatisfactory situation created by her neglectful parents. "Instead of simply submitting to the inherited" situation or "imposed complication" of her life, James adds, the child contributes "to the formation of a fresh tie, from which it would then (and for all the world as if through a small demonic foresight) proceed to derive great profit." The child's power to renew and transform an otherwise unhealthy situation flows from what James later calls, with redoubled emphasis, the "freshness" of Maisie's nature: her ability "to remain fresh, and still fresh, and to have even a freshness to communicate" (*Art of the Novel* 142, 146).

To survive and finally to flourish in her distinctively modern environment, James's child calls on the resources—freshness, spontaneity, and wonder—that she, like Dickens's literary children, has inherited from the novelist's Romantic predecessors. At the same time, however, James drops a sly hint when he remarks parenthetically on Maisie's "demonic foresight." Here he insinuates that the child's amazing freshness or potency may also be linked to the powers of darkness. With this glancing remark, James merely hints at this shadowy aspect of the child's nature; readers of *The Turn of the Screw* can better appreciate the extent to which he explored those latent ambiguities. The tantalizing link between a child's youthful freshness, the veritable emblem of human *potential,* and his or her demonic *potency* is one that maddens, as we shall see, not only James's famous governess but also Nabokov's infamous narrator in *Lolita.*

Marveling at the world, Maisie, says James, "treats her friends to the rich little spectacle of objects embalmed in her wonder." Her ability to serve as a wonder-working agent apparently derives from the creative force of imagination. Wonder—the child's distinguishing characteristic for Wordsworth, Blake, and others—evinces the human being's creative potential and, most particularly, the gift of artistic imagination. As soon as James sounds this Wordsworthian note, however, he qualifies or complicates it; in the next sentence, he makes a decisive break with Romantic nostalgia: "She wonders, in other words, to the end, to the death—the death of her childhood, properly speaking." In Maisie "wonder" implies not only innocent rapture but also logic, intelligence, curiosity. Noting what Maisie does "for appearances in themselves vulgar and empty," James adds, "she has simply to wonder, as I say, about them, and they begin to have meanings, aspects, solidities, connexions—connexions with the 'universal'!" (*Art of the Novel*

146–47). The child's wonder *about* as well as *at* the world inevitably leads, James implies, to knowledge that culminates in the experience and responsibility of adulthood.

For James, unlike Wordsworth, the death of childhood marks a necessary, even fortunate termination that is also a culmination. *What Maisie Knew* opens by announcing its theme as this very death. When, at the outset, a distant relative realizes she can do nothing to rescue young Maisie from the internecine war being waged by her estranged parents, she exclaims, "Poor little monkey!" Her "words were an epitaph for the tomb of Maisie's childhood," James's narrator inserts, underscoring the reference to Shakespeare: "Now God help thee, poor monkey!" Lady Macduff says to her son, just before they are viciously murdered by Macbeth's men (*Macbeth* act 4, scene 2). The allusion, while vividly recalling *Macbeth*'s slaughter of the innocents, does not inspire any great pathos here. Instead, James's narrator states matter-of-factly, Maisie "was abandoned to her fate" (19). The death of Maisie's childhood, though premature and therefore regrettable, does not occasion overriding grief, a sense of loss, or even nostalgia. Human growth and maturity, James suggests, are the not inconsiderable benefits every adult should reap from the death of childhood, which is also a beginning.

Innocence, James elsewhere writes, both dawns and dies in the "morning twilight of childhood." This remarkable phrase, which occurs in his 1891 story "The Pupil," comes to the main character Pemberton's mind as he contemplates the startling depth and "lucidity" of his young pupil's "sensibility." In this oxymoronic stage of life, nothing, not even the child's ignorance or innocence, is clear-cut: "he perceived that it was never fixed, never arrested, that ignorance, at the instant one touched it, was already flushing faintly into knowledge, that there was nothing that at a given moment you could say a clever child didn't know" (598). This observation could well serve as an epigraph to *What Maisie Knew*, just as it might offer a helpful, if ironic, introduction to *The Turn of the Screw*. In each of these works James focuses on the fascinating, if inevitable, process by which innocence exposes itself to knowledge and dies—laying to rest, in the process, the Victorian image of childhood.

In *What Maisie Knew* James's narrator implicitly announces this oxymoronic morning twilight of childhood at the opening of the novel's first chapter. Here James instructs the reader to discover what is new in *What Maisie Knew,* the image of childhood itself: "It was to be the fate of this patient little girl to see much more than she first understood, but also even at first to understand much more than any little girl, however patient, *had perhaps ever understood before*" (emphasis added). James's use of the word "before" places Maisie squarely in literary history. Never before in the history of the novel, he implies, has a child's understanding been rendered in so penetrating a manner, to so full an extent. Emphasizing the daring of Maisie's literary-historical mission, the narrator compares the young heroine to "a drummer-boy in a ballad or a story" who finds himself "in the thick of a fight" (23).

The fight refers, of course, not to a military but to a marital conflict. In the thick of this battle Maisie proves inventive and courageous in a way that previous literary children do not—not even Huck Finn, whose resistance to authority I discuss in chapter 5. For all his energy and ingenuity, Huck is passive in regard to the social order; his destiny, as Leslie Fiedler says, is "to suffer and evade" adult strife. Ultimately, Huck does not "take a hand in the affairs of the world, [does not] make something *happen*." His "decision to light out at the end [of the novel] must be understood . . . as the acceptance of his fate, which means to be without regrets what he was from the start: neither hero nor citizen, neither son nor brother—but a stranger and outcast." The novel ends as it began, with "a refused adoption and a flight," a flight from the very knowledge—of evil, sexuality, and death—that threatens the idyll of childhood.[3]

Maisie, by contrast, is impelled by the desire to know—even if the knowledge she seeks spells the death of childhood. Eager to enter the fray, to assume an active role in the world, she proves as worthy a heroine as any of James's adult characters. "The Jamesian child," Muriel Shine observes, "has all the attributes of the distinctive Jamesian heroine—and this is true of his little boys as well as his little girls; adult and child, therefore, tend to become one undifferentiated being."[4] In James the border between childhood innocence and adult experience is remarkably permeable. Shot through with knowledge, the silky wonder of Maisie's innocence is open to experience. As she struggles to cope with "her terribly mixed little world," she is already implicated in "the confusion of life" (*Art of the Novel* 143).

The complex sensibility of James's "interesting small mortal" intrinsically complicates and challenges the Victorians' rarefied image of children—those "genderless angels," in James Kincaid's words, whose "purity" and "harmlessness" function as "cleansing negations," wiping the image of childhood clean of human complexity and leaving "a blank." Singling out David Copperfield as a prime example of childhood made "wonderfully hollow," Kincaid does not mean, I think, that little David's (or Oliver's or, for that matter, Huck's) imagination, fears, loneliness, and longing do not ring true. Rather, he pinpoints the telling "absence of harmfulness"—of willfulness, drive, sexual energy, and identity—in the Dickensian child. Emptied of knowledge, assertiveness, and desire, the "blank image" of the child, Kincaid paradoxically argues, is prey to invasion, manipulation, and eroticization by prurient adults—among whom he includes a considerable number of contemporary as well as Victorian readers.[5]

In contrast to those Victorian children emptied of will, desire, and sexual potency, Maisie participates in the ambiguous confusion of life. No clear and categorical divide exists between her youthful innocence and the knowledge that she, at the age of six, has already embarked on acquiring. Children, James suggests in his preface, very early acquire knowledge of life's contradictions and paradoxes. They recognize the "close connexion of bliss and bale, of the things that help with the things that hurt, . . . [of] somebody's right and ease and the other somebody's pain and wrong." He adds, "Small children have many more perceptions than they have terms to translate them; their vision is at any moment much richer, their apprehension even constantly stronger, than their prompt, their at all producible, vocabulary" (*Art of the Novel* 143, 145).

While complicating the late-Victorian version of childhood, moving it beyond the domain of sentimentalized purity and sexless simplicity, James does not forfeit the Dickensian theme of compassion. Children are vulnerable; they suffer at the hands of harsh and cruel, stupid and selfish adults. Philip Weinstein notes, for example, the many "abrupt and coercive gestures made toward Maisie" by adults who have no regard for her autonomous being.[6] Instead of wagging their fingers and leveling threats like Dickens's self-righteous Pumblechook, James's modern sophisticates blow smoke in Maisie's face and pinch "the calves of her legs till she shriek[s]" (*What Maisie Knew* 24). On occasion, Maisie's rejection by her parents is tinged, though never saturated, with Dickensian pathos. An example occurs in the following passage, in which her mother's sudden show of affection startles Maisie with its heartrending contrast to Ida's customary behavior: "'My own

child,' Ida murmured in a voice—a voice of sudden confused tenderness—that it seemed to [Maisie] she heard for the first time. She wavered
but an instant, thrilled with the first direct appeal, as distinguished
from the mere maternal pull, she had ever had from lips that . . . had
always been sharp" (123).

In a way that also owes something to Dickens, James uses comedy to
relieve the sad and gloomy spectacle of child neglect. In *Great Expectations* part of Mrs. Gargery's comical equipment is the "square impreg-
nable" apron bib she wears "stuck full of pins and needles," successfully
warding off any bid for affection by Pip or Joe (14). The more elegant
bosom of Maisie's mother is similarly bolstered by an array of sharp-
edged jewels and trinkets. When Maisie tries to approach her mother's
breast, sequestered in "a wilderness of trinkets, she [feels] as if she ha[s]
suddenly been thrust, with a smash of glass, into a jeweller's shop-front,
but only to be as suddenly ejected with a push" (123). Dickens's novels
are filled with mothers like Ida Farange whose self-obsession poses a
threat to the child's well-being. In *Bleak House* Mrs. Jellyby, whose zeal
for her charity work lifts her gaze to faraway Borrioboola-Gha, takes
no notice when one of her children gets his head stuck in the porch
railings and another falls down the stairs (70–72). Nor does Mrs.
Pocket, distracted by *her* great expectations, bother to look up from
her book while various Pocket children tumble headfirst over the
footstool hidden beneath her voluminous skirts (*Great Expectations*
204). Only rarely, however, does James expose Maisie's situation, with
heartrending clarity, to the light of Dickensian pathos: Maisie "could
only face doggedly the ugliness of seeming disagreeable, as she used to
face it in the hours when her father . . . called her a dirty little donkey,
and her mother . . . pushed her out of the room" (131).

More frequently, Maisie exhibits amazing resilience in the face of
rejection. Part of her resilience springs, I would suggest, from the
ambiguity and complexity that distinguish her from a host of Victorian child victims. Maisie, for one, sees beyond her years: "There was
something in him [Maisie's father] that seemed, and quite touchingly,
to ask her to help him to pretend—pretend he knew enough about
her life and her education, her means of subsistence and her view of
himself, to give the questions he couldn't put her a domestic tone."
Instilling the blank image of Victorian childhood with the active
element of knowing and wanting to know, James celebrates, in the
words of his narrator, an "innocence so saturated with knowledge and

so directed to diplomacy" that the word takes on new meaning and vitality (148–50).

Maisie's innocence is so saturated with knowledge of what experience entails that even a quarrel with her mother can spark "a vision ominous, precocious" beyond a child's years: "there was literally an instant in which Maisie fully saw—saw madness and desolation, saw ruin and darkness and death" (180). One function of James's narrator, as this passage makes clear, is to supply on Maisie's behalf the language and vocabulary she lacks, in order to convey the full significance of her vision and what awaits her upon the death of her childhood. Thus in a later scene the narrator comments on the "momentary pang" Maisie experiences when she realizes that the absence of Sir Claude's belongings from a table spells his absence from the house: "She was yet to learn what it could be to recognise in some lapse of a sequence the proof of an extinction, and therefore remained unaware that this momentary pang was a foretaste of the experience of death" (228).

In the same way that Maisie remains innocent but prescient, inexperienced but capable of gleaning what experience entails, she transcends the Victorian image of "genderless angel," to recall Kincaid's term. The gendering of the child's image, James makes clear in his preface, was a necessary and deliberate step in the novel's conception and composition. For the "light vessel of consciousness" operating at its center, he chose "a slip of a girl" rather than "a rude little boy." To James the choice was inevitable because, he says, "the sensibility of the female young is indubitably, for early youth, the greater"; and his plan for the novel "would call, on the part of my protagonist, for 'no end' of sensibility" (*Art of the Novel* 143–44). In the novel Maisie's gender proves a defining factor in her relationship with Sir Claude and in the conflict over her guardianship. "The essence of the question," Maisie's stepmother, Mrs. Beale, maintains, is "that a girl wasn't a boy: if Maisie had been a mere rough trousered thing, . . . Sir Claude would have been welcome" to take charge (236). The difficult choice of a guardian, which Maisie makes at the end of the novel, signals the flowering of her mature insight. While James's readers have cause to admire Maisie's precocity, they also recognize in the burden of knowledge she assumes the unambiguous death of her childhood.

The strong attachment between Maisie and Sir Claude paves the way for her ultimate understanding of his weakness for women. It is clear, moreover, that Maisie's attachment to him comprises various

interlocking threads of affection: the "more than filial" attraction of
male and female is as important as the filial bond of stepfather and
child (209). At the outset Sir Claude's beauty as much as his kindness
wins Maisie's heart. And Maisie's own beauty, of character as well as of
countenance, draws the handsome young man to her—as he inadvertently confesses. Their friendship, Sir Claude admits to her, might not
have developed so strongly "if you [Maisie] hadn't had the fatal gift of
beauty—!" (112). As the bond between them develops over the
years—years during which Maisie, of course, is also growing up—Sir
Claude finds himself confiding more and more in his stepdaughter.
Alluding to the dangerous nature of sexual attraction without actually
naming it, he admits to Maisie that he is *afraid* of being adored by his
female friends. When she candidly asks him why he is not, then, afraid
of her (for the obvious reason that she, too, adores him), he spontane-
ously replies, "I *should* be in fear if you were older"—and then breaks
off, embarrassed by what he has said. "See," he quickly adds, "you
already make me talk nonsense" (101).

Sometime later, seated in a cab with Sir Claude, Maisie speaks to
him about her father, Beale Farange. There is nothing obviously sexual
in Maisie's sudden realization that she has been "placing in an inferior
light, to so perfect a gentleman and so charming a person as Sir
Claude," her own father. Only her sense of loyalty, of having betrayed
"so very near a relative as Mr. Farange," causes her to blush "to the
roots of her hair." The depth of Maisie's "unexpected shame" at having
been disloyal to her father is conveyed, nonetheless, in language suggestive of passionate feeling: "at this moment colouring to the roots of
her hair, [Maisie] felt the full hot rush of an emotion more mature
than any she had yet known." It is the violent effect of Maisie's emotion, rather than its specific cause, that in turn embarrasses Sir Claude:
"the violence with which she had just changed colour had brought
into his own face a slight compunctious and embarrassed flush. It was
as if he had caught his first glimpse of her sense of responsibility" (104).
Nothing improper or untoward passes between the young man and
the little girl. Sir Claude does not glimpse a preadolescent's nymphic
limbs or rosebud breasts. What he glimpses, rather, is Maisie's sense of
responsibility—which implicitly announces her approaching maturity.
That sign of maturity also announces the steadily narrowing gap separating Sir Claude's adulthood from Maisie's childhood. By his own
admission, only this gap of years protects the young man from fearing—

that is, desiring—the woman Maisie will become. The border between innocence and experience, the novel again suggests, is not as
absolute or impermeable as that constructed in Victorian versions of
childhood.

As though sensing the relative rather than absolute gap that separates (and protects) him from Maisie, Sir Claude begins, playfully, to
deny her gender. As their mutual affection grows, he frequently addresses her in familiar locutions, alternately calling her "dear boy," "old
man," "my dear old man," and "old chap." At one point Sir Claude and
Maisie are strolling along the harbor of Boulogne when he, having just
addressed her as "dear boy," turns to watch "the fine stride and shining
limbs of a young fishwife who ha[s] just waded out of the sea with her
basketful of shrimps." As Maisie grows aware of her stepfather's "absent
gaze—absent, that is, from *her* affairs"—the reader simultaneously
grows aware of two distinct planes of Sir Claude's identity: virile
young man and fond stepfather (188). One does not have to cite Freud
on the sexual elements in parental love to recognize that the boundary
between those two planes is relative, not absolute.

Both the passing of time, signaling Maisie's maturation, and the
steady growth of her knowledge continually blur the border between
the shades and sources of affection that constitute her bond with Sir
Claude. The passage in which Sir Claude takes leave of Maisie in
Boulogne, to return to Mrs. Beale in England, is couched in suggestive
language that is not obscured by his addressing her as "Maisie boy":

> He turned to his stepdaughter as if at once to take leave of her and
> give her a sign of how, through all the tension and friction, they were
> still united in such a way that she at least needn't worry. "Maisie
> boy!"—he opened his arms to her. With her culpable lightness she
> flew into them and, while he kissed her, chose the soft method of
> silence to satisfy him, the silence that after battles of talk was the best
> balm she could offer his wounds. They held each other long enough
> to reaffirm intensely their vows; after which they were almost forced
> apart by Mrs. Wix's jumping to her feet. (207–8)

Like a young woman clinging to her sweetheart, Maisie rushes into Sir
Claude's open arms with "culpable lightness." Her eagerness to be
kissed as well as to satisfy him complicates the innocent gesture: eagerness quickens her movements and makes culpable their lightness. As
the two cling to each other, intensely reaffirming their vows, Maisie's

governess, Mrs. Wix, only manages to force them apart by violently jumping to her feet.

Mrs. Wix breaks off the embrace not because she detects anything unseemly between the young man and Maisie but because she is violently opposed to his returning to the "immoral" Mrs. Beale. While Sir Claude "wavers," casting about for a way to extricate himself from Mrs. Wix's demands, the situation is resolved, significantly, by Maisie's *female* identity and devotion. As Sir Claude meets "the more than filial gaze of his intelligent little charge," he recognizes a possible exit from the situation: Maisie's gaze "gave him—poor plastic and dependent male—his issue. If she was still a child she was yet of the sex that could help him out. He signified as much by a renewed invitation to an embrace. She freshly sprang to him and again they inaudibly conversed. . . . On which, without another look at Mrs. Wix, he somehow got out of the room" (209).

Later, after Sir Claude returns to Boulogne, where Mrs. Beale has already arrived, Mrs. Wix explains to Maisie that no woman on earth has the power to dislike her charming stepfather. When Maisie argues that her mother must be the exception, having left Sir Claude, Mrs. Wix promptly corrects her, saying, "She loves him—she adores him. A woman knows." To this statement the narrator adds, "Mrs. Wix spoke not only as if Maisie were not a woman, but as if she would never be one" (245). The extent to which Mrs. Wix is mistaken about Maisie's gendered identity is underscored in subsequent scenes. First, having heard that Sir Claude has arrived back in Boulogne, Maisie seeks him out; she finds him in the salon adjacent to the room where his mistress, Mrs. Beale, is presumably asleep. After addressing her—"My dear child, my dear child!"—"he kissed her, he laughed, she thought he even blushed." Embarrassed, even blushing to be found in this way, Sir Claude insists that he has not yet seen Mrs. Beale. But Maisie, alert and suspicious of her female rival, has "the faintest purest coldest conviction that he wasn't telling the truth." Finding it impossible to explain to the child the precise difference between his affection for her and for his mistress, Sir Claude instinctively falls into the role, doubtlessly familiar to him, of guilty lover. Trying to convince Maisie that he loves only her, he cannot help but distort the truth. Thus he says of the beautiful Mrs. Beale, "I don't care about her. I want to see *you*" (248–49).

Later, in the café to which he takes Maisie for breakfast, she queries him on this point. Insisting, once again, that it is "really and truly you

I wanted to see," Sir Claude does not explain his full purpose. As Maisie later discovers, he wants to win her without giving up his mistress; he wants the child to live, as he says, "with me and Mrs. Beale." Admitting that such an arrangement—"I mean the little household we three should make together"—would be "quite unconventional," Maisie's stepfather glosses over the full impropriety of his "proposal," as he later calls it. For Maisie such a domestic arrangement—sharing a household with her stepfather and his mistress—would be further complicated by the fact that, as Mrs. Wix reminds her, Mrs. Beale is not yet divorced from Maisie's father. Further improprieties, only latent at this point, are subtly suggested when, in the process of confiding his scheme to his stepdaughter, Sir Claude suddenly says: "I'm always talking to you in the most extraordinary way, ain't I? One would think you were about sixty and that I—I don't know what any one would think *I* am. Unless a beastly cad!" (259, 274).

Realizing that he is talking to Maisie not as a child but as an equal, Sir Claude draws attention to that steadily narrowing gap between his adulthood and her status as a child—a gap further eroded by Maisie's mental precocity. By rushing to say that Maisie resembles a sixty-year-old, might he be trying to skirt the treacherous abyss lurking beneath this narrowing gap? Or, to put it another way, by verbally whisking Maisie safely past womanhood onto the relatively sexless plane of old age, is Sir Claude unconsciously seeking to maintain the "decent" distance between them? If so, his conscience cannot hold him to it. Despite his "frank pretension to play fair with her, not to use advantages, not to hurry or hustle her," Sir Claude cannot refrain, in subsequent scenes, from using all of his seductive charms to win Maisie over: "It was true that once or twice, on the jetty, on the sands, he looked at her for a minute with eyes that seemed to propose to her to come straight off with him to Paris" (262, 265).

Tempted by those charms, and by her love for Sir Claude, Maisie yields to the fantasy of running away with him. Contrary to the terms of his proposal, however, her fantasy entails leaving the two other women behind—*other* being appropriate here, given that no clear line is drawn between Maisie's identity as a child and her soon-to-be-realized role as a woman: "she even had a mental picture of the stepfather and the pupil established in a little place in the South while the governess and stepmother, in a little place in the North, remain linked by a community of blankness" (265). To the very end of the novel, when Maisie rejects Sir Claude's proposal and offers her guardian the chance to come away with her and leave Mrs. Beale behind, Maisie's moral struggle is couched in romantic terms—terms that Gustave Flaubert's Emma Bovary would surely understand, although she might not comprehend Maisie's power to resist their appeal. Experiencing the temptation to run off with Sir Claude on the train to Paris but refusing to give in to it, Maisie finally sees that she will "have to give him up. It was the last flare of her dream" (272).

Although by giving him up Maisie demonstrates the force of her moral sense to Sir Claude and Mrs. Wix, even that triumph is complicated rather than sentimentally idealized by James's rendering. It is Sir Claude, not James's narrator, who lapses into an "ecstasy" of admiration at Maisie's good sense. Praising her to Mrs. Wix, explaining how the little girl refused to give up her governess and go away with him, Sir Claude offends Maisie's sense of honesty as well as devotion (to him). "I didn't refuse," she insists. "I said I would [give up Mrs. Wix] if he'd give up [Mrs. Beale]." In response, Sir Claude praises Maisie for making "her condition—with such a sense of what it should be! She made the only right one." His "fine appreciation" of her "exquisite" moral sense and "sacred" innocence is now redoubled. Resisting Sir Claude's idealized image of her—as "some lovely work of art or of nature . . . set down among them"—Maisie appears determined to reject the image of herself as sacred icon or divine innocent (273–75). She has powerful feelings and selfish desires, and she declares them in no uncertain terms to Mrs. Wix and Mrs. Beale: "I love Sir Claude— I love *him*," she repeats, making clear that giving him up has been the most painful thing she has ever done (277). Insisting on her own complicated identity, Maisie rejects the efforts, even of the person she loves most, to sentimentalize and idealize her—to erase all contradiction and ambiguity from her nature. Here again James ensures that his image of childhood is not a blank, not emptied of human complexity by those "cleansing negations" of Victorian child worship.

The negation or denial of ambiguous humanity is, in Geoffrey Carter's view, a dominant feature of Dickens's children, especially in their relationship to adults. Carter points out the distinction between Dickens's intuitive understanding of "distorted sexuality," such as Tulkinghorn's "unhealthy passion" in *Bleak House,* and his blindness to "the ambivalence of normal relationships," particularly "those between parents and children." Carter adds, "Often when Dickens writes about the filial relationship, an element of fantasy appears to float in." The "parent is given or offered total love, all-suffering and all-sufficing," regardless of his or her responses or behavior. "At times [Dickens] takes this fantasy a step further and seems to contemplate a sexless marriage between 'father' and daughter," such as "the union of Annie Strong" with "white-haired" Dr. Strong in *David Copperfield* or "the contemplated union of Jarndyce and Esther Summerson" in *Bleak House.* In such instances—which hardly constitute all of the relationships depicted by Dickens—the novelist, says Carter, manifests his age's "determination to believe in false stereotypes of impossible purity as the standard for normal healthy people." No "modern writer," he adds, "has been likely to do this kind of thing"—to uphold, that is, the Victorian standard of impossible purity—since Freud exposed the ambiguities of both parental and filial devotion.[7]

Just as Maisie fixes a more than filial gaze on the handsome young stepfather she adores, she reflects in every aspect of her innocence the complexities, contradictions, and ambiguities intrinsic to our current understanding of human nature and sexuality. Along with the other innovations by which James advanced fiction writing and shaped the twentieth-century novel, he was instrumental, as Shine says, "in stripping the veil of hypocrisy from contemporary representations of children. . . . James gave the child a psychic identity he had rarely had before. Dickens' children had been 'vessels of grace'; with James, they become 'vessels of consciousness.'" So up-to-date is James's rendering of human nature and consciousness that critics, when discussing his turn-of-the-century fiction, tend to forget how many years were to pass before Freud's work would be widely available in English. Thus Maxwell Geismar, discussing *The Sacred Fount* (1901), attributes to James's narrator the stereotypical posture of a mid-twentieth-century Freudian analyst: "He becomes the perfect proto-Freudian analyst, as it were, who is always right, who . . . can rationalize away any action which contradicts his own 'conclusions.'"[8]

By the end of the nineteenth century, as I have suggested, both Freud and James had embarked on their separate but culturally related projects of revising the image of childhood to reflect a more complex appreciation of the nascent human self. As Freud argued in his revolutionary essay on infantile sexuality, altering the child's image is necessary if we are to arrive at a new understanding of fundamental human nature: "One feature of the popular view of the sexual instinct is that it is absent in childhood and only awakens in the period of life described as puberty. This, however, is not merely a simple error but one that has had grave consequences, for it is mainly to this idea that we owe our present ignorance of the fundamental conditions of sexual life."[9] Although James and Freud were both engaged, at virtually the same time, in dismantling this popular view of the child's sexless simplicity, their premises for doing so were as different as their methods.

In *What Maisie Knew* James celebrates an image of the child's inner resourcefulness and resilience that controverts Freud's more deterministic vision: "If there are quarrels between the parents or if their marriage is unhappy," Freud predicts, "the ground will be prepared in their children for the severest predisposition to a disturbance of sexual development or a neurotic illness."[10] Implicitly defying such prognostications, Maisie finds within herself that wonder-working magic— the creative gifts of imagination, spontaneity, curiosity—through which she enlivens and renews a dismal environment of domestic quarrels and parental dissension. Having succeeded, as James says in his preface, in establishing a new domestic "order" and "a fresh tie" for herself— first with Mrs. Beale and then with Sir Claude—Maisie is most remarkable when she proves capable of giving them up. In contrast to her charming stepparents, the child possesses sufficient will and strength of character to forsake the lovely order of a world she helped to create.

Maisie's decision at the novel's close to stay with Mrs. Wix rather than join Sir Claude and Mrs. Beale bespeaks the extent of both her moral sense and her knowledge—knowledge of human weakness as well as of sexual attraction. As she stands on the deck of the steamer that is carrying her and Mrs. Wix back to England, Maisie assures her governess of how much, indeed, she knows. Having glanced back at the shore while the steamer was pulling out, she explains that Sir Claude had already disappeared from view. As she frankly puts it, "He wasn't there." With an adult's surmise, Mrs. Wix answers, "He went to *her.*" To which the child quickly replies, "Oh I know!" (280). Then, in a final tribute to the child's prodigious insight, James closes the novel on the following lines: "Mrs. Wix gave a sidelong look. She still had room for wonder at what Maisie knew."

CHAPTER

3

The Child at a Turning Point
James's *The Turn of the Screw*

In the novella James published a year after *What Maisie Knew,* two prodigious children appear to possess, like Maisie, an innocence both
"saturated with knowledge" and "directed to diplomacy" (*What Maisie
Knew* 150). In this case, however, the children's complexity is more
ominous than charming, inspiring not only wonder but dread in their
governess. In *The Turn of the Screw* Miles and Flora's governess is loath,
indeed horrified, to recognize that children have complex, elusive
inner lives that remain largely hidden from adults. As their governess
grows increasingly invasive of their privacy, the children resort to the
same order of tact and diplomacy that Maisie employs when coping
with adults, particularly her mother and father. To Miles and Flora's
far more attentive guardian, however, the children's naive diplomacy
appears, increasingly, like "hideous" deceit (*Turn of the Screw* 39–40).

The ability to remain silent, to look blank or stupid when adults
make contradictory and impossible demands, is a talent that helps
Maisie survive in the troubled atmosphere of her libertine parents.
Miles and Flora's governess, on the other hand—whether she is acting
from repressive instinct or acute insight—cannot abide the children's
silence and reserve. Insisting at first on their absolute innocence and
purity, she is shocked to learn that they "know," as she later says, "all
that *we* [adults] know—and heaven knows what more besides!" (30).
To many critics, therefore, the governess offers a prime example of
what James Kincaid calls the absolutist impulse of Victorian "child-
loving." The "absolutism amounts to a demand," he says, "that the child
have no reservations, no withholding some secret part of itself." The

cult of childhood ends, paradoxically, by dispossessing the child not only of "things like strength, knowledge, corruption" but also of his or her "being." Even when the governess is forced to relinquish her ideal of childhood innocence, she tries to save Miles and Flora from further knowledge and corruption. She ends by harming and, in Miles's case, destroying the very innocence she worships. Kincaid thus finds, in the only reference he makes to James, that Miles is a perfect example of "the dispossessed child": having given himself "over to purity," he has "nothing left and nothing left to do but to die."[1]

In his preface to *The Turn of the Screw* James alludes to the conflicting interpretations that his "independent and irresponsible little fiction" tends to provoke in its readers and critics (*Art of the Novel* 169). Turning to the tale, we discover that our image of, and assumptions about, the child is central to them all. *The Turn of the Screw* opens with a kind of prologue to the narrative proper; on Christmas Eve, a merry group of adults gather around the fire to enjoy some holiday cheer. With only a week left of the year—and only a few years left of the century—the assembled party is seeing out the old year by exchanging ghost stories. Delighting in terrifying themselves, they testify to the Victorian cult of childhood innocence while they signal its waning influence. Nothing, the houseguests agree, could be more "horrible" (and delectable in the telling) than to imagine a "ghost, or whatever" appearing before a tiny child. It is frightening enough to imagine some emissary from the unknown confronting a startled adult. But how much more "gruesome" (and riveting), more startling (and suggestive) "such a visitation" from the underworld would be if, as one guest enthusiastically remarks, that visit were to "fall on a child." The myth of natural innocence, having played so dominant a role in Victorian literature and culture, adds an exotic flavor to the year-end festivities—notching up the excitement, as James puts it, with yet another "turn of the screw" (1).

Two nights later, Douglas, one of the guests, produces for the assembled company an old manuscript he has been inspired to send for. Written "in old faded ink and in the most beautiful hand," the document arrives from a time already vanished. Now sixty, Douglas explains that he first met the author of the manuscript when he was a young man in college. When Douglas met her, a decade *after* the events narrated in her manuscript had transpired, the author was his sister's governess. Ten years the governess's junior, Douglas admits to having been a little in love with this "charming person," who made so "agreeable" an impression on him and was so "awfully clever and nice." Yet another twenty years were to pass before the governess, on the verge of death, sent him the written account of her tale for safe-keeping. Having kept the manuscript in a locked drawer of his desk for years, Douglas unveils its contents to others for the first time. The story evokes that remote, mid-nineteenth-century era when Douglas was but a small boy and the long-dead governess only twenty years old (2).

The governess was scarcely more than a child herself when she arrived at the estate of Bly to take up her first post, though she recounts her story from the perspective of a woman many years older and wiser. The narrator knows herself to have been, at the mere age of twenty, impressionable and "easily carried away." She describes her young self, arriving at Bly on "a lovely day" in June, as brimming with romantic dreams—dreams that appear, at first glance, delightfully fulfilled by the fairy-tale charm of the estate. From her "present older and more informed" perspective, she qualifies such youthful fancy, admitting that the estate and its surroundings would now have "a very reduced importance" in her eyes. To the young dreamer, however, the world of Bly is enchantment itself. Bathed in "summer sweetness," the surrounding countryside greets her with a show of "bright flowers" and a "golden sky" full of twittering birds (9, 7). The estate and its environs enchantingly re-create, as Reinhard Kuhn observes, that mythically "perfect childhood paradise" evoked by Rousseau in his *Confessions*.[2]

Enchantment redoubles when the governess beholds her two young wards for the first time. Eight-year-old Flora, with her sweet face and "hair of gold," strikes the young woman as "the most beautiful child I had ever seen"—a "vision" of "angelic beauty" evoking spiritual as well as physical perfection. Like "one of Raphael's holy infants," the child gazes up at her new teacher with "placid heavenly eyes"—creating in the latter the impression of a romantic as well as Renaissance ideal: "a castle of romance inhabited by a rosy sprite" (7–8). Similarly, Flora's ten-year-old brother, Miles, turns out to be "incredibly beautiful." His image radiates a "great glow of freshness, the same fragrance of purity," the governess adds, "in which I had from the first moment seen his little sister." Most "divine" of all is Miles's air of absolute "innocence"—an "indescribable air of *knowing nothing* in the world but love" (13, emphasis added).

Such a vision of innocent perfection—the blank purity of child-hood—is by this time, however, somewhat vexed. The governess already knows that Miles has been abruptly dismissed from school. Although the school officials "go into no particulars," the boy's dismissal is irrevocable; it is "impossible," they state in a letter, "to keep him" at school. That, as the governess says, "can have but one meaning": Miles has proved "an injury" to his schoolmates (10, 11). Still, the young woman is an ardent disciple of Rousseauian faith; she declares the officials' action "grotesque." Nature, the world she beholds with her eyes, cannot be so deceitful. The proof of the matter, she insists, lies in the limpidity of the child's beauty—"the real rose-flush of his innocence." Appealing to Mrs. Grose, the housekeeper, for confirmation, the governess declares, "My dear woman, *look* at him!" Miles, she adds, is simply "too fine and fair for the little horrid unclean school-world" that has rejected him (14, 19).

When the governess spies the first of a series of ghostly apparitions, the idyllic spell is again interrupted: "the rooks stopped cawing in the golden sky and the friendly hour lost for the unspeakable minute all its voice" (16). But enchantment quickly resumes, and she again takes up her charmed life with the two "cherubs," luxuriating in "the romance of the nursery and the poetry of the schoolroom." All the vexing qualities of mundane existence seem magically suspended—all signs of the customary "grind," tedium, and "grey prose" banished from the poetry of this classroom (19). As the narrator later realizes, there is something rash and even unhealthy in her eagerness to retreat. Her behavior draws attention to the romantic decline noted by Peter Coveney: from the mid-nineteenth century the "original romantic" vision of Wordsworth and Blake was gradually devolving into the "debased-romantic, Victorian concepts of innocence." Originally an "active image" emphasizing the human being's "potency," the innocent child was gradually becoming a static symbol of "withdrawal" from life. As the emphasis shifted away from creative celebration to "negative assertion," the romantic image of childhood became associated not with renewal but with moral and psychological "retreat."[3]

Certainly there is more than a little negative assertion in the governess's own need to retreat. As she points out, "disturbing" messages keep arriving at Bly "from [her] home, where things were not going well," but she staves them off: "with this joy of my children what things in the world mattered?" In hindsight, however, she acknowledges the "spell" in which she was caught up and admits that it was to a great extent self-induced: "Of course I was under the spell, and the wonderful part is that, even at the time, I perfectly knew I was. But I gave myself up to it; it was an antidote to any pain, and I had more pains than one" (20). Identifying the spell as drug or antidote to life's pain, the governess as narrator implicitly indicts the debased-romantic nature of her idyllic retreat.

It is the governess's curiosity, an eagerness to *know* worthy of Maisie, that speeds the demise of the romantic idyll. Miles's dismissal from school and the mystery shrouding his departure ultimately goad her to find out more about the child—no matter how divine his air of unknowing innocence. Her initial denial of any fault on Miles's part proves logically too flimsy for a young woman of her intelligence. If the school from which he was sent down is as horrid and unclean as she declares it, the grounds for his dismissal must be equally extreme. Whatever Miles may have done or "said," as he himself later admits, his behavior has been judged substandard by a headmaster and staff undoubtedly inured to the crude pranks and nasty habits of young boys (86). As the governess's investigations uncover, in her eyes at least, a wealth of clues pointing to some unhealthy influence on the children, she becomes vigilant in her determination to protect them. Eventually convinced that they know all about the illicit sexual relationship between the now dead Peter Quint and Miss Jessel, the governess tries to shield Miles and Flora from their ghostly influence, which she perceives as contaminating the children from beyond the grave. Shouldering her terrible burden of knowledge—of the passion, fury, and possible murderousness "between the two wretches"—the governess registers the collapse of her romantic faith in the drastically altered image that the children subsequently assume in her eyes (36).

The Rousseauian paradise begins to seem uncanny even when the ghosts are not around. The children are too perfect, too well behaved, too eager to *appear* perfect in the governess's eyes. Performing prodigious feats of memory and mimicry, they strike her as a parody or caricature of innocence rather than its authentic embodiment. As the governess watches Miles and Flora get "better and better" at "diverting, entertaining, surprising her," she sees how clever they are at "reading her passages, telling her stories, acting her charades, pouncing out at her in disguises, as animals and historical characters, and above all astonishing her by the 'pieces' they had secretly got by heart and could interminably recite." They are cunning performers indeed, as they play at being everything from tigers and Romans to Shakespeareans, astronomers, and navigators (39). Discovering a "grotesque" disparity between semblance and reality, the governess scans the faces of her wards for signs of their duplicity. Mirroring her own altered vision, "their false little lovely eyes" stare back at her with falsely "innocent wonder." Their innocence now strikes her as a "fraud" or contrivance— not natural innocence but "unnatural goodness" (58, 48). Once the governess loses faith in the children's innocence, she rapidly arrives at more dire conclusions. Behind their artificial gestures and elaborate games she begins to detect more dreadful forms of unnatural—that is, abnormal and perverse—behavior. Although never precisely defined, the children's apparent complicity with the ghosts comes to signify, for the disillusioned young woman, something terrible, even "monstrous" about reality.

The image of the child—that once limpid vessel of purity and inno-cence—now yields a cracked mirror reflecting the grotesqueness of a world that can never be made whole. Gazing at Miles's countenance, the governess says, "I seemed to see in the beautiful face with which he watched me how ugly and queer I looked" (55). In the child's serene and lovely gaze the adult senses what she can read not *there* but only in herself: ugly suspicion and awkward distress. Despite its surface loveliness, moreover, there is something grotesque about Miles's beau-tiful face as the governess now perceives it. Far from reflecting the state of his soul, his countenance serves as a kind of optical device with which, as she puts it, he surveys the world and cannily watches her. How rapidly she has lost the idealized world of romance and assumed our disenchanted condition. If nature offers members of contemporary Western society a mirror, it is a mirror irrevocably cracked, distortive, fragmentary. What we find in its prisms is not a single trustworthy image, a stable and coherent universe, but endless uncertainty, confu-sion, duplicity. The more we look, the more ambiguity we discover: the culture in the creature, the guile in the child.

The appearance of Quint's and Jessel's ghosts is the most obvious catalyst for the governess's drastically altered vision. When she perceives the ghosts communicating with the children, she becomes thoroughly "disenchanted," divested of her romantic vision. The appearance of these strange figures is not the only apparition to influence her youth-ful perception, however. On her first day at Bly, she comes face-to-face with another compelling image: her head-to-toe reflection in the mirror. Describing the impact that Bly's richly appointed rooms make on her, she singles out the "long glasses in which, for the first time, I could see myself from head to foot." She has never beheld such a vision before because, as the daughter of a poor country parson, she has not had access to such domestic luxuries as full-length mirrors (7, 4).

Only when she arrives at Bly does she find herself the proud inhabitant of a large, impressive, and richly furnished room boasting not one but several "long glasses." What must this provincial young woman think when first she gazes, at length and in private, at the head-to-foot image of herself in the mirror? It would hardly be seemly for the Victorian narrator to tell us—but her reference to her "first time" invites readers to ponder the significance of the young woman's sensual, if not sexual, awakening. At the heart of Bly's refinements and luxuries, the governess discovers nature—in the guise of both the children's altered image and her own. In the latter alteration she sees herself for the first time not as she appears to others but as a naked form: a body as defined and developed as the "figured full draperies" adorning her room (7). So graphic an encounter with, or exposure to, one's body signals that new stage of awareness that Gérard Vincent, borrowing a term from psychoanalysis and applying it to modern culture, calls the "historical 'mirror stage.'" This new stage in Western culture and consciousness, he suggests, began at the end of the nineteenth century, when wider availability of the full-length mirror allowed great numbers of people "to view the body not as it appeared in society but in total nudity."[4]

This altering experience on her first day at Bly serves as a fitting announcement of the startling revelations to follow: her imminent discovery of the ghosts' haunting presence and the revelation that the children are not what they seem. In a sense, the altered image of the children in the governess's eyes acts as a reflection, a kind of picture in reverse, of the new self-image she acquires in Bly's "long glasses." Both of these altered images suggest that nothing is what it seems or what she has thought. The mirrors in the governess's room cunningly report her existence as a body in nature. At the same time, what she took for nature in the children, their absolute purity or natural innocence, now appears a construct, or crafted illusion. Without art, moreover—the artifice of the mirror or the children's cunning performance—neither of these natural-seeming images would be perceptible.

Like the officials who dismiss Miles from school, the governess is reticent about the exact nature or extent of the children's perceived corruption. Even if readers are convinced that the children were contaminated by their relationship with the living Quint and Jessel— and many of James's critics are not—they still must formulate the precise nature and degree of that contamination. As James says in the preface, the novella contains "no eligible *absolute*" by which the "action" of the "haunting pair" can be judged. The nature or extent of the "wrong" committed "remains relative to fifty other elements, a matter of appreciation, speculation, imagination—these things moreover quite exactly in the light of the spectator's, the critic's, the reader's experience" (*Art of the Novel* 176). Less subject to doubt and uncertainty than the source or nature of the children's perceived corruption is the *effect* of this discovery on the governess. Withholding any objective knowledge of the causes of the perceived contamination, James supplies plenty of tantalizing evidence of its effects. Readers may speculate about those causes, in other words, only *after* assessing their effects.

One obvious effect on the governess is her growing obsession with the beings whose contaminating influence on the children she resolves to destroy. As she endeavors to "save" Miles and Flora from these ghostly "demons," she becomes increasingly "haunted" by them (85). When bleak autumn arrives, the change of season announces a much more permanent change in her subjectively perceived universe. "The spring of gay, bright human innocence," as Robert Heilman puts it, "has given way," in both senses, to "the dark *fall.*"[5] Knowledge of passion, sexual jealousy, tragic death now permeates her psychic landscape. In the arcadian world where she had sought refuge from disturbing reality, she comes face-to-face with harbingers of human guilt and suffering. Sex and death, anguish, bitterness, and fury announce themselves in the figures of Quint and Jessel. With the demise of the pastoral dream, the governess steels herself to confront "the very worst that was to be known" (52).

In the short time since the governess's arrival at Bly on that "golden" summer day, eternity has collapsed. In the children's altered image she reads the end not only of childhood but of faith, her faith in original innocence. The sweet "fragrance of purity" no longer wafts from the children's angelic presence; their image is bereft of any "glow of freshness" in her eyes (13). Despite his tender age, Miles is no longer young; in a few swift months he has become "an older person."

Similarly, observing Flora in communication with the figure she identifies as Miss Jessel's ghost, the governess comments: "She's not alone, and at such times she's not a child: she's an old, old woman"—an observation she repeats a short time later (69, 71–72). The daughter of a clergyman, the governess experiences the loss of innocence as an expulsion from paradise—a fall into experience, time, history. She has lost that ideal world mythicized by Rousseau and cultivated by her romantic imagination.

This terrifying fall, an event staged primarily within the governess's consciousness, accounts for the sudden and awful aging of the children in her eyes. It is as though, thrust outside the paradise they were perceived to inhabit, Miles and Flora must assume the burden of human history. It is the governess's growing awareness of Miles's "previous life," as she puts it, that signals his expulsion from the perfect world of childhood. Registering the shock of that discovery, she recalls to Miles "the first hour I saw you," when "you seemed so perfectly to accept the present" (63). Like Adam and Eve, the "angelic" children, perceptibly tainted by shame and self-consciousness, are now subject to time and mortality.

Narrating from an "older and more informed" perspective her version of paradise lost, the governess speaks of the "trap" that those first enchanted days at Bly presented to her "imagination" and "vanity." Whereas she now acknowledges, as narrator, how rough a future life holds for any child, no matter how seemingly pure and perfect, she admits that at the time she could not imagine any ordinary "rough future" for Miles and Flora. The only "form" that their "afteryears" took in her young "fancy" was "that of a romantic, a really royal extension of the garden and the park." With another note of self-irony, the grown-up narrator points out the glaring difference between the "charming" figure of a man she dreamed of meeting on her walks at Bly and the dreadful apparition she saw instead (15–16). Though "dangerous" and finally fatal to romantic vision, this figure is the "detestable presence" she must acknowledge as part of the mortal, or human, scheme of things. Thus she says, when describing her third encounter with Peter Quint's grim ghost, "He knew me as well as I knew him." Their meeting "was as human and hideous as a real interview: hideous just because it *was* human" (41).

Later in the narrative, when the figure of Miss Jessel, "seated" at the governess's "own table," appears to her in the schoolroom, it wordlessly reminds her of the bond between them. Jessel used to occupy the governess's position: "in her black dress, her haggard beauty and her unutterable woe, she had looked at me long enough to appear to say that her right to sit at my table was as good as mine to sit at hers. While these instants lasted indeed I had the extraordinary chill of a feeling that it was I who was the intruder." In feeling herself an intruder, the governess subliminally acknowledges Miss Jessel's right to occupy her place in this schoolroom and at Bly. At the same time, she registers her keen understanding of the dead woman's suffering and unutterable woe. Expressing both sympathy and hostility for this "tragic" figure, she cries out to the ghost, "You terrible miserable woman!" But the ghost's "awful image" has already vanished, and the governess might as well be speaking to herself (59). Knowledge of suffering and evil brings the young woman face-to-face with an altered image not only of the child but of herself—an implication borne out by her affinity with that dreadful other.

Among the disclosures the narrator makes, one is especially telling: "In going on with the record of what was hideous at Bly," she says, "I ... challenge the most liberal faith" of the auditor—a rudeness or rupture about which "I little care" (40). James's narrator is candid about her indifference to the romantic faith she once held and to the distress, or incredulity, her story may provoke in others who still enjoy such liberal faith. By no means a tragic figure in the full sense of the term, she evinces, all the same, the "tragic consciousness" that, according to Erich Heller, marks "the end of a tradition" and "a new departure." To "live within a tradition means to enjoy," says Heller, "the privileges of innocence": to agree "not to ask certain questions, to narrow the domain of the questionable, and grant the mind a firm foundation of answers." James's self-declared fairy tale rings changes in a minor key on this age-old theme of paradise lost. At Bly as in Eden, knowledge spells the death of innocence; its privileges give way to a new vision of reality. In the governess's altered gaze the image of the child, of the self, of the world—all enter the domain of the questionable.[6]

Everything about the design and composition of *The Turn of the Screw* constructs this domain of the questionable. Even if readers accept that the ghosts are "real" rather than figments of the governess's mind, the source of their influence on the children remains enigmatic. Faced at every turn with the questionable, each reader participates in creating the novel's meaning by building on the elusive and ambigu-

ous image of childhood. That is why, in surveying the voluminous
criticism on this novella, one can learn as much about a critic's construction of childhood as about the governess's. For the reader as for
the narrator, the image of childhood is crucial: it is the nexus or axis
on which meaning accretes and events acquire significance. When a
critic like Mark Spilka, for example, interprets the story, his Freudian
assumptions are candidly put forward. In "Turning the Freudian
Screw," he says, "The appearance of such ghosts to children suggests
one of the most basic Freudian principles, that of infantile sexuality,
which James clearly anticipates."[7] What the governess perceives as
evidence of the ghosts' corruption of the children, Spilka regards as
natural, as innate in all children.

Developing this line of argument, other critics have pointed out
that the governess seems to *know* intimately, to recognize immediately,
these mysterious apparitions of forbidden sexuality. When, for example,
she encounters Quint's ghost for the second time, she says, "it was as if
I had been looking at him for years and had known him always" (20).
In discovering the children's intimate acquaintance with these "sex-
ghosts," Spilka contends, the governess is forced to confront nothing
less than the facts of human nature. Knowledge of the child's sexuality
is what she has both known and repressed for years—years going back
to the time when she was a child.

From a less sanguine perspective, however, what happens to the
children seems every bit as horrifying as the governess finds it, even
though Victorian reticence keeps her from naming the dread thing
that she knows. Many contemporary readers, exposed to the massive
literature on and media coverage of child abuse, are less likely to assume,
as does Spilka, that the children's contact with Quint and Jessel has
been normal or healthy. Are there not sexual overtones in the "deep
and hard" stare of Quint's ghost as it "hungrily hover[s]" in search of
Miles (46)? In a "flash" the governess realizes "that it was not for me
[that Quint's ghost] had come. He had come for someone else." It is
this terrible "knowledge," which comes to her "in the midst of dread,"
that sparks her sense of "duty" and steels her to protect the children
from further interference (20–21). At one point Mrs. Grose all but
confirms the sexual nature of Quint's relationship with Miles, saying
to the governess, "It was Quint's own fancy. To play with [Miles], I
mean—to spoil him." After a brief pause, she adds, "Quint was much
too free." At this moment the governess has a "vision of [Quint's] face,"

whose deep and hard stare has filled her with such dread, and suffers "a sudden sickness of disgust." When she asks Mrs. Grose whether Quint was "too free with *my* boy?" the housekeeper answers, "Too free with everyone" (26).

The governess assumes that by "everyone" Mrs. Grose means both males and females. "I forbore for the moment," says the governess, "to analyse this description further than by the reflexion that a part of it applied to several of the members of the household, of the half-dozen *maids and men* who were still of our small colony" (26, emphasis added). The suggestion that Quint had sexual relations with people of both sexes is underscored later in the story; once again the reader is reminded of the mixed composition of the household staff—"the maids and the men" from whom Quint apparently chose his sexual partners (79). In this context Mrs. Grose's repeated references to the inclusive nature of Quint's choice of victims—"everyone" and "them all"—take on pointed significance. On yet another occasion the housekeeper says of Quint's "infamous" and "dreadful" conduct, "I've never seen one like him. He did what he wished." Here the governess assumes the reference to be both person- and gender-specific. Referring to Miss Jessel, she asks, "With her?" Once again Mrs. Grose is ambivalent in her reply: "With them all" (33).

To contemporary readers the "deadly view" that the governess keeps "forbidding [her]self to entertain" seems obvious. Among those "secret disorders" and "vices" practiced by Quint is pedophilia (37, 28). What else are we to make of Mrs. Grose's statement to the governess that "for a period of several months Quint and the boy had been perpetually together." It was Miles's habit, moreover, to deny those occasions, so obvious to Mrs. Grose, "when [he and Quint] had been about together quite as if Quint were his tutor . . . and Miss Jessel only for the little lady. When he had gone off with the fellow, I mean, and spent hours with him." Miss Jessel's complicity in these lies is also apparent to the housekeeper, who says that the former governess "didn't mind. She didn't forbid [Miles]." While Miles "was with the man," Mrs. Grose continues, "Miss Flora was with the woman." Then she adds in yet another ambivalent reference, "It suited them all!" (36–37).

That Miss Jessel may have had her own (sexual) reasons for going along with Quint and Miles's relationship is also implied in the text. Just before the governess holds this conversation with Mrs. Grose, she walks with Flora by the large pond or lake on Bly's grounds. Seated with the child next to the water, the governess suddenly realizes that Flora is being watched by "an interested spectator" whose "identity" quickly becomes clear to her. Dressed in black, the "pale and dreadful" figure is no other than Miss Jessel's ghost. Later, discussing what she has seen with Mrs. Grose, the governess describes the terrifying manner in which the apparition "fixed the child" in its gaze, a "fury of intention" blazing from its "awful eyes." Although Flora fails to give any "sign either of interest or of alarm," the governess says that "all spontaneous sounds from her had dropped." Having "turned her back to the water"—and to the ghostly spectator—Flora appears ignorant of the apparition's presence (29–32). The governess is convinced, however, that Flora is merely playing her customary game of innocence.

At this point the governess describes to the housekeeper the exact manner in which Flora pretends to busy herself: "She had picked up a small flat piece of wood which happened to have in it a little hole that had evidently suggested to her the idea of sticking in another fragment that might figure as a mast and make the thing a boat. This second morsel, as I watched her, she was very markedly and intently attempting to tighten in its place" (29–30). Although the child seems to be fashioning a little boat out of fragments of wood, the language of the governess's description evokes a far more telling pattern of gesture and meaning. In Flora's sticking a tiny wooden shaft into the little hole of another piece of wood, contemporary readers are likely to detect another game, as the child imitates the motions of sexual intercourse. The language James assigns to his narrator, whether or not she is conscious of it, is freighted with sexual implication. The word "morsel" charges the image of dead matter with a kind of fleshy pliancy associated not with bits and pieces of wood but with delectable tidbits of food—or, extending the association, with the parts of a body. While the details of Flora's little game are visually striking, the source or cause of these suggestive gestures remains unclear. Confronted once again by the domain of the questionable, James's readers must decide whether the sexual act suggested by Flora's handling of the wooden pieces is, as critics from Edmund Wilson to Shoshana Felman maintain, a projection of the governess's own repressed sexual impulses.[8] If not, they must decide whether Flora may have witnessed Quint and Jessel having sex; whether Miles may simply have "said things" to his little sister about his own sexual activity—as he claims to have "said things" to his classmates (things sufficiently scandalous to bring on his dismissal from school); or whether Flora may have been subjected by Jessel, Quint, or even Miles to the physical manipulations she graphically delineates.

Whether the governess is blind to or represses the full import of what she sees—and what her language so vividly conveys—readers alert to the signs of child abuse can hardly disagree with the conclusion she reaches: that, as she tells Mrs. Grose in the following scene, the children "know, they know . . . all that *we* know—and heaven knows what more besides!" (30). When Mrs. Grose asks her whether the gaze that Jessel fixes on Flora is full of "dislike," the governess promptly answers, "God help us, no. Of something much worse." The ghost's "fury of intention," she implies, expresses not dislike but desire—desire "to get hold of" the child. Visibly shaken by the suggestion that the ghost's intense stare may have expressed the dead woman's passion or lust for the child, Mrs. Grose can only respond with a silent "shudder" (32).

Silent but eloquent, Mrs. Grose's involuntary shudder is a fitting tribute to the "unnamed" horror emblematized by James's apparitions, who emanate from that "forbidden ground" of unspeakable desire. Impelled to acknowledge that secret terrain, the governess cannot bring herself to name it. She gives the reader to understand, however, that what she once described as "the very worst . . . to be known" falls short of the unspeakable truth. In the end she is convinced that "whatever I had seen, Miles and Flora saw *more*—things terrible and unguessable and that sprang from dreadful passages of intercourse [with Quint and Jessel] in the past." As the dense "element of the unnamed" accretes, permeating the governess's experience at Bly, it forms an atmosphere of doubt and suspicion that darkens and finally obliterates her original vision of the child (50–53). In much the same way, that element of the unnamed charges and changes the meaning of what is spoken.

Take, for example, the passage in which the governess expresses her relief at being temporarily spared the ghosts' presence: "I continued unmolested; if unmolested one could call a young woman whose sensibility had, in the most extraordinary fashion, not declined but deepened" (52). Given the atmospherics provided by the element of the unnamed, the word "unmolested"—as neutral as it might seem in another context—here carries an explosive charge. By associating the oppressive presence of the ghosts with molestation, the governess calls attention to those unspeakable vices and disorders of which Quint is "more than suspected" but which she cannot name. Only near the end of her story, after she resolves to wrest Miles away from Quint's demonic influence, does the governess come close to naming the "hideous" truth: "the truth," as she says, "that what I had to deal with was, revoltingly, against nature" (80). In this telling little phrase, "against nature," a proper Victorian young lady sums up—as best she can and as explicitly as she dare—all that is monstrous, abnormal, *unspeakable* in her restricted universe.

The element of the unnamed carries such dreadful connotations that many critics have sought to dissociate the children from its corrupting influence. According to some, the ghosts that the governess perceives do not implicate the children in any dark or corrupting experience because they are mere figments or hallucinations of her overwrought, neurotic mind. While the arguments made in favor of Miles and Flora's innocence run to great length and complexity (critics of this camp must explain, for example, why the governess can describe Quint's red hair and other features to Mrs. Grose *before* she is told who he was and how he looked), the children tend to be treated as static images of innocence, passive victims of the governess's fears and fantasies.[9]

Vexing the various, often ingenious arguments seeking to remove the troublesome ghosts from the fictional landscape and install them in the governess's mad mind is the unresolved question of genre. Why, if the ghosts clearly and unambiguously do *not* exist within the frame of the fiction, did James take pains to emphasize his reasons for writing a contemporary "ghost-story"—one, he pointedly added, that would elicit the reader's "conscious and cultivated credulity"? In his preface James describes the specific difficulties as well as the "irresistible" appeal of trying to create his own modern version of a "sinister romance." What he was patently *not* interested in writing, James says, was a ghost story in name only: the "mere modern 'psychical' case, washed clean of all queerness as by exposure to a flowing laboratory tap." By displaying the "credentials" of a modern education, with all its scientific underpinnings, a contemporary writer of "ghost-stories" would be tempted to render his "apparitions" in the clear light of reason, analysis, and documented case histories. Instead of rousing "the dear old sacred terror," hygienic reason would produce a "respectably certified" account of once fertile mysteries and resonant "night-fears" (*Art of the Novel* 169–70, 174).[10]

Commenting, a decade after James published his preface, on the author's masterful achievement in *The Turn of the Screw,* Virginia Woolf expressly admires the way he managed to avoid this pitfall. Noting the inevitable urge of twentieth-century readers to "reason away" James's mysterious ghosts, she maintains that, "for all our reasoning," they "return" to haunt us. Their mystery is their meaning, Woolf suggests, for they make us "afraid of something unnamed, of something, perhaps, in ourselves." They are "present whenever the significant overflows our powers of expressing it; whenever the ordinary appears ringed by the strange." In their comments both Woolf and James are perceptibly wary of the cleansing operations of scientific reason, which reifies the "sacred terror" of the "unnamed" and does away with the "peculiar *frisson,*" as Millicent Bell puts it, that the "tale's built-in ambiguity" induces in the reader.[11]

Ironically, and exactly in the manner the author refutes in his preface, many critics have tried to cleanse James's ghost story of its ghosts. Subjected to a stream of scientific analysis, these troubling apparitions dissolve into mere figments of the governess's disturbed mind—which the critic proceeds to diagnose. The modern reader's preference for the apparatus, or "flowing laboratory tap," of clinical analysis thus exposes an unforeseen connection between two cultures often characterized as polarized opposites: the Victorians, with their moralistic insistence on the child's sexual simplicity, and twentieth-century readers, with their reliance on the no-less-rigid codes of scientific analysis. Both may be seen to share a common source. Perhaps for this reason James Kincaid provocatively echoes James's metaphor of the flowing laboratory tap when he comments—without specific reference to James, however—on the "cleansing negations" of Victorian prudery and child worship. In each case the observer's hygienic intent, if you will, is to eradicate mystery: to cleanse the image of the child and of perceived reality of *haunting* ambiguity.

By cleansing James's ghost story of the ambiguous presence of ghosts—attributing their appearance to the unstable, hallucinatory, or demented perceptions of the governess—contemporary critics, like their Victorian predecessors, venture to cleanse the child's image of any impurities. As if by magic, in this case the magic of analysis, the child is restored to angelic purity and innocence. Thus, as Mark Spilka points out, both Freudian and non-Freudian interpretations of the story often prove "oddly Rousseauistic." By insisting that the children are "passive or unwilling victims without positive desires," these critics, Spilka adds, betray a surprising "belie[f] in Original Innocence."[12]

If, as suggested earlier, James's "perfectly independent . . . little fiction" tends to undermine the myth of childhood purity, the story also testifies to the enduring power of that idyll. As so much of the critical commentary demonstrates, the most sophisticated and knowledgeable of James's readers often prove as susceptible to the romantic myth of the child as the idealistic young governess. Even Peter Coveney, though he describes with persuasive authority the decline of "Victorian concepts of innocence" into static sentimentality and the desire for "withdrawal," succumbs to some of the "debased-romantic concepts of innocence" he categorically deplores. In contrast to those who would deny any contamination of the child's image, however, Coveney finds Miles and Flora clearly implicated in the ghosts' corrupt history. Not only do the children communicate with the ghosts, but they are *absolutely* ruined by them. In Coveney's view the "depravity of the children is a given fact." The figure Coveney holds responsible for the children's "corruption," however, is neither the governess nor the demonic ghosts. Instead, James alone is to blame for having created the "given facts" of the tale, for having written it the way he did. *The Turn of the Screw,* Coveney concludes, "is not a significant work of James's art, but the product of a seriously disordered sensibility. It is not really a piece for literary analysis at all; but something patently for the psychiatrist."[13]

Shocked by the writer's failure to foster faith in the child's absolute purity and sexual innocence, the critic in his response strangely echoes the initial, horrified reaction of James's governess, whom, ironically, Coveney deems "neurotic." Uncertain to the end about what the children may in fact *know,* the governess cannot tolerate the possibility that they are implicated in that dark, forbidden world of sexuality represented by the ghosts. Convinced, as Coveney puts it, of the "corruption" such knowledge spells for the children, she attempts to "save" them from those dark "demons"—and inadvertently brings on young Miles's death. Read from this vantage, James's tale reveals the terrible price that "debased-romantic concepts of innocence" exact from the children whose innocence they exalt. As Coveney argues, the Victorians, having "taken to themselves the romantic image of the child, . . . negated its power. The image is transfigured into the image of an innocence which dies. It is as if," he adds, "so many [Victorians] placed on the image the weight of their own disquiet and dissatisfaction, their impulse to withdrawal, and, in extremity, their own wish for death."[14]

With the full weight of her own dread and disquiet, the governess bears down so heavily on Miles that he dies. The effort either to keep his secret or to be free of her controlling influence proves too much for his frail body. The motive for Miles's resistance remains enigmatic, but the effect is clearly fatal. By refusing to release the child in her grip, the governess dispossesses him of life. In contrast to Coveney's negative assessment, Spilka finds that James's ghost story speaks with the power of a nineteenth-century "fable" in which "two lovely children . . . are exposed to outside evil in the form of sex-ghosts": "To their rescue comes a maternal young lady, full of domestic affection and attuned to sexual evil, saintly and prurient in the Best Victorian manner. The young woman proceeds to fight the invading evil in the name of hothouse purity and domestic sainthood. That she destroys the children in saving them is understandable: her contemporaries were doing so all around her, and would do so for the next six decades."[15]

Spilka's reading has the advantage of acknowledging, rather than explaining away, the central theme and presence of ghosts in James's self-declared ghost story. In reading *The Turn of the Screw* as a Victorian fable, however, one in which the governess is assigned the role of hothouse prude, Spilka may be subjecting the story's ambiguous effects to the same cleansing operations that, in his view, "oddly Rousseauistic" critics use to declare their faith in "Original Innocence." Not the governess's role, nor Quint's and Jessel's sexual influence on the children, nor the meaning of this alleged fable is as clear-cut as he assumes.

Rather than viewing the story as a fable of Victorian sexual repression, contemporary readers are likely, as mentioned earlier, to regard it as a subtle exploration of the forbidden world of child–adult sexual relations and the fog of ambiguities and contradictions that enshrouds it. To adults or social authorities who, like the governess, endeavor to interrogate the suspected victims of this formerly unnamed evil, the child's silence or ambivalence can present the greatest obstacle and source of frustration. As so many court cases and conferences dealing with charges of child abuse demonstrate, the battalions of psychological experts hired by lawyers on each side often leave the observer, or jury, with as great an appreciation of problematic reality as *The Turn of the Screw* leaves James's readers. On the other hand, to maintain that James's ghost story says as much about the most timely issues and ambiguities of contemporary culture as it does about Victorian repression will not bring us any closer to fixing the image of childhood it reflects. To those familiar with Michel Foucault's reading of modern history and sexuality, for example, James's novella presents not a fable about child abuse but, quite the opposite, a precocious indictment of modern culture—where open inquiry into human sexuality has worked not to liberate but to codify and control its energies.

This inquiry or "discursive explosion," Foucault maintains in *The History of Sexuality*, began at the end of the eighteenth century and continued expanding into the twentieth, when it mushroomed into a social force or power of devastating proportions. Never before in the history of the West, he argues, has the "sexuality of children" as well as adults come under such massive scrutiny. By the nineteenth century, Foucault notes, authorities in charge of the social order believed "it was time for all these figures, scarcely noticed in the past"—"children, mad men and women, and criminals"—"to step forward and speak, to make the difficult confession of what they were." From this perspective James's governess simply takes up the charge that, according to Foucault, sundry social authorities were defining as their sacred duty: "to protect" society from the "perils" of sex, "everywhere" to be "driven out of hiding." For the governess, as for other guardians of health and welfare, sexuality becomes "something akin to a secret whose discovery is imperative, a thing . . . dangerous and precious to divulge."[16]

Just as the governess comes to view the children as corrupt, so her peers in real life, a Foucauldian reading might suggest, came to identify those whose sexual conduct could not be regulated as sick. Not only Miles and Flora but their alleged predators, the former manservant and governess, fit rather precisely into the social drama Foucault describes. These "scandalous, dangerous victims" and "outcasts" were regarded, he says, as *"prey to a strange evil that also bore the name of vice* and sometimes *crime.* They [included] *children wise beyond their years, precocious little girls, ambiguous schoolboys, dubious servants and educators"* (emphasis added). Concluding with a statement that uncannily evokes the central device of James's ghost story, Foucault observes that, once identified, these dangerous victims and outcasts were removed from society—placed in houses and asylums, which they "haunted" like ghosts, eking out a "shadow existence."[17]

Foucault's remarks highlight the distinctively modern consciousness at work in James's seemingly old-fashioned ghost story. If the fictional landscape is haunted (and why deny James's work the central feature of any ghost story?), it is the power of the subliminal rather than the supernatural that charges the ghosts' presence with significance. The psychosexual apparitions of the dead lovers testify to the hidden but pervasive force of sexuality operating at every stage and level of human existence. To exclude children from the implications and operations of human sexuality may prove tantamount, as the governess's overzealous actions graphically demonstrate, to depriving them of life.

As the governess approaches the end of her tale, she recounts her final efforts to make ten-year-old Miles confess his secret history. He resists, and the contest between the stubborn child and the insistent adult ends in death. In hindsight the governess condemns her youthful blindness and vanity: "I was infatuated—I was blind with victory." In her candor she also articulates a nagging sense of doubt that perhaps she got it wrong—perhaps the children were as ignorant and innocent as she first believed. This haunting doubt, her brush with the ambiguous nature of reality, surfaces on the penultimate page of her narrative. Here she repeats to the reader the terrible question she asked herself at the time: "if [Miles] *were* innocent what then on earth was I?" (87). This lack of certainty, and of self-knowledge, casts a dubious light on her self-styled role as the children's protector and should not be ignored. Neither, however, can we ignore that she herself articulates these reservations. Many critics have commented on the arrogance of her self-proclaimed desire "to serve as an expiatory victim," pointing out that her desire "absolutely [to] save" the children from evil leads, like all repressive morality, to guilt and suffering (26). Still, the first person to recognize her blindness, failure, and vanity is the governess herself. In resolving to reveal not only her story but her mistakes— "to push [her] dreadful way through it to the end"—she suggests more about human resilience in the face of uncertainty than many of James's critics allow (40).

However we attempt to solve the enigma of this story, one feature remains indisputable: the tantalizing ambiguity at its core. At every turn of the narrative *The Turn of the Screw* draws attention to the subjective nature not only of human experience and perception but of the shifting cultural constructions of childhood they create. The enigma of the child's role and image, like the contradictions arising between the children's statements and the governess's suspicions, is never resolved by an outside authority or observer. Miles's death ends the tale but offers no solution, assigns no fixed cause to the story's richly ambiguous effects. In her extensive analysis of the tale Shoshana Felman reminds us that the lack of an "outside" reference or authority is paradigmatic of all literary texts, that "one is always, necessarily, *in* literature."[18] Still, what distinguishes *The Turn of the Screw* from most fiction—particularly that produced at the end of the nineteenth century—is the way it teases (one might even say torments) its readers into awareness of their trapped condition. As mentioned earlier, James slyly states in his preface that the novella contains "no eligible *absolute*" by which its "action" can be judged. Only by bringing our own constructions of childhood to bear on this cunningly wrought domain of the questionable can we discover its meaning and significance.

The Child and the Novel at a Turning Point

If the meaning and effects of James's novella remain forever ambiguous, its success with generations of readers is patently clear. In his preface James is candid about his intent: "to catch" in the web of his narrative those "fastidious" readers "not easily caught" (*Art of the Novel* 172). The author's triumph seems assured: it is virtually impossible to read *The Turn of the Screw* without getting caught in the act of interpretation. To make sense of the narrative, readers must determine what *happens,* an act of interpretation that inevitably reveals the nature and extent of our cultural concepts, our image of the child, our understanding of evil and innocence, our forms of romantic or rational faith.

Secret longings, private fears, unspoken anxieties also color the canvas that springs before each reader's inner eye. Just as an audience becomes aware, while viewing *Hamlet*'s play within the play, that they are engaged in a process analogous to that of Shakespeare's characters, so James's readers discern how their progress through the text mirrors the narrator's subjective journey through the landscape.[19] Just as the governess envisions, then drastically re-envisions the nature of her wards, so readers ponder and revise their initial perceptions of the characters and the apparent meaning of events. The self-consciousness that the governess acquires at Bly is a condition both underscored and repeated in the act and process of reading her narrative. The emphasis James increasingly placed, during his novelistic career, on a character's "web of consciousness" is well known; and this emphasis inescapably draws attention to the way that the reader's own consciousness perceives, shapes, and distorts phenomenal as well as textual reality.

As the governess tries to fathom the apparitions and images surrounding her, the subjective, highly ambiguous, and ultimately uncertain nature of her perceptions mirrors the readers' own. If this provincial young woman may be said to have entered the historical mirror stage of Western culture, contemporary readers must admit how deeply entrenched they are in its development. Gazing into the ubiquitous mirrors of postmodern culture, we meet ourselves everywhere: in an endless succession of domestic, department-store, and rearview mirrors; on television and video screens stationed in every room of the house as well as at the office, the airport, the restaurant, and the bar; on gigantic posters, billboards, and movie-house screens; in glossy magazines, newspapers, family photo albums; on licenses, permits, and passports toted in wallets stuffed with pocket-size snapshots of friends, relatives, property, and pets.

Caught in an endless series of reflections and replications of reflections, we cannot extricate our countless images from the prisms of self-consciousness that James made a hallmark of his fiction. In *What Maisie Knew* and *The Turn of the Screw* he implicates the image of childhood in that grammar of reflexivity and ambiguity from which hereafter it cannot be effectively separated. His emphasis on the web of modern consciousness and self-consciousness elicits our awareness that every new image of childhood is also another ambiguous, infinitely questionable reflection of the self.

Nabokov's Novel Offspring
Lolita and Her Kin

So far-reaching was James's vision of the child's ambiguous, impure image that we must skip forward half a century to take up where he left off. We arrive at that cunning work of aesthetic enchantment created by an exiled Russian writer who, in middle age, transformed himself into a formidable American master. Vladimir Nabokov's most famous, and infamous, novel exhibits and carries to a new stage of development that same impulse or drive toward self-reflection, ambiguity, and paradox that characterizes James's innovative turn-of-the-century fictions. The slyly allusive, intensely parodic structure of *Lolita* can by now claim to have provoked as many contradictory interpretations, and caught out as many readers, as James's cunningly ambiguous fairy tale. In the 1950s, when *Lolita* was published first in France and then in the United States, its volatile subject matter—the sexual passion of a middle-aged European for a twelve-year-old American kid—set off a flurry of scandal.

Nabokov's novel has never fully recovered from the charges of obscenity that greeted it, despite the fact that they were quickly dismissed by the courts as well as by prominent critics. In the popular mind the name Lolita has come to signify the cynical sophistication and sexual precocity, bordering on lewdness, of American—and Americanized—youth. Marie Winn, a social critic concerned with the fate of contemporary children, thus says, "Once upon a time a fictional twelve-year-old from New England named Lolita Haze slept with a middle-aged European intellectual named Humbert Humbert and profoundly shocked American sensibilities. It was not so much the idea of an adult having sexual designs on a child that was appalling. It was Lolita herself, unvirginal long before Humbert came upon the scene, Lolita, so knowing, so jaded, so *unchildlike,* who seemed to violate something America held sacred." As Winn goes on to say, however, only "a single generation after *Lolita*'s publication," Nabokov's vision appeared prophetic: "There is little doubt that schoolchildren of the 1980s are more akin to Nabokov's nymphet than to those guileless and innocent creatures with their shiny Mary Janes and pigtails, their scraped knees and trusting ways, that were called children not so long ago."[1]

Winn's statement is rife with implicit as well as explicit information about the contemporary image of childhood. As a social critic, she purports to be discussing real children, not literary types like the "fictional twelve-year-old" called "Lolita Haze." Yet in distinguishing between past and present generations, she contrasts Nabokov's young heroine with another fiction, or construction, of childhood: the innocent in Mary Janes and pigtails. We note how *her* costume, stance, and physiognomy (those scraped knees bespeaking such guileless pastimes as roller-skating, hopscotch, and jumping rope) assure the adult— as little Flora's golden hair, placid face, and charming frock initially assured James's governess—of the child's sexual ignorance.

The passage says much, as well, about the way Nabokov's novel has been construed (and misconstrued) not only by the general public but by critics and reviewers. Having made her way into popular culture, Lolita has given rise to a cultural icon and a popular canard. Just as the name Frankenstein has come to signify, erroneously, the unnamed creature whom Victor Frankenstein, the protagonist of Mary Shelley's 1818 novel, conceives in the bowels of his scientific laboratory, the nymphet Lolita, conjured in the depths of Humbert's ardent imagination, gives rise to a case of mistaken identity. (Other revealing parallels between Shelley's novel and Nabokov's will be discussed later in this chapter.) To the popular misconception of the nymphet as sexy teenager decked out in tight jeans and bright lipstick, both the book jackets of various paperback editions and the cinematic image of Sue Lyon—the star of Stanley Kubrick's 1962 film adaptation of *Lolita*— have undoubtedly contributed.[2] (Adrian Lyne's 1997 film version features a less vampish but even more strapping teenager, fifteen-year-old Dominique Swain, in the title role.) More surprising is the number of professional critics who, like Winn, cleave to the image of a jaded, supremely knowing twelve-year-old who has lost all claim to innocence long before Humbert comes on the scene. Apparently misled by the adolescent's stance of cool sophistication, such critics fail to note how flimsy, indeed how tragically futile, a defense it proves against Humbert's violation of both her childhood and her body.

Winn unwittingly draws attention to the perceptual haze surrounding Nabokov's child when she dubs the little girl Lolita Haze. This misnomer contradicts what the narrator already reveals in his opening lines, as he launches a hymn to the beauty of his bewitching nymphet: both her name and her image are creations of Humbert's rhapsodic imagination. Like the goddess Athena, who sprang fully formed from Zeus's brow, Lolita is a mythical being. A figment of Humbert's dreaming mind, the fantasized nymphet can claim no earthly genealogy or surname.[3] Dolores Haze—the child with whom Humbert conflates the nymphet—is, on the other hand, the daughter of Charlotte Haze and her deceased husband, Harold. The identity of Dolores, or Dolly as she is known at school, is largely a matter of indifference to ardent Humbert; only sporadically does he glimpse, through the "rosy, gold-dusted" haze of his desire for the nymphet, the poignant image of the child (62).

Humbert's belated recognition of the child's identity occurs, significantly, not in the heat of passion but at a distance—recollected, so to speak, in Wordsworthian tranquillity. Only after Dolly escapes her captor, depriving him of his cherished object of desire, does Humbert begin to recognize the autonomous being—the "North American girl-child named Dolores Haze," as he ultimately identifies her—whose tender flesh was sacrificed on the altar of his obsession (285). In pursuit of his "mythopoeic nymphet," romantic Humbert can only possess, in the physical or sexual sense, the *body* of a child he has imaginatively transformed into the figment of his dreaming mind (188). That Humbert consummates his passion for the nymphet in The Enchanted Hunters hotel is apt, for he is the enchanted hunter of his own romantic tale.

The Romantic Legacy: Enchanted Hunters and Poor Children

Like so many romantic dreamers before him, Humbert is captivated by an ideal image or vision: one infinitely more real to him than the American youngster whose childhood he destroys. Here Humbert's true precursors are not the pedophiles of psychiatric case history but

those ardent disciples of romance—from Emma Bovary to Edgar
Allan Poe, Don Quixote to Jay Gatsby—who in countless novels and
poems suffer the fatal affliction of infinite longing, transcendent desire.
Romantic love—as Poe writes in his poem "Annabel Lee," whose
lines resonate throughout Humbert's narration—aspires to "a love that
[is] more than love." The power (and poison) of romantic love springs
from the paradox of ideal vision wedded to sheer impossibility. It is
Humbert's longing for the unattainable, for ideal perfection—what he
calls "the great rosegray never-to-be-had"—that fires his imagination
and fuels his desire for nymphet beauty. As he admits, "it may well be
that the very attraction immaturity has for me lies not so much in the
limpidity of pure young forbidden fairy child beauty as in the security
of a situation where infinite perfections"—those that can only be
dreamed of or dreamed up—"fill the gap between the little given and
the great promised." The vision is perfect because it remains "out of
reach, with no possibility of attainment to spoil it" (266).

Only the power of imagination can "fill the gap" between the ideal
and the actual. To possess his nymphet, Humbert must first eclipse the
child; only when she has been, as he says, "safely solipsized"—subjugated,
in other words, to the dreamer's private world of imagination—is
sexual bliss assured. Only then does the nymphet worshiper enter
"a plane of being where nothing mattered, save the infusion of joy
brewed within [his] body." After Humbert experiences, surreptitiously
and onanistically, his first sexual ecstasy with Lolita—as the child,
munching an apple, lies casually sprawled on his lap—he identifies the
psychic maneuvers by which he has achieved physical relief: "I had
stolen the honey of a spasm," he boasts, "without impairing the morals
of a minor. . . . I had delicately constructed my ignoble, ardent, sinful
dream; and still Lolita was safe—and I was safe. What I had madly
possessed was not she, but my own creation, another, fanciful Lolita—
perhaps, more real than Lolita; . . . and having no will, no consciousness—indeed, no life of her own."[4] That Humbert's clandestine maneuvers cannot ensure the child's safety is foreshadowed by the imperial
nature of his fantasies. Having successfully obliterated her autonomous
identity, Humbert, like "a radiant and robust Turk," can delay "the
moment of actually enjoying the youngest and frailest of his slaves";
but he is clearly poised for invasion (62–64).

In thrall to his imagination, Humbert is at once captor and captive,
predator and prey. Inadvertently testifying to the imagination's power

to bewitch and enchant, readers of *Lolita* often fall prey to the spell cast by the narrator's mythical fantasies. Further disoriented by the abrupt shifts in narrative tone—as Humbert's voice alternates between pathos and farce, rapturous evocation and mocking self-denigration—many readers fail to heed his warning: "You can always count on a murderer for a fancy prose style" (11). In a statement at once telling and teasingly ambiguous, the narrator announces his efforts to conceal, in the very act or pretense of revealing, crucial aspects of his story. All art, like that "good cheat" nature, is deceptive, Nabokov maintains (*Strong Opinions* 11). But Humbert's language is particularly duplicitous because he figures prominently among those he would deceive. Only gradually and with great difficulty can he bear to reveal the truth of the tale he has to tell: that at the age of thirty-seven he conceived a passion for a twelve-year-old child whom he subsequently begged and bribed, cajoled and tyrannized into sexual cohabitation—until, at the age of fourteen, she managed to escape.

All the self-reflexive devices for which *Lolita* is famous—most particularly, its parody of literary conventions—signal the epistemological gap between narrator and reader, between Humbert's romantic obsession and the reader's more independent perspective. But here, too, the radical nature and effects of the narrative are often misconstrued, as decades of critical commentary demonstrate.[5] In an early review of the novel, for example, Leslie Fiedler was so taken with its innovative design that he overlooked what Nabokov, in his comments on the novel, called "my little girl's heartrending fate" (*Strong Opinions* 25). Fiedler finds, by contrast, that *Lolita* "is the final blasphemy against the cult of the child." "Nowhere," he adds, "are the myths of sentimentality more amusing[ly] and convincingly parodied." In *Love and Death in the American Novel* Fiedler takes his point further: "it is the naive child, the female, the American who corrupts the sophisticated adult, the male, the European." Nabokov's child, he concludes, is Poe's "Annabel Lee as nymphomaniac, demonic rapist of the soul."[6]

Underlying Fiedler's hyperbolic response is an assumption highly surprising in a critic long identified with cultural radicalism: the child shown to have a sexual nature or identity must be perverse. Here he serves as unwitting spokesman for that ethical conservatism or "rigorism" that Ian Watt attributed, only a few years after *Lolita* was published, to the Puritan influence on English and American culture. In *The Rise of the Novel* Watt discusses the "tremendous narrowing of the ethical scale, a redefinition of virtue in primarily sexual terms," which took hold of the eighteenth century and reached its peak during the Victorian era. As part of the Puritan legacy, "resistance to the desires of the body became the major aim of secular morality; and chastity, instead of being only one virtue among many, tended to become the supreme one."[7]

Watt's discussion sheds light on an odd but telling affinity between Fiedler's harsh language, charging Nabokov's child with nymphomania and rape, and the equally dramatic, if more sincere, expressions of outrage by James's Victorian narrator in *The Turn of the Screw*. As soon as the governess detects implications of sexual knowledge in her previously angelic wards, she assumes their absolute contamination. For all the cultural distance separating Fiedler's postwar cynicism from the governess's repressive morality, their reactions evince a mutual inflexibility, an all-or-nothing construction of the child's image: allow the child to tumble from the pedestal of blank (sexless) purity, and evil or corruption (or its modern equivalent, psychopathology) rushes in to fill the void. James Kincaid characterizes this either/or view of the child's innocence as the "dualistic" vision contemporary culture has inherited from the Victorians. Focusing on nineteenth-century literature and culture, Kincaid does not mention *Lolita* in *Child-Loving*, yet his argument sheds light on Fiedler's implicit assumption: that, in Kincaid's words, the "child is either free of any whiff of sexuality or is, somehow, saturated with it."[8]

To that either/or formulation even so knowledgeable a critic as Alfred Appel Jr. appears to subscribe. "Satirized" in the novel, Appel asserts, is "the romantic myth of the child, extending from Wordsworth to Salinger.... *Lolita* marks its death in 1955." In his view *Lolita*'s debut was at once fatal and salutary. By the time this remarkable novel arrived on the scene, the romantic myth of the child was already moribund; in one swift blow *Lolita* relieved us of this tiresome tradition. As Appel was the first to point out, however, Nabokov's art "records a constant process of *becoming*," analogous to metamorphosis.[9] The aesthetic and linguistic process by which his fiction transforms a theme, cluster of images, or literary myth suggests—like the metamorphosis of a caterpillar into a butterfly—not so much an end as a beginning, a culmination that gives rise to new forms and images. Rather than sounding a death knell to the romantic myth of the child, I shall argue, *Lolita* renews and reinvigorates the myth, rendering the image of childhood with fresh resonance and complexity.

Before focusing on the intricacies of *Lolita's* narrative, it may prove helpful to consider some of Nabokov's other writing, both fiction and nonfiction, that treats the image of childhood. Largely ignored by his readers thus far, the persistence of the child theme in his thought and work highlights *Lolita's* unexpected affinities with some of Nabokov's literary predecessors—specifically, Dickens and Mary Shelley. While Nabokov openly expressed his admiration for Dickens's literary image of childhood, his debt to Shelley's *Frankenstein* remains implicit; yet the parallels between her best-seller and his are striking. As I will show later in this chapter, the poignancy of *Lolita,* like that of *Frankenstein,* largely derives from its vision of the child's sacred innocence. To point out Shelley's debt to the English Romantic poets, whose ranks included her husband, is only to repeat what scholars and critics have long re-marked. It is common knowledge that Percy Bysshe Shelley was a major influence on his wife's intellectual and artistic development and that he collaborated with her on the text of *Frankenstein.* Because *Lolita* was published a century and a half later—by a writer notorious for his parody of literary conventions and his disdain for sentimentality—the case for its romantic inheritance requires a more thoroughgoing defense. For clinching evidence, we must turn, of course, to the novel. By initially contemplating a larger frame of reference, however, readers may be better equipped to assess the evidence amply, and eloquently, provided by the text.

The earliest challenge to the widespread critical assumption that *Lolita* deliberately sabotages the romantic myth of the child comes from the author himself. Nearly five years before the novel appeared in print, Nabokov, with characteristic precocity, had already under-mined the position his future critics would adopt. Publicly repri-manding those who "denounce" the theme of the child's innocence as "sentimental," he forthrightly accused "such people" of ignorance; they are, he declared, "unaware of what sentiment is" (*Lectures on Lit-erature* 86). The forum for these remarks was a course on European fiction that Nabokov inaugurated at Cornell University during the academic year 1950–51, the period during which he began to com-pose *Lolita* in earnest.[10] In one series of lectures Nabokov paid annual tribute for nearly a decade to the novelist who translated Romantic faith in the child's innocence into some of the finest prose fictions of the nineteenth century, Charles Dickens. Singling out *Bleak House* for detailed analysis, Nabokov drew special attention to the child theme that resonates throughout its pages.

Each year during his lecture on *Bleak House,* Nabokov took pains to criticize the casual manner in which modern readers and critics dismiss as so much "sentimentality" the theme of childhood innocence. No doubt, Nabokov told his students, the "story of a student turned shepherd for the sake of a maiden is sentimental and silly and flat and stale." In regard to Dickens's evocation of "the plight of children," however—the "strain" of "specialized compassion" and "profound pity" that "runs through *Bleak House*"—Nabokov flatly rejected "the charge of sentimentality." Instead, he praised Dickens's "striking" evocation of innocent children—"their troubles, insecurity, humble joys, and the joy they give, but mainly their misery." The "most touching pages," he avowed, "are devoted to the child theme" (*Lectures on Literature* 86–87, 65). In language that deliberately echoes Dickens's incantatory rhythms, Nabokov delivered a veritable litany of "poor children" who inhabit the novel (*Lectures on Literature* 91; see also 70, 74, 88). Significantly, he would later claim that epithet for *his* literary child, referring to Lolita in a 1966 interview as "my poor little girl" (*Strong Opinions* 94).[11]

Nabokov's Offspring, Lolita's Kin

The affinities between Nabokov's and Dickens's visions of the child confirm what careful readers of *Lolita* may discover for themselves: far from sounding a death knell to the romantic myth of the child, Nabokov breathes new life into that resonant myth. For him as for his literary precursors, the child—whose innocence has not yet been ravaged by experience, whose wonder at the world is still fresh— emblematizes the human being's creative potential. In a manner that recalls Wordsworth's immortality ode, Nabokov marvels in his autobiography at "the dark-bluish tint of the iris" in his infant son's eyes. Their depth of color seems "to retain the shadows it had absorbed of ancient, fabulous forests ... where, in some dappled depth, man's mind had been born." The birth of human consciousness, he postulates, was a sudden, glorious flowering—an intuitive leap, a "stab of wonder" by which the dreaming mind awakened to the world. Each child, in turn, repeats the miracle of that original awakening—which Nabokov calls "the initial blossoming of man's mind" (*Speak, Memory* 227–28). To borrow from F. R. Leavis's comments on Dickens, Nabokov "can feel with intensity that the world begins again with every child."[12]

As a youth and fledgling poet, Nabokov already subscribed to the luminous vision of childhood that informs his oeuvre. In 1921, while still a student at Cambridge, he wrote the following in a letter to his mother: "This little poem [I enclose] will prove to you that my mood is radiant as ever. If I live to be a hundred, my soul will still go round in short trousers."[13] For Nabokov, to gaze wide-eyed at the world as children do—and poets must—is not sentimental; grief, death, and loss are never far from view. Drawing on one of English literature's most famous children to illustrate his point, Nabokov says, "In a sense, we are all crashing to our death from the top story of our birth to the flat stones of the churchyard and wondering with an immortal Alice in Wonderland at the patterns of the passing wall. This capacity to wonder at trifles—no matter the imminent peril—these asides of the spirit . . . are the highest forms of consciousness" ("Art of Literature" 372–74). Our childish ability to wonder at the world is, then, a form not of escape but of courage in the face of imminent peril and death.

Blessed with this capacity to wonder at trifles, Nabokov's most insightful and creative protagonists glimpse beauty and truth even in the darkest corners of their world. Though virtual prisoners of nightmarish reality, the heroes of his two most political novels, Cincinnatus C. in *Invitation to a Beheading* and Adam Krug in *Bend Sinister*—along with Fyodor in *The Gift,* Pnin, John Shade in *Pale Fire,* Sebastian Knight, even tormented Humbert and Van Veen in *Ada*—experience those liberating asides of the spirit that constitute, for their author, the highest forms of consciousness. Nabokov's novels always describe a tension or healthy conflict between collective and individual life, between the conventional world that runs on common denominators and the singular consciousness of the individual. But at certain historical moments—as this Russian émigré and fugitive from Hitler well knew—the forces governing collective life become onerous. Seeking to suppress, manipulate, or control the creative exercise of human consciousness, the ruling powers may conspire to destroy the individual altogether. In Nabokov's fiction this unhealthy state of affairs is often signaled by the plight of children, who are inevitably the most vulnerable and easily victimized.

As *Lolita* testifies, Nabokov did not require the conditions of a police state to depict the crimes committed against society's frailest members. Still, a cursory look at his most politically explicit novels, *Invitation to a Beheading* and *Bend Sinister,* may help to clarify the significance of the child in his imaginative universe. In the grotesque police states depicted in these works, Nabokov dramatizes the intrinsic connection between a totalitarian regime's hostility to individual freedom and its lethal effect on the child. In the farcical and shoddy world of *Invitation to a Beheading* Cincinnatus C. is the only surviving representative of creative human consciousness, the only being who harbors an "exceptionally strong, ardent and independent" inner life. Although Cincinnatus possesses the age and experience of an adult, he looks "extraordinarily youthful," even maddeningly *childlike* to his jailors (120–21, 211). Everything about him—from his "small and still young" face to his delicate limbs and "slender feet"—expresses the "impossible, dazzling freedom" of a vital imagination and memory.[14]

An active and unique inner life constitutes Cincinnatus's only crime against the state that holds him prisoner. Taunted by the radiance of an inner life they can neither possess nor control, his jailers long to "destroy utterly [his] brazen elusive flesh" (122). Betraying their hostility to consciousness at every level, the prison officials throw a party to celebrate their prisoner's impending execution. Even the food and decorations gleefully announce the doomed man's scheduled demise. As guest of honor at the banquet, Cincinnatus notices, for example, the "heaps of apples" decorating the festive table. Each bloodred apple, he observes, is "as big as a child's head" (185). This seemingly casual reference abruptly announces the sentence of beheading to both Cincinnatus and the novel's readers. In the vivid image of slaughtered children, tyranny delivers its message.

In *Bend Sinister,* another novel reflecting the nightmarish world of a totalitarian regime, collective life proves so hostile to the individual and his nascent creativity that an innocent child—the philosopher Adam Krug's eight-year-old son, David—is senselessly butchered. Instead of taking him to "the best State Rest House, as had been arranged," the officials accidentally remove David to the Institute for Abnormal Children. Here he is mistakenly identified as an orphan. That mistake proves fatal to David, because the Ekwilist regime regards parentless children as a social and economic burden. From time to time, therefore, officials at the institute use a helpless orphan as a "'release-instrument' for the benefit" of the most violent criminals, who, as one medical official explains, vent "their repressed yearnings ... upon some little human creature of no value to the community" (218). Assigned to protect Krug's son, the officials bungle the job. In a larger sense, however, David's murder is a logical outcome of this brutal regime, which denies any intrinsic value to the "human creature."

As these brief examples from Nabokov's political fictions suggest, the child's image is often implicated in the efforts of human consciousness and imagination to confront the extremes of human cruelty and suffering. Thus, in a letter Nabokov wrote to his sister at the end of World War II, he reveals how recent information about the Nazi death camps instantly evokes, in his mind and heart, an image of the children who died there. "There are things that torment too deeply," he writes: "the German vilenesses, the burning of children in ovens,—children as funny and as strongly loved as our children."[15] To Nabokov the horrific image of those burning children brings home a terrible truth: that each of those unnamed legions consumed by the camp incinerators was as unique, playful, and fiercely loved as his own young son. That Nabokov repeatedly referred, in statements like those cited earlier, to his most famous literary offspring as his "poor little girl" suggests a similar sympathy for her plight. More conclusive than any external authorial avowal, of course, is the rich evidence provided by the novel itself. Lolita is, without doubt, Nabokov's most extensive exploration of the child's betrayal by a world of adults.

Nabokov's "Poor Little Girl"

Set in prosperous, postwar America, Lolita is remote, both politically and geographically, from the nightmarish worlds of Invitation to a Beheading and Bend Sinister. The novel testifies to the ways collective society can, even in the name of free enterprise and progressive education, conspire against the child's essential welfare and freedom.[16] In the end Dolores Haze loses not only her childhood but her life; the first of these deprivations already implies, in Nabokov's universe as in Dickens's, a betrayal of human consciousness and its creative potential.

Humbert's rhapsodic desire for his nymphet notwithstanding, Dolores Haze's experience reflects that of countless *actual* children whose plight is broadcast daily in the media: children who are sexually exploited by adults claiming to be their guardians. Like those children who are the subjects of innumerable psychological and sociological case studies, Dolly begins by receiving little attention and less love from her mother; falls prey to notions of romance propagated by movies and magazines; succumbs to the blandishments of a handsome, adult male who adopts the role of her substitute father; and, orphaned by the death of her only surviving parent, learns to put up with her stepfather's routine sexual demands. As Humbert accurately recalls, "she had absolutely nowhere else to go" (144).

True, adolescent Lo is not a virgin when Humbert has sex with her for the first time. But Dolly Haze's experimental forays at summer camp with thirteen-year-old Charlie Holmes, the son of the camp's director, are, if not particularly savory, entirely predictable. While the adolescents' clumsy activities satirically comment on the adults who claim to be supervising them, what Charlie and Dolly get up to in the bushes is little more than child's play (138–39). Touching and vulnerable as children may be, Nabokov does not seek to portray them as genderless angels. Quite the opposite: by restoring sexual vitality to the image of childhood, he rescues it from those "debased-romantic conceptions of innocence" (to recall Peter Coveney's formulation) by which late Victorianism had all but killed it. Like James's Maisie, Nabokov's children are vigorous creatures in whom the seeds of adult energy and sexuality, will and intelligence are firmly rooted.

That innocence should not be equated with sexless simplicity—a point that Fiedler and others patently ignore—is recognized even by scurrilous Humbert. When, on the road from Camp Q to The Enchanted Hunters hotel, Lolita offers her stepdad a naive imitation of a Hollywood kiss, Humbert, despite the thrill, warns himself to be careful. Wary of exceeding what he calls "the limits and rules of such girlish games," he tells the reader: "I knew, of course, it was but an innocent game on her part, a bit of backfisch foolery in imitation of some simulacrum of fake romance" (115; the German word *backfisch* means an immature, adolescent girl). Even after Humbert and young Lo have "technically," as he says, become "lovers," the adult cannot pretend ignorance of the child's vulnerability. Only in the most literal, and puritanical, sense can twelve-year-old Dolly be said to have seduced middle-aged Humbert. "While eager to impress me with the world of tough kids," Humbert says of Lolita's initial invitation to have sexual intercourse, "she was not quite prepared for certain discrepancies between a kid's life and mine. Pride alone prevented her from giving up." Naive Lo, he adds, "saw the stark act merely as part of a youngster's furtive world, unknown to adults. What adults did for purposes of procreation was no business of hers" (134–36).

Lolita's brand of naïveté—which leaves her more vulnerable, in some ways, than a child who lacks her pretense of knowing sophistication—poignantly attests to the intrusive power of the media. Forming her notions of reality from images projected on the silver screen, she has no idea that adult experience transcends the Hollywood gestures and ritual movie kiss she has learned to imitate. By the time Humbert arrives on the doorstep of the Haze household, the forces of consumer culture have clearly made inroads on the child's limited experience. Spreading false cheer and empty promises, the philistine art of advertising and the mass media exert a hypnotic influence on her trustful and dreamy nature. Above all, Hollywood's images of fake romance glamorize handsome Humbert and his dark shadow, Clare Quilty, in her eyes. At once starstruck and naively trusting, Lolita, like her mother, is an easy mark for promoters and predators.

With the same naïveté that makes her prey to the media's versions of romance, twelve-year-old Dolores Haze accepts those of the adman: "She believed, with a kind of celestial trust, any advertisement or advice that appeared in *Movie Love* or *Screen Land*. ... If some café sign proclaimed Icecold Drinks, she was automatically stirred, although all drinks everywhere were ice-cold." An avid consumer, Dolly confirms Neil Postman's observations on modern advertising, which employs "the symbols and rhetoric of religion" to deliver its message. To these "idols" that bear no "burden of logic or verification," children are particularly vulnerable.[17] Dolly Haze's unwitting faith in the adult's version of reality makes her as susceptible to the claims of the billboard as to Humbert's ploys. "She it was," Humbert explains, "to whom ads were dedicated: the ideal consumer, the subject and object of every foul poster" (150). What he fails to point out, however, is that the success of his own foul designs depends, like the poster, on the child's inherent gullibility.

Just as Hollywood teaches Dolly Haze how to kiss, Clare Quilty's celebrity status thrills her adolescent heart. Years later, Quilty's promise to make her a starlet turns out to be a ruse; when she refuses to join in the orgies he stages for his amusement, Quilty loses interest in her. Yet even after she leaves him, Lolita cannot think of this "famous" man or his "sensational name" without awe (273). In the final analysis, however, it is her miserable bondage to Humbert that schools Dolores Haze in depravity and deceit. On Humbert's shoulders rests the prime responsibility, as he ultimately acknowledges, for her ruined innocence. From the moment he tells the orphan that her mother is dead and that she must comply with his sexual demands, the game is truly up: Lolita's childhood is over.

In *Lolita* as in *Ada* Nabokov reveals the process by which blind passion can poison the wellsprings of love—just as "the invisible worm" corrupts the rose in Blake's poem "The Sick Rose." The poet might well be speaking of Humbert or Van Veen when he writes in another poem from *Songs of Experience:*

> Love seeketh only Self to please,
> To bind another to its delight;
> Joys in another's loss of ease,
> And builds a Hell in Heaven's despite.
> ("The Clod & the Pebble," ll. 9–12)

Just as Blake contrasts the cruel reality of self-serving passion with the hopeful innocence of love (invoked in the poem's previous stanza), Nabokov contrasts Humbert's youthful ardor for Annabel Leigh with his destructive passion for Lolita, which "builds a Hell" for them both. Humbert's love for Annabel is mutual and trusting—innocent not of sexuality but of tyranny, rancor, and deceit. She is Humbert's willing and equal partner, not the solipsized object of his self-serving fantasy. Although Annabel, like Dolores, meets an untimely death, it is not Humbert but typhus that robs her of her childhood (15).

The fatal erosion of innocence begins the moment Humbert deprives the child of her rightful protection. Gradually, and inexorably, Lolita must assume the only role left her, as the slave of Humbert's desire. But since Humbert is also in thrall to his passion, she shrewdly begins to counter his demands with her own. Thus he balks, but quickly pays up, when she exacts a "bonus price" of "four bucks" for a particularly "fancy [sexual] embrace." An irony writ large in the novel is the public pretense so necessary to their relationship: that Humbert is Lolita's guardian and protector. At times Humbert even allows himself to be taken in by the convenient deceit. Faced "with the distasteful task" of recounting their increasingly mercenary sexual negotiations, he even acts the pained father, bemoaning a "definite drop in Lolita's morals" (185–86).

Humbert's professed concern for Lolita's morals is painfully ironic.

Canceled by his rapture for the nymphet is any real sense of responsibility for the child. Voicing his indifference to her early in the novel, Humbert says of young Dolly: "Mentally, I found her to be a disgustingly conventional little girl" who loved "gooey fudge sundaes" and equally gooey "movie magazines." Despite his disdain for American popular culture, the conventions it fosters have something in common with the "system of monetary bribes" he eventually devises to keep his Lolita in tow. In both cases the child's desire for gooey sweets and attractive toys is manipulated by adults for their private gain. With a note of condescension that suggests the disdain all con men have for their dupes, Humbert describes the twelve-year-old Dolly as "a simple child," one easily brought under "submission" by his threats (150–51).

Orphaned by her mother's death, Lolita is especially vulnerable to threats of abandonment. Humbert makes this clear in his description of their first cross-country car trip: "A simple child, Lo would scream no! and frantically clutch at my driving hand whenever I put a stop to her tornadoes of temper by turning in the middle of a highway with the implication that I was about to take her straight to [a] dark and dismal abode." As Dolly grows more obdurate, Humbert's "methods of persuasion" increase in intensity (151). Suppose she does report him to the authorities, he tells her: "Okay. I go to jail. But what happens to you, my orphan? Well, you are luckier," he pronounces with heavy irony, you "will be given a choice of . . . the correctional school, the reformatory, the juvenile detention home." As Humbert wraps up this portion of his account with a final display of rhetorical prowess, his method of persuasion speaks for itself. Syntactically tucked away in his parenthetical asides is eloquent confirmation of his victim's total surrender: "You will dwell, my Lolita will dwell (come here, my brown flower) with thirty-nine other dopes in a dirty dormitory (no, allow me, please) under the supervision of hideous matrons. This is the situation, this is the choice" (153).

Using adult knowledge and power to undermine the choice he pretends to offer her, Humbert succeeds, as he says, "in terrorizing Lo, who despite a certain brash alertness of manner and spurts of wit was not as intelligent a child as her I.Q. might suggest" (153). Here Humbert patently confuses the child's intelligence with inexperience. His blindness is wholly in keeping with his transgressions against her—his violation, as he ultimately admits, of the sacred rights of childhood. Inexperience, not stupidity, is what makes the child gullible; an older, more seasoned Lolita would not be so easily taken in by Humbert's false claims. It is only a matter of time, in fact, before Lolita learns to trade lies with her captor. "Eventually," as he acknowledges, "she lived up to her I.Q." (184).

At the heart of Humbert's exploitation of Lolita is an irony that gradually reveals its tragic dimensions: having explored every particle of his nymphet's face and body—from the gleaming "baby folds of her stomach" to the "peppermint taste of her saliva"—he remains blind to the child's inner life and being (164, 115). Such blindness is both deliberate and self-serving: "I recall," he later says, that "it was always my habit and method to ignore Lolita's states of mind while comforting my own base self." In a brief but telling passage near the end of the novel, a remorseful Humbert recollects one of the rare times when "I knew how [Lolita] felt, and it was hell to know it" (289, 286–87). The revelation occurs when the father of Lolita's school friend Avis Chapman comes to take his daughter home. In contrast to the beautiful nymphet, Avis is "a heavy, unattractive, affectionate child" for whom Humbert feels not the slightest shudder of attraction. Invited to sit down, "Mr. Byrd" (Humbert puns on the Latin meaning of Avis's name) chats politely with Humbert while Avis "perche[s] plumply on his knee" and Lolita looks on with a smile.

Suddenly, however, "as Avis clung to her father's neck and ear [and], with a casual arm, the man enveloped his lumpy and large offspring," Humbert watches "Lolita's smile lose all its light and become a frozen little shadow of itself." Holding back her tears with a grimace, the orphan rushes out of the room—to be followed, Humbert adds, "by Avis who had such a wonderful fat pink dad and a small chubby brother, and a brand-new baby sister and a home, and two grinning dogs, and Lolita had nothing" (287–88). As he recollects this scene, which sets him to "squirming and pleading" with his conscience, a remorseful Humbert concedes, in hindsight, the child's right to a dad and a dog and a chubby brother—all the "conventional" elements of an impossibly ordinary (for her) childhood. For once Humbert's mask of disdain slips, exposing his recognition of the child's plight.

The Monster and the Nymphet: *Frankenstein* and *Lolita*

For most of his narrative guilty Humbert plays on that all-or-nothing vision of childhood innocence exemplified by James's Victorian governess. Claiming to have the "utmost respect" for "ordinary children," Humbert—who, in an effort to claim Rousseauian faith in natural innocence, even calls himself Jean-Jacques Humbert—contrasts "their purity and vulnerability" with the nymphet's sexual allure (126, 21). Turning that alleged purity to his self-serving advantage, Humbert insists that the nymphet is not really a child at all: her true nature "is not human but nymphic (that is, demoniac)." Among the "innocent throng" of "wholesome children," he explains, the ardent nympholept searches for "the little deadly demon"—and finds, with a shiver of delight, a bewitching young "Lilith" (18–22). Through this elaborate twist of rhetoric, the impossibly chaste child is supplanted by her dark alter ego—a cruel enchantress, or *belle dame sans merci*—and the pedophile transported, on wings of imagination, to that "enchanted island" where the "laws of humanity" conveniently do not obtain (308). Taking refuge in fancy's "mossy garden" or "pubescent park," as he puts it, Humbert feels free to dally and disport at will (18, 23).[18]

The language Humbert uses to justify his conduct exposes the dark underside of his professed reverence for the child: "Humbert Humbert tried hard to be good. Really and truly, he did. He had the utmost respect for ordinary children, with their purity and vulnerability, and under no circumstances would he have interfered with the innocence of a child, if there was the least risk of a row" (21–22). Here, as though unable to bear the weight of its own false logic, Humbert's argument instantaneously collapses. In one swift aside the speaker bares his true motives, admitting that he would interfere with a child's innocence—that is (when the euphemism is decoded), he would tamper with her body—*only* if he could get away with it.

Betraying him at every turn, the narrator's rationalizations are as intriguing in their self-exposure as those of his literary precursor Victor Frankenstein. Humbert's striking kinship with the protagonist of Mary Shelley's novel appears to have gone unnoticed—perhaps because the characters appear to have little in common.[19] Frankenstein, who endlessly delays marriage to his betrothed, is almost comically indifferent to the force of sexual passion that torments and consumes Humbert. Probing beneath this disparity, attentive readers may discover a telling analogy between Humbert's "deadly demon," the alluring nymphet, and Frankenstein's dreaded "daemon," the monster he laments having conceived (*Lolita* 19; *Frankenstein* 39, 40, 56, 78, and passim). Monster and nymphet—each of these "marvels" of creation, offspring of Promethean imagination, provokes torments in its creator. The true disaster, however, is one to which Frankenstein wholly and Humbert partially remain blind: the tragic betrayal of the child's original innocence. Just as Frankenstein's creature is trapped in the monstrous shape his maker fashions for him—a shape that alienates him from all humanity—the child Dolores Haze is trapped within the nymphic guise conjured by Humbert's imagination.

Conceived in the depths of Frankenstein's scientific imagination, the creature is no sooner brought to life than his maker rejects him. Recoiling in shock from the creature's grotesque appearance, Frankenstein cannot accept responsibility for the "filthy mass" of flesh and bone that he has brought to life (121). Blinded by disappointment as he formerly was by ambition, Dr. Frankenstein does not recognize what *his* author, Mary Shelley, makes clear to her readers: ugly as the creature appears, he begins life as an innocent child in a benign state of nature. With a grotesque grin wrinkling his yellow cheeks, the trusting newborn instantly stretches out a hand to his parent, as Frankenstein, overcome by repulsion, rushes out of the room (40). Much later, after suffering the misery of rejection, the creature still insists to his horrified parent that at birth he "was benevolent; my soul glowed with love and humanity" (78). Frankenstein's creature, U. C. Knoepflmacher observes, is a "genuine Wordsworthian child" who delights as much as "any Romantic" in the wonders of nature.[20] As Shelley reveals, however, innocence is no proof against experience—particularly experience as cruel as that imposed on the creature not only by strangers but by the man who gave him life.

Like Frankenstein, who spurns his offspring, Humbert betrays the covenant between parent and child while exploiting his role as her self-styled guardian. When, as mentioned earlier, Humbert adopts an absurdly paternalist note, lamenting the "definite drop" in young Dolly's "morals," readers are invited to consider the monstrous irony of his pretense. The perverse logic of Humbert's moral stance as paterfamilias is worthy of his literary precursor. Giving voice to his own brand of solipsistic fervor, Victor Frankenstein conceives of himself as "creator" not only of a single offspring but of a "new species" to follow in the wake of his initial experiment. Casting himself in the role of divine patriarch, he grandiosely declares, "No father could claim the gratitude of his child so completely as I should deserve theirs" (36).

His sudden volte-face, once the supposed paragon of this superior species comes to life, is brutally comic.[21]

Cursing the "demoniacal corpse" he has brought to life, Frankenstein condemns his unfortunate offspring to isolation, misery, and, finally, rage against humanity (39). The process by which Shelley's Promethean hero projects his own "daemonic" energies—both creative and de-structive—onto his creature exposes in a sharper light Humbert's hazy references to demonic enchantment. Take, for example, the scene in which Humbert, having consummated his desire for the nymphet, stands at the hotel desk waiting to check out with his "little mistress." His "every nerve," Humbert comments, is alive "with the feel of her body—the body of some immortal daemon disguised as a female child" (141). Here, as in Frankenstein's case, the narrator's rhetoric is more self-revealing than he knows. Humbert's evocation of the nymphet's mortal disguise draws attention to his own need to disguise his guilt.

Standing in the lobby of The Enchanted Hunters, Humbert strains to conceal what just took place in the hotel room upstairs, where he and the "female child" had "strenuous intercourse three times that very morning." As if that were not enough, Humbert is hiding other dreadful secrets. Not until he has safely removed Lolita from the hotel and its onlookers will he dare to tell her the truth: that he has lied to her about their destination as he has lied to her about her mother. Charlotte Haze is not eagerly awaiting her daughter's arrival in some "hypothetical hospital" in a nearby town (141–42). She is dead. Lolita is a hapless and helpless orphan.

As he and the "lone child" drive away from the hotel, Humbert is suddenly gripped by a feeling of "oppressive hideous constraint as if I were sitting with the small ghost of somebody I had just killed." Temporarily awaking to the fact that the little "waif" seated next to him is no "immortal daemon," Humbert reluctantly voices his guilt. In contrast to Frankenstein, whose little brother, William, is eventually murdered by the creature, Humbert has no hideous monster to blame for the violence perpetrated against a helpless child. There is only the "heavy-limbed, foul-smelling adult" seated next to her in the car (142). No wonder he feels haunted by a small ghost: only a shade, or shadow, remains of Dolly Haze's brief childhood. The true demon is the "pentapod monster," as Humbert later describes himself, who has defiled the offspring in his charge.[22]

No sooner does this revelation occur than the processes of deflection, and self-serving projection, once again take over—as Humbert begins to feel "somewhere at the bottom of [his] dark turmoil . . . the writhing of desire again, so *monstrous* was [his] appetite for that *miserable* nymphet" (142, emphasis added). Here the narrator's language offers a direct parody of Frankenstein's, as the scientist blames the "miserable monster" for what he himself has wrought (39). In those moments, however, when Humbert's monstrous appetite temporarily abates, he again suffers "pangs of guilt." In realizing his "lifelong dream" by having sexual intercourse with a child, he has, he admits, "plunged" them both "into nightmare" (142).

A similar descent into nightmare is traced by Shelley's narrator. Like Humbert, Frankenstein pursues his lifelong dream with solipsistic fervor—having "desired it," as he says, "with an ardour that far exceeded moderation." He, too, observes "the beauty of the dream" plunge into nightmare, a living "hell" that "even Dante could not have conceived" (39–40). (In a similar allusion to Dante's *Inferno,* Humbert describes the nympholept's strange admixture of guilt and rapture, heaven and hell as the "first circle of paradise" [285].) Seized by the Promethean ambition to create life, Frankenstein does not pause to consider the potentially disastrous consequences. Blindly he assumes that the gigantic creature he is patching together out of bits and pieces—the flesh and bones collected in charnel houses—will be "beautiful." Only after he assembles the severed limbs and body parts, stitches them together, and jolts them into life can he perceive what a dreadful "thing" he has wrought (36, 39–40). Even so, Frankenstein does not accept responsibility for the nightmare that follows. Only after his infant brother and old father, his best friend, and his bride have all died does he fathom the extent of the destruction he has wrought.

The parallels between Frankenstein's "miserable monster" and Humbert's "miserable nymphet" help to clarify, as we have seen, the relationship of each protagonist to the child he victimizes. In addition, both protagonists suffer tremendous feelings of guilt, which they project onto others. Frankenstein curses the creature for the murderous actions he has set in motion; Humbert reserves his purest hatred for the "fiend" who steals Lolita from him (*Lolita* 255, 261). At a deeper level, however, both characters recognize in their hated adversaries a mirror image of themselves. Frankenstein's hideous monster mirrors, first as a physical shape and then in his vicious actions, the scientist's monstrous disregard for moral and natural laws. By the same token, Quilty, the pervert and pedophile, serves as a nasty, even more brutish reflection of Humbert's "monstrous" lust (142). The passion enflaming both protagonists—one to usurp nature and create life, the other to usurp a child's life for his own pleasure—is monstrous in the most fundamental sense: a transgression, as Humbert ultimately admits, of "all laws of humanity" (308).[23]

Referring, near the end of Shelley's novel, to the "hideous narration" he is about to complete, Frankenstein appears, at least temporarily, to take full measure of his guilt. Repeating one of the terms he has used to deplore the creature, "hideous," he now claims this epithet for the story he has set in motion (42, 56, 166, and passim). With a similar sense of the hideousness he has wrought, Humbert draws his tale to a close: "This then is my story. I have reread it. It has bits of marrow sticking to it, and blood, and beautiful bright-green flies" (310). Humbert's narration, like Frankenstein's, issues from the ruins of death and decay; it resembles, metaphorically, the monster Frankenstein created—a kind of living corpse.

That the text is a body, or monstrous offspring—one that each writer, like a modern-day Frankenstein, constructs and sends out into the world—is a notion that Shelley asks her readers to contemplate. In her preface to the 1831 edition of the novel, she says with a paradoxical flourish: "And now, once again, I bid my hideous progeny to go forth and prosper. I have affection for it, for it was the offspring of happy days" (197, 192). Implicitly linking her own acts of creation—both as a writer and a mother—with those of her Promethean narrator, she hints that, as Peter Brooks observes, art is "a kind of controlled play with the daemonic." Significantly, however, Shelley embraces the relationship that Frankenstein spurns—avowing her affection for the "hideous" offspring she has delivered into the world. Like a maternal expression of unconditional love, Shelley's affection for her "hideous progeny" implicitly comments on her protagonist's outright rejection of his: Frankenstein's failure to acknowledge, in Brooks's phrase, "the destructive potential of the creative drive."[24] Both *Frankenstein* and *Lolita* testify to the destructive as well as the creative power of imagination and the terrible beauty it engenders. In the "controlled play with the daemonic" that each text invites its readers to enter, we discover the profound extent to which imagination and will can wreak havoc with nature and human nature. Entering into a relationship with the demonic that is wildly out of control, each narrator produces his "hideous" story: hideous not because his desires are grotesquely thwarted but because human hope and innocence—embodied for both Nabokov and Shelley in the image of childhood—have been monstrously abused.

Describing the cross-country journey on which he and Lolita embarked, Humbert sadly acknowledges that despite having "been everywhere" they "had really seen nothing." He adds, "And I catch myself thinking today that our long journey had only defiled with a sinuous trail of slime the lovely, trustful, dreamy, enormous country that by then, in retrospect, was no more to us than a collection of dog-eared maps, ruined tour books, old tires, and her sobs in the night—every night, every night" (177–78). Humbert's account concretely renders the metaphysical process by which, in Nabokov's expressed view, a world emptied of good becomes a fitting habitation for evil.[25] Indifferent to everything but his desire, Humbert has seen *nothing* of the innocent and dreamy landscape, the beneficent order of reality through which he passed like a blind man. For him this lovely country was only a grid, a blueprint, a series of marks on a map. Such an abstract universe, emptied of love and meaning, signifies the moral vacuum that evil rushes to fill—just as the child's miserable sobs filled the silence every night. Recognizing that he has defiled both the child and the pristine beauty of the unspoiled countryside, Humbert faintly gleans the connection between the radiant source of reality and the child's innate innocence. To have robbed Dolores Haze of her childhood constitutes nothing less, in Nabokov's universe, than a crime against the cosmos.

The Romantic Legacy Qualified

Humbert's fierce but blinkered imagination leads, paradoxically, to his transgressions against the source and symbol of creative imagination: the child. For Wordsworth and Blake, Dickens and Nabokov, the child's wonder, innocence, and spontaneity constitute the image and embodiment of human freedom and creativity. In striving to attain his perfect world or paradise, Humbert deprives Lolita of her rightful childhood—and betrays the principles of romantic faith and freedom. Significantly, his capacity to transcend his solipsistic vision entails not wholesale abandonment but searching renewal of romantic faith.

In a passage near the end of the novel Humbert recalls a time when, overhearing Dolly talking to a school friend about death, he first realized how little he knew about the child. "And it struck me," he says, "that I simply did not know a thing about my darling's mind and that quite possibly, behind the awful juvenile clichés, there was in her a garden and a twilight, and a palace gate—dim and adorable regions which happened to be lucidly and absolutely forbidden to me" (286). Employing the fairy-tale formulas of a remote and enchanting kingdom—one that faintly echoes the refrain of Poe's "Annabel Lee," with its "kingdom by the sea"—Humbert is not, for once, lamenting his lost paradise. Instead, the romantic evocation of a walled garden, or private kingdom, pays homage to the child's inner life, forever inaccessible to him.

Only in hindsight, in the process of recounting his love and loss of Lolita, does Humbert glean an image of the child as an autonomous being, an individual with the right to her own kingdom, her own universe of hopes and dreams, feelings and flights of fancy that have nothing to do with his desire. Only this gradual, painful recognition of the child's independent reality secures Humbert the moral and imaginative insight that makes his story so compelling to the reader—even a reader as wary of treating Nabokov as a "plodding moralist" as Michael Wood, who says: "if Humbert has not evoked the substantial American child as well as the solipsized . . . nymphet, there is no novel here that matters." At the end of his story Humbert's wish to protect Lolita's privacy—his instruction that his memoir "be published only when Lolita is no longer alive"—is one manifestation of his belated recognition of her autonomous being (311). That she inhabits his narrative not only as a bewitching nymphet but as a victimized child testifies, in a much more telling way, to his moral growth as well as his guilt.[26]

Only through the medium of art can Humbert restore to the child he tyrannized—the child whose "life," as he says, he "broke"—some semblance of the freedom and autonomy he otherwise denied her (281). But as he makes clear, the consolation of art is no compensation for what she has lost: "Unless it can be proven to me . . . that in the infinite run it does not matter a jot that a North American girl-child named Dolores Haze had been deprived of her childhood by a maniac, unless this can be proven (and if it can, then life is a joke), I see nothing for the treatment of my misery but the melancholy and very local palliative of articulate art" (285). In stark language that abruptly departs from the "fancy prose style" in which most of his narrative is cast,

Humbert evokes the child's right to her own life and liberty. Significantly, he now eschews the temporal terms reserved for his nymphets, grounding the child's autonomy in space: the boundless space of the North American continent, whose geographical extension and history patently invoke a universe beyond Humbert's dominion.

Humbert's admission that "Dolores Haze had been deprived of her childhood by a maniac" implicitly affirms a central tenet of romantic faith: "the conviction that," as David Grylls says, "children being innocent, the wickedest thing one can do to them is to rob them of their childhood."[27] In Dickens's *Dombey and Son* Edith Skewton accuses her conniving mother of this very crime: "What childhood did you ever leave to me?" she demands. "I was a woman—artful, designing, mercenary, laying snares for men—before I knew myself. . . . Look at me, taught to scheme and plot when children play" (406). Victim of still fouler manipulations at the hands of her stepfather, Dolores Haze might well lay this charge at Humbert's feet. Schooled by her "mercenary" relationship with a man who pretends to be her protector, she, too, is forced to scheme and plot when she should be at play.

Tyrannized by a vicious adult, Dolly Haze's young life, like that of so many of Dickens's "poor children," is prematurely cut off by death. Humbert, at least, is spared the recriminating knowledge that, as John Ray Jr. says in the novel's foreword, Mrs. Richard F. Schiller (Lolita's married name) dies at seventeen "in childbed, giving birth to a stillborn girl" (6). The reader's discovery of this grim fact adds a final note of pathos—what Nabokov calls, in his lecture on *Bleak House,* "divine" pity—to the theme of abortive childhood and thwarted innocence. As much as any work by Dickens, *Lolita* owes its poignancy, and a good deal of its poetry, to the vision of the child reflected in its depths. Here and throughout Nabokov's imaginative universe, the child's image shines like a beacon: a beacon that serves, among other things, to highlight this writer's unique position in the development of twentieth-century fiction. Nabokov's novels are as involuted and self-reflexive as any work of postmodernist fabulation; at the same time, however, they evoke a mysterious connection, impalpable as a shaft of light, to a world that lies beyond the alleged prison house of language and the confines of the text. Readers who detect this connection can appreciate the way the novelist's art both engages and defies appearance. Like the magician whose deft fingers pluck a live bird from his hat, Nabokov beckons the real in the very act of creating illusion.

Ambiguous Constructs

Kosinski's Child as Painted Bird

Lolita's midcentury American landscape bears little trace of World War II's traumatic influence. Even in Nabokov's earlier dystopian novels, *Invitation to a Beheading* and *Bend Sinister,* the nightmarish worlds of political tyranny fail to eclipse the luminous image of childhood and the optimistic faith in human nature it expresses. Evincing the author's self-avowed "irrational belief in the goodness of man" and the child's original innocence, Nabokov's fiction offers a fascinating exception to much of the writing produced in the postwar era. A more timely representative is the first novel that a young Polish émigré, living in the United States and writing in English, published a decade after *Lolita*. In *The Painted Bird*—which first appeared in 1965 and was followed by a revised edition in 1976—Jerzy Kosinski produced a best-seller that shocked readers with its horrific account of a child's wartime experience.[1]

Part of the appeal of *The Painted Bird* "when it first appeared," Naomi Sokoloff suggests, "was that it contributed to the vogue for the violent, the bizarre, and the absurd in American fiction of the sixties." Her statement begs the question regarding the historical and cultural conditions giving rise to such a trend. For fostering a sense of existential absurdity and meaningless suffering, the impact of World War II can hardly be overstated. Knowledge of genocide and the Holocaust led many members of the postwar generation to question, in the words of one commentator, "the sanity of organized and developed societies."[2] Having spawned radical doubts about human nature and civilization, World War II helped to create a cultural divide that separates

most postwar novels from their prewar counterparts. From Kurt
Vonnegut's *Slaughterhouse-Five* to Joseph Heller's *Catch-22* and Thomas
Pynchon's *Gravity's Rainbow,* postwar fiction has registered the effects
of this disaster and the shock waves it set in motion. Drawing on the
spectacle of global warfare, mass genocide, and nuclear holocaust,
these novels depict the devastating power of the group or collective to
crush the individual. Such catastrophic events, eclipsing any residual
faith in original innocence, have intensified—to a degree Rousseau
could not have anticipated—the Romantics' perception of society as
repressive, indeed destructive, of the individual.

For *The Painted Bird* Kosinski drew on his traumatic wartime childhood to depict in the starkest terms the vicious power of the collective
over the individual. As he says in an essay, he deliberately chose to portray the threatened individual "as a child, and society in its most deadly
form, in a state of war. I hoped," he adds, "that the confrontation between the defenseless individual and overpowering society, between
the child and war, would represent the essential anti-human condition"
(*Passing By* 34, 186). Its focus confined to a single character, the unnamed
boy through whose eyes the events of the novel unfold, *The Painted Bird*
appears deceptively simple: a chronicle, based on the author's personal
history, of an Eastern European child's experience of World War II.[3]
The nature of that experience, and its impact on the reader, is so immediate and graphically horrifying—and the style in which it is couched
so transparent, as though the text were a window through which
the reader might gaze directly at the unmediated "real" world—that the
novel's most suggestive and ambiguous implications tend to escape
the reader's attention.[4]

Some of *The Painted Bird*'s most provocative passages, structurally
and thematically, are also the most concretely explicit and repellent.
(Only the most determined reader is likely to focus, for example, on
Kosinski's style in a passage that starkly depicts the devouring of a human
corpse by starving rats.) Such nightmarish images—the extraction of a
peasant's eyes with a tin spoon or the coupling of a peasant girl with a
goat—suggest that the author's treatment of the child's wartime experience, however concretely rendered, is styled to shock. As Kosinski
avows, every "writer constructs one curtain after another" between
"external reality and his own imagination." The "locale and setting"
of *The Painted Bird,* he admits, are "metaphorical": the "whole journey
could actually have taken place in the mind"—with the image of the

painted bird serving as a "symbol" of the novel's protagonist (*Passing By* 201, 206, 211). In this war-torn landscape fraught with terror and violence, the bombs raining destruction on unnamed cities, the anonymous trains dispatching cramped carloads of groaning human beings through the Eastern European countryside, the skull and crossbones on an SS officer's uniform all testify to the crushing force of the collective bearing down on the fragile individual.

Separated from his parents by the accidents of war, the six-year-old protagonist of *The Painted Bird* arrives friendless and alone in a provincial landscape mined with dangers. It is the fall of 1939, and the unnamed countryside is identified, without further specificity, as lying "east" of a "large city in Eastern Europe" where the boy formerly lived with his parents. Bewildered by their disappearance, the boy at first expects them "to come for me any day": "Wasn't I their child?" he asks himself. "What were parents for if not to be with their children in times of danger?" Soon he discovers that his "parents were nowhere" and that he has "to find people" to help him survive (3, 12–13).

Haphazardly wandering from desolate village to village, the six-year-old struggles to find food and shelter among an "isolated and inbred" peasantry, whose habitual suspicion of strangers has developed, under wartime conditions, into lethal hostility. In contrast to the peasants' Slavic features—their "fair-skinned" complexion, "blond hair and blue or gray eyes"—the boy is "olive-skinned, dark-haired." Further marking him as an alien or outsider whom the country people immediately identify as a Gypsy or Jew, the boy's language is that of the urban, "educated class," a language "barely intelligible to the peasants" (1–2). Bartering his labor for food and shelter, the orphaned child experiences—to an extent unimaginable in Twain and Dickens—the heartless cruelty, violence, and depravity of which human beings are capable. Very little of humankind's sordid behavior remains unknown to the child, who witnesses everything from the mundane spectacle of village boys torturing a squirrel to the most diabolical forms of cruelty, the most sadistic kinds of slaughter.

Kosinski's Boy versus Twain's Boy

Struggling to stay alive in a death-saturated universe, Kosinski's boy evinces many of the qualities of the traditional picaresque hero, for whom cunning and guile are necessary means of survival. Like Huckleberry

Finn, he takes advantage of his insignificant size and presence to beat a hasty retreat whenever adults become too threatening or murderous. His inventiveness at escape also recalls those resources of creative imagination that Huck and his romantically inspired peers summon to the cause of innocent adventure. But the traditional echoes Kosinski's novel sounds ultimately reveal the radical differences between his novel's image of childhood and that of his literary predecessors. To clarify these differences, I should like to recall briefly the nature of Twain's boy Huckleberry Finn and his adventures on the Mississippi.

One of Huck's remarkable talents lies in the way he can improvise an identity at the drop of a hat, effortlessly fabricating a past for himself or, with the help of some fresh hog's blood, staging the scene of his ostensible slaughter. Clever and observant, Huck takes on various guises and disguises—at one point dressing up as a girl, at another posing as the child of a family riddled with smallpox—to elude his would-be captors. But for Huck these confinements are only temporary. All the social trappings he adopts, all the different suits of clothing he dons, are part of the protective coloration that the natural mimic assumes to elude vicious predators. Like a moth whose wings bear intricate markings that resemble those on a leaf or a fish lying rigid as a rock at the bottom of a pond, Huck inevitably reverts to his original identity or state: Rousseau's state of nature. Here Huck is always himself, an innocent boy whose innate decency, kindheartedness, and loyalty win out over every cultural habit, convention, institution—virtually all of them devised, in Twain's view, to transform innocence into greed, hypocrisy, lust, and vengeance.

Shedding the trappings of civilization, Huck finds himself back on the raft; stripping off his (cultural) clothing, he drifts naked as a newborn down the river. Together with the runaway slave Jim, the runaway white boy resumes the idyll of innocence, reenters the world of nature. Unimpeded by the constructs of collective life, Huck is free to follow the dictates of his innocent heart, to discover the startling fact that Jim, a black man and a runaway slave, is not only a fellow human being but a noble, exemplary one. For a southern white boy in the 1830s who has been taught from birth and from the Bible to regard slavery as righteous and to despise the abolitionist, the revelation is both stunning and shattering. The moment Huck resolves to "*go to hell*" rather than to turn Jim in is a resounding testament to Rousseau's idyll of childhood (206). The "ceremony of innocence," to recall

William Butler Yeats's dire prophecy in "The Second Coming," is not yet "drowned." The celebration of innocence—the child's natural and humanity's original innocence—sounds a resonant, if nostalgic, chord in this novel, completed when romantic idealism had all but disappeared. When Huck declares his love and loyalty to Jim, Twain's readers can almost hear Blake's little babes, all "naked & white," laughing and "leaping" in their heaven ("The Chimney Sweeper," ll. 17, 15).

The freedom and unfettered innocence that Huck discovers on the river—and that he sets out to regain at the end of the novel—are only a faint glimmer, the shards of a broken dream, for Kosinski's twentieth-century child. Yearning like Huck for a world of pure freedom, the boy also identifies that freedom with the world of nature, the "primitive kingdom of birds and forests where everything was infinitely abundant, wild, blooming" (*Painted Bird* 48). For the boy, however, this world of freedom—this world forever "clashing with the human world"—remains torturously out of reach. Only once, after being buried to the neck in earth and remaining there for hours "like an abandoned head of cabbage," does he joyfully believe that he can merge with this wonderful world, return to the source, and reenter the state of nature (21). Then he begins to hallucinate in earnest: "I gave up. I was myself now a bird. . . . Stretching my limbs, I joined the flock of ravens. Borne abruptly up on a gust of fresh, reviving wind, I soared straight into a ray of sunshine . . . , and my joyous cawing was mimicked by my winged companions." In his "crazed" condition, the boy believes he is free; in fact, he is on the verge of death. Alert to his moribund condition, those so-called winged companions show their true colors. As the boy subsequently tells the reader, "Olga found me in the midst of the swarming flock of ravens. I was nearly frozen and my head was deeply lacerated by the birds. She quickly dug me out" (24).

No matter how solitary and rootless his existence, the boy cannot find his way back to that original state of nature of which he dreams. On the level of plot, the boy cannot escape the tyranny of the group or collective in all its forms: whether it is the primitive master-servant relationship inflicted on him by the peasants, the welfare policies of the orphanage where he eventually winds up, the Roman Catholic liturgy in a rural church, or the marxist ideology taught him by soldiers of the Red Army. On the level of narrative and thematic structure, the world to which the boy dreams of escaping proves not only inaccessible but nonexistent. There simply is no original source of innocence or existence to which the human being can return. Just as the boy quickly forgets his immediate past—the world he shared with his parents—so that it begins to seem a dream, the reader fails to discover in the child any image, source, or essence of the human that controverts or transcends his immediate environment. Everything about *The Painted Bird,* from the ambiguity of its eponymous symbol to the events it depicts, undermines the conventional polarities of nature and culture, animal and human, innocence and experience.

Even the distinction between past and present is ambiguous: as the boy's memories of early childhood fade, he notes that "this past of mine was rapidly turning into an illusion like one of my nanny's incredible fables" (8). But as the past retreats and the present takes over, the boy seems, paradoxically, to be progressing backward in time. From a sophisticated urban world, where even his remembered toys—"the airplane with the turning propellers," the "small easy-moving tank, and the fire engine with its extending ladder"—bespeak the technical progress of postindustrial society, he enters an archaic world of superstition, magic, and primitive religion. It is well known in this world, for example, "that even a single lost hair, if spied by an evil eye, could be the cause of serious throat trouble" (8). If this archaic world bears traces of humanity's childhood, the ignorance and brutality of the childlike peasants demolish any Rousseauian notions of the innate nobility of human beings living close to their natural state. So fearful are these illiterate peasants of the unknown that the sight of a stranger, even a six-year-old stranger, prompts them to savage attack. The first time the destitute boy enters an unfamiliar village, the peasants, women and children included, begin to prod and poke him. When he begins to cry, the crowd becomes more lively, pelting him with everything from dried cow dung to moldy potatoes and small stones. As the attack is stepped up and one man begins kicking the boy, another whacking him with a whip, "the children and adults howled with laughter" (14–15).

In his desire to escape human cruelty, the boy dreams of finding refuge in nature, but he is thwarted there as well. Both kingdoms, the animal and the human, are riddled with conflict; there is no refuge from the world's strife and struggle, no pastoral retreat. Just as two peasants will go at each other "with their teeth like enraged dogs," the "woolly mosses hanging from the boughs of great trees" recall "graying, half-frozen rabbit skins." Similarly, the bloodstains on the walls of a room where a murder has been committed become "a dark rust-colored fungus embedded in the wood forever" (76, 86, 88). The pristine "kingdom of birds and forests" to which the boy, like a modern-day Huck, yearns to escape is an illusion: the faint memory of a once cherished ideal. The idyll is sounded, and shattered, early in the novel with the introduction of Lekh, the bird catcher, and the novel's eponymous symbol, the painted bird.

The Ambiguities of Nature and Culture

A lover of birds who also traps and kills them, Lekh is enthralled by a strange and wild woman known as Stupid Ludmila. A vagrant who lives in the forests, Ludmila, the boy explains, "was Lekh's great love. He made up tender songs for her in which she figured as a strange-colored bird flying to faraway worlds, free and quick, brighter and more beautiful than other creatures." For the boy, Lekh and Ludmila's rhapsodic lovemaking sounds a momentary pastoral note as their bodies imitate the swaying of "the grasses around them, almost growing into each other like two tree trunks rising up from a single root" (48). Soon, however, erotic love turns to war, in much the way that Lekh's love of birds leads to envy and malice. Like his delight in Ludmila's unfettered existence, admiration for the apparent freedom of birds led Lekh, as a young man, to abandon his home and village for life in the forest, where he lives "like a wild and abandoned bird" (42). In the forest the bird lover has gradually transformed himself, through study and imitation of his subject, into a bird catcher—at one moment "speaking soothingly" to his birds, at another "threatening them with death" (45). Even more conflicted is the expression of Lekh's love for Ludmila. The birdlike freedom of her solitary existence is the source of both his admiration and his resentment.

When, as the boy says, Ludmila "would disappear in the undergrowth like a starling," Lekh, the frustrated lover, would wait for her, lonely and bereft. If her absence is prolonged, the bird catcher's longing turns mean, his mood ugly. Then, to vent his frustration and anger, Lekh singles out a scapegoat for punishment. (The parallels are obvious: the countryside through which Lekh and Ludmila roam is crisscrossed by trains transporting carloads of Jews, Gypsies, and other "undesirables" to nearby concentration camps, where the ideological fury of German society is being unleashed on its victims.) Each time that Lekh, "possessed by a silent rage," must endure the torments of thwarted desire, he picks out "the strongest bird" from the many he has captured. After preparing some "stinking paints of different colors," he methodically applies them to his chosen scapegoat. When the task is completed, Lekh carries the newly painted bird "into the thick of the forest," where he releases it into the air. Then the bird lover waits until his victim attracts "a flock of the same species," whose members attack and finally kill him (49–50). Even after Lekh traps and sacrifices a large raven—which, apparently so "happy and free," is torn apart by the other birds after he is released into the sky—his wrath is not assuaged. He orders the boy "to keep setting new snares and catching new birds." When, weeks later, Ludmila reappears, her contrary display of emotions more than matches that of her lover. Finding that Lekh has gone away, "she alternately sobbed and laughed"—first pressing Lekh's old cap affectionately against her cheeks, then trampling it furiously with her feet (51–52). With mercurial rapidity, laughter dissolves into tears; and Ludmila's love, like Lekh's, descends into disappointment, rage, and hate.

Later in the novel the boy has occasion to observe another pair of adults engaged in sexual intercourse. This time, however, the pastoral note is significantly absent. So imbued are the actions of human beings with the boy's experience of war that the "trembling woman" now strikes him as yet another helpless victim. Buried under the man's crushing weight, her body does not sway with unfettered life; rather, her "legs resemble the wings of a bird crushed under a stone." As the boy looks on "with disgust at the two intertwined, twitching human frames," he sees nothing to distinguish lovemaking from fighting: "So that's what love was," he thinks. "This love was like a brawl in which man and woman wrested pleasure from each other, fighting, incapable of thought, half stunned, wheezing, less than human" (174).

Even in rare moments of apprehended beauty and apparent tranquillity, the Darwinian struggle for survival quickly eclipses the fleeting sense of harmony. When, for example, the coming of spring announces itself in the melting of the river's ice, the blue dragonflies hovering above the current engage in a life-and-death "struggle" against "the sudden bursts of cold, wet wind." And when the eagerly expected warm weather finally arrives, the boy observes, it brings "along a plague. The people whom it struck wriggled with pain like transfixed earthworms, were shaken by a ghastly chill, and died without regaining consciousness" (20). Here human beings, rather than animals, are the prime victims, but the simile used to describe their symptoms calls attention to the endless struggle against disease and death futilely waged by the animal kingdom. To human beings this struggle may appear less dramatic than their own but only because those victims, like the transfixed earthworms, tend to be silent, anonymous, invisible. The world of nature is no less implicated in vicious strife than the human world, whose cataclysms have driven the boy to seek refuge in the countryside.

In a passage that ambiguously melds the human world with its presumed opposite, the inanimate and nonhuman, the boy recalls "the first days of the war, when a bomb hit a house across the street from my parents' home." He remembers how the deafening roar of collapsing walls became fused with "the screams of unknown dying people." The nightmarish spectacle of chandeliers falling apart and "grand pianos opening and closing their lids in flight" discloses a universe of inorganic objects in animated flight from the blast, while the organic bodies of human beings are reduced to rags made sticky and red by blood:

> Limp human bodies lay tossed over the jagged edges of the broken floors and ceiling like rags covering the break. They were just beginning to soak in the red dye. Tiny particles of torn paper, plaster, and paint clung to the sticky red rags like hungry flies. . . . Then came the groans and screams of people pinned down by the falling beams, impaled on rods and pipes, partially torn and crushed under chunks of walls. Only one old woman came up from the dark pit. She clutched desperately at bricks and when her toothless mouth opened to speak she was suddenly unable to utter a sound. (75)

As civilization proceeds to destroy the material objects it has devised (pianos, houses, chandeliers), Kosinski's metaphors reveal how the human reverts to mere matter. Still more gruesome and ironic, the blood-soaked bodies dwindle into sticky red rags so lifeless, so lacking in human identity that the bits of torn paper and paint sticking to them appear furiously alive by comparison. With all the zeal of the living, these bits of inert matter cling "to the sticky red rags like hungry flies."

In the universe of *The Painted Bird* culture neither alters nor transcends the savagery of nature. It simply paints over it, superficially altering appearances, just as Lekh distorts the appearance of the bird whose feathers he paints with man-made colors. Such distortions are sufficient to confuse the rest of the brown flock, which ultimately attacks and kills the painted bird—just as superficial differences in physiognomy provoke the peasants' rage against the boy (50). Ultimately, however, the dead bird's blood dissolves, as it merges with, the paint applied to its feathers and wings. Similarly, the savage conflict of global war—which each side regards as a battle to maintain its distinct heritage and identity—dissolves the veneer of cultural difference, as well as civilized order, in the massive flow of blood. Far more vicious than the birds Lekh dupes into killing one of their own, human beings devise the bombs and other weapons that reduce members of their species to bits of inert matter. (For readers recalling other events of World War II, Kosinski's description of those "tiny particles"— bits of "torn paper, plaster, and paint" clinging like hungry flies to human flesh—is particularly dreadful to contemplate. Once the atomic bomb was unleashed on Japan, dread of such microscopic particles would reign supreme in the civilized world. Like so many parasites or hungry flies, they forever threaten to reduce organic life to bits of dead matter.)

Powerfully dissolving distinctions between animate and inanimate matter, *The Painted Bird* metaphorically exposes the ambiguous border between nature and culture, savagery and civilization. As mentioned earlier, in one of the novel's most horrific passages starving rats swarm in a concrete bunker, "murdering and eating one another" for lack of other food (61). The link between animal and human murderousness —between the greedy cannibalism of the rats inside the bunker and the ideological war raging outside—is vividly suggested through the stylized yoking of natural and cultural images: "The moving rumps of the rats became stained with brownish red blood. The animals . . . [were] panting, twitching their tails, their teeth gleaming under their half-open snouts, their eyes reflecting the daylight as if they were the beads of a rosary" (63–64). As vivid as it is shocking, this passage fuses images of savage nature, red in tooth and claw, with those suggesting humankind's lofty desire to transcend animal instinct through worship and prayer. Kosinski's evocation of the rats' bodies, "stained with brownish red blood," resonates with the image of those "sticky red rags" of inert human flesh created by man-made bombs. The passage also recalls the novel's central image and symbol: Lekh's painted bird viciously pecked to death by its fellow creatures until "the blood seeped through its colored wings," staining its feathers with a darker hue (49–50).

The Child as Painted Bird

Much later in the novel, after the child's years of wandering draw to a close at the war's end, the boy (now on the verge of adolescence) continues to associate his own "drive for freedom" with the "primitive kingdom" of nature. When his parents finally locate their son, now twelve years old, at an orphanage and arrive to take him home, he sadly recalls the "powerful leaps, playful tumbles, and swift escapes" of a magnificent hare that one of his ephemeral masters, Makar the peasant, had caught and caged. Days after his capture, the hare discovers its chance to escape; but despite the boy's help and encouragement, it cannot leave its cage. "Freedom," the boy realizes, had "left him like the wind-driven fragrance evaporating from crushed, dried clover." The hare "now carried the cage in himself." The image of the defeated hare, "suddenly aged and shrunken," expresses the boy's dismay at his own caged condition as he realizes he cannot run away from those two forlorn beings, his parents—even though, after so many years on his own, he feels trapped by the filial bond. Some "inner force restrained me," he observes, "and forbade me to fly off. I suddenly felt like Lekh's painted bird, which some unknown force was pulling toward his kind" (241–42).

Here, as the novel draws to a close, its eponymous symbol is transposed. The central analogy between the boy and the painted bird has focused until now on the fatal effects of difference in a world based on collective identity and conformity. The brightly colored wings of Lekh's painted bird spark hostility in the brown flock, which attacks the solitary alien and kills it. Similarly, the blond, blue-eyed peasants demonize the boy's dark features and treat him as the enemy. The Germans' Nazi ideology lethally fuses with the peasants' primitive superstitions, particularly their fear of the devil.

In the novel's final allusions to the symbol, however, the emphasis is not on dangerous difference but on imprisoning likeness—on the fetters binding one member of a species, community, or family to the others. The boy now suffers the pain of belonging rather than of alienation. He finds himself succumbing to the same "unknown force" that draws the painted bird "toward his kind." Unlike the murderous brown flock, the boy's kin, or kind—his parents—want only to protect him; but it is too late. Having spent so much of his childhood surviving on his own, he views them as a threat to his independence. The capacity for love—celebrated in Dickens, Twain, and even Nabokov as a potential source of moral regeneration—is to the boy only another trap or snare. All his suffering at the hands of cruel adults does not end, as it does for the Dickensian child, in youthful martyrdom or loving reconciliation; it ends, as we shall see, in the victim's thrilling discovery of his own power to victimize. Reared in a world of murderous conflict, the boy is "disappointed" when he realizes that the war is now over (191).

Although Kosinski's child proves extremely resourceful, he lacks those inner resources, that metaphysical resilience of the Wordsworthian child—to whom even Dolly Haze, still kind and trusting toward the world despite her entrapment by Humbert, is heir. In rendering his image of childhood, Kosinski focuses not on the latent resources of human nature but on the painted product: the way the individual is shaped and finally determined by the collective.

Admittedly, Kosinski's child, in contrast to Lekh's painted birds, survives the alienation and persecution to which he is subjected. His plight, while symbolized by that of the painted bird, is hardly identical to it. Obviously, what happens to Lekh's painted birds could not happen without the bird catcher's spiteful interference. In the boy's world the relationship between cause and effect is more complex and ambiguous. Whereas the artificial colors that Lekh imposes on the painted bird can be traced to a single source, the physiological traits that make the boy appear alien derive from a complex network of sources. No colors have to be applied to the child to make him stand out from the blue-eyed, fair-haired peasants who view him with suspicion. The boy naturally looks different from them; but as Kosinski's novel reveals, it is the cultural construction of difference—not the physical traits in themselves—that makes the boy's features so dangerous to his survival. In another cultural context, at a different historical moment, the boy's dark hair and eyes might be perceived differently, especially if the ruling powers happened to possess such features themselves.

At one point in the novel the boy wonders "what gave people of one color of eyes and hair such great power over other people" (93). The phrasing of his question implicitly underscores the relative insignificance of the content or color of particular features. Even at his young age he appears to understand that for human beings there is no way of distinguishing the image or construct from its presumed origin. Separated from his kind by the man-made disasters of war, wandering through a world that has deprived him and so many others of warmth, shelter, food, and adequate clothing, the boy is still fully dressed: a creature clothed in culture. By establishing, through the symbol of the painted bird, an analogy between a man-made product—paint—and the natural or physiological hues of skin, eyes, and hair, Kosinski collapses the traditional opposition between nature and culture. He suggests, furthermore, that it hardly matters whether the boy is actually (that is, ethnically) a Jew or a Gypsy. Like the bird whose wings have been painted a different color, the boy's superficial resemblance to another ethnic group is sufficient cause for his extermination. In this nightmarish world, where the lives of untold numbers of men, women, and children are being snuffed out as easily as candles, distinctions between appearance and reality, essence and identity have no meaning.

A world of nightmare is often invoked by critics to describe the atmosphere of this novel, in which extreme visual and emotional effects are interwoven with a naturalist's sharp rendering of concrete detail. As Naomi Sokoloff points out, *The Painted Bird* creates the "impression of an equivocal reality" located "somewhere between a reliable account of a specific historical moment and a purely fictive parable of evil." This effect, she observes, largely derives from Kosinski's handling of the child's point of view. To the boy, who has "little experience or memory beyond the terrors of the moment," horror "has come to seem ordinary," atrocity routine.[5] The child's inexperience and lack of historical insight create a perspective at once vivid and myopic. As Kosinski says of this novel, "Events to the child are immediate: discoveries are one-dimensional. This kills, that maims, this one cuffs, that one caresses" (*Passing By* 208).

Interestingly, the child's lack of historical and social perspective does not detract from his emblematic status as a painted bird, or creature clothed in culture. Having, as Sokoloff says, little "memory beyond the terrors of the moment," the boy's psyche is clearly formed or constructed by his environment. In contrast to the Nazi ideology that demonizes the boy and celebrates racial purity, *The Painted Bird* undermines the notion of human purity or essence. As the historical setting of Kosinski's novel demonstrates, such notions are easily exploited, turned against the very humanity they purport to celebrate. Taking it on themselves to cleanse the human race of its impurities, the self-appointed guardians of essence decimate the human and natural landscape, littering city and countryside with "limp human bodies." The sordid spectacle of those broken bodies in every stage of desiccation and decomposition—like the images captured on film that still haunt us half a century later, as they promise to haunt posterity—may well betray the ultimate degradation of the romantic spirit.

In our collective memory of World War II and the Holocaust, Kosinski's novel reminds us, all the "limp human bodies," all the maimed and the dead, look eerily alike. Stripped of their cultural clothing or identity, blond and brunette, the fair and the swarthy fuse into heaps of anonymous matter, bits of sticky red rags. The mask or facade of civilized order dissolves in the red dye of spilled human blood, revealing the ubiquitous face of death. Far from resembling that "glittering death's head and crossbones" emblazoned on the Nazi officer's uniform—to the boy a "symbol of might and majesty"—death's true face proves as indistinct as the "formless chunks" to which starving rats reduce a man's body (119, 64). Such formlessness bespeaks not mastery over death but the subjugation of all living things to its law.

To the child's myopic view, however, the Nazi insignia symbolize superhuman authority and power. Worship of power, Kosinski suggests, is the inevitable result of victimhood: in the Nazi officer's "resplendent" presence, says the boy, "I felt like a squashed caterpillar oozing in the dust, a creature that could not harm anyone yet aroused loathing and disgust" (118–19). Subjected to the brutal exercise of power by those who torture and try to kill him, the boy is eager to escape pain and injury in any way he can. Persuaded for a time by the teachings of a local priest, he momentarily believes he has found "the governing principle" of reality: "there was order in the human world, and justice too. One had only to recite prayers, concentrating on the ones carrying the greatest number of days of indulgence" (132). But the prayers to which he devotes himself as a form of protection do not prevent him from being tortured and beaten by his master. Then, on Corpus Christi Day, the ten-year-old is pressed into service as an altar boy at Sunday mass. When he accidentally drops the heavy missal the assembled peasants, convinced he is a "Gypsy vampire," drag him outside and hurl him into an enormous manure pit. After this the boy loses both his power of speech and his "faith" in the Almighty (143–47). Henceforth the priest's cassock seems "a miserable thing in comparison with the uniform adorned by the death's-head, crossbones, and lightning bolts" (120).

The boy's abrupt change of faith—his turning from God to the devil, from prayer to revenge—has little to do with the ancient struggle between good and evil. It signifies, rather, his attempt to survive in a world defined by conflict and Darwinian struggle. Even in the midst of a brief respite from strife and struggle, when a young peasant woman named Ewka awakens his budding sexuality, the boy, though only eleven, dreams of sexual conquest and domination: "There was nothing I would not do for Ewka. I forgot my fate of a Gypsy mute. . . . In my dreams I turned into a tall, handsome man, fair-skinned, blue-eyed. . . . I became a German officer in a tight, black uniform. Or I turned into a bird-catcher. . . . In these dreams my artful hands induced wild passions in the village girls, turning them into wanton Ludmilas" (153).

When the boy observes—in a scene packed with vivid details and grotesque effects—the fair-haired Ewka lustily coupling with a goat, his love turns to lust for revenge: "the more harm, misery, injury, and bitterness a man could inflict on those around him, the more help he could expect. If he shrank from inflicting harm on others, if he succumbed to emotions of love, friendship, and compassion, he would immediately become weaker. . . . I felt annoyed with myself for not having understood sooner the real rules of this world" (158–59). The "extraordinary success" of the Germans is now clear to him as well. In league with the powers of evil, they were "invincible"; they "contaminated others with hatred. . . . This was the source of their power and strength" (160).

By the summer of 1944, however, it is clear to everyone that the Germans are losing the war. After a series of bloody conflicts in which "brother fought against brother" and the Kalmucks, "deserters from the Soviets," join forces with the Germans "to loot and rape" the local peasantry, the boy is injured, taken to a regimental hospital, and subsequently billeted with the Soviet troops (182–84). Predictably, his allegiance shifts to the victorious Red Army. The boy's admiration for the Soviet uniform is based on the same impulse that led to his worship of the German officer's: the desire of the weak and helpless for liberating power, the longing of the victim to dominate others. From Mitka, the Soviet sharpshooter and hero, he absorbs the teachings not of marxism but of vengeance: a man's "worth" is based on "his ability to take revenge on those who wronged him" (227).

Growing up in a world ceaselessly engaged in violence and conflict, the boy views virtually everyone as his enemy. His understanding of freedom is based on the lessons of war: freedom to avenge himself on others. In the orphanage for "lost children," where he is sent at the end of the war, he meets other children, survivors of "ghettos or concentration camps" who, like him, have been "exploited" and victimized by "brutal and greedy" adults: "We all looked at one another with loathing and fear," and every "fight drew blood." One night "several boys raped a nurse in the basement," practicing on her the "elaborate" lessons "they had learned in various places during the war" (221, 226–28). What goes on in the orphanage is a direct reflection of the adult world outside its walls: "a girl reckless enough to have ventured out alone" is raped in "the ruins of a bombed house," while "a fight broke out in a nearby tavern." In this troubled universe, which appears deceptively "at peace" in the "daytime," the "war continued at night" (246).

In the final pages of *The Painted Bird* the boy assumes the full-fledged identity that years of suffering and brutality at the hands of adults have carved out for him. The alien and outcast—victim of untold injustices, persecution, and cruelty—proves but a reflection or product of his victimizers. As he and a cohort from the orphanage silently await the destruction of numerous unnamed and unknowing passengers on a train they have arranged to derail, the boy is "overcome by a great sense of power," which he overtly identifies with those who have demonized him:

> I recalled the trains carrying people to the gas chambers and crematories. The men who had ordered and organized all that probably enjoyed a similar feeling of complete power over their uncomprehending victims. These men controlled the fate of millions of people. . . . All they had to do was issue orders and . . . trained squads of troops and police would start rounding up people destined for ghettos and death camps. . . . To be capable of deciding the fate of many people whom one did not even know was a magnificent sensation. I was not sure whether the pleasure depended only on the knowledge of the power one had, or on its use. (233–34)

In the final grim sentence of this passage the boy suggests that he will continue to seek the *use* of deadly power over others.

The novel's closing lines bear out this grim prophecy. Having recovered his power of speech in a skiing accident, the boy resolves to wield language as a weapon to dominate and control others. When, after the accident, a telephone rings in his hospital room, the boy lifts

the receiver, feels "an overpowering desire to speak," and does so for
the first time in years: "I spoke loudly and incessantly like the peasants
and then like the city folk, as fast as I could, enraptured by the sounds
that were heavy with meaning, . . . convincing myself again and again
and again that speech was now mine and that it did not intend to
escape through the door which opened onto the balcony" (249–51).
Several critics have gleaned an optimistic note in these lines, pointing
out that the boy's overwhelming desire to speak to the person on the
other end of the line reveals a desire to communicate with others.
Immediately before this scene, however, the boy expresses his disdain
for those who fail to accept alienation; he is convinced that "every one
of us stood alone" against the others, that "everyone knew only himself" (249).

The boy's exultant discovery of the power of speech does not necessarily mean that he desires communication with others—even though
Paul Lilly Jr. interprets the novel's ending in this optimistic light. "The
Boy's movement away from silent victimization toward the power of
eloquence," Lilly contends, "is also a tale of a writer's slow progress
from silence to spoken to written words." The writer in question, however, was far less sanguine about his protagonist's motives. Kosinski
points out in a letter that a balcony is "the place reserved for those who
speak to the masses (leaders, political figures, mob crusaders, etc.)."
Citing a sentence from the passage quoted above, he adds, "The Boy's
speech 'did not intend to escape through the door which opened onto
the balcony.' Perhaps the communication will be 'to' others rather than
'with' them."[6]

That the boy identifies with those who use language as a form of
propaganda rather than communication, who seek to dominate the
minds of others rather than to share their thoughts with them, is
evinced by the lack of interest he shows the few adults who have
sought to help him. The boy is overcome by admiration for the SS
officer, his "soot-black uniform" embellished by the death's-head and
crossbones (117–19). For the elderly German soldier who spares his life,
on the other hand, he has little regard. Ordered by a young officer to
execute the captured boy, the "elderly bespectacled soldier" takes him
to a clearing; there, having untied the youth and signaled him to run
away, the kindly soldier fires two shots into the air. Both his advanced
age and his weak eyesight bespeak his lack of significant rank or authority; in contrast to the SS officer's imposing outfit and insignia, the

rank-and-file soldier wears a "faded" uniform and "battered boots."
Thus, despite the deliverance he receives, the boy remains unimpressed
by the man and his conduct (72–78).

Cut off from the child's romantic heritage, Kosinski's boy reveals
no innate store of innocence by which to transcend the conditions of
a harsh and fallen world. Exposed to cruelty and injustice, he cannot
find within nature or his own nature what that other quintessential
boy, Huckleberry Finn, discovers on the mighty Mississippi, in his bond
with Jim, and within the depths of his heart: a more profound reality
than anything the sad, sorry state of human affairs can conjure. Unable
to shed the cultural clothing painted to his skin, Kosinski's boy cannot
see beneath, or beyond, the conditions in which others are also
clothed. Unlike Huck or Dickens's Pip, he lacks the inner resources to
detect—beneath the black skin of a runaway slave like Jim or the
rough clothing and language of an escaped convict like Magwitch—
the essential truth and goodness of a loving heart. Only a child who
bears a trace of the human being's divine origins enjoys the privilege
of transcendent vision: a vision from which Kosinski's boy appears
permanently estranged.

Orphaned and victimized by a society at war, Kosinski's boy is
alienated by a world that strips him, as Humbert strips Lolita, of parental love and protection. But the boy is its creature—its product—in a
way that Dolly Haze, for all her starstruck allegiance to popular culture,
is not. Just as Humbert remarks the ease with which Dolly casts off,
"like a bit of dry mud caking her childhood," their "poor romance,"
Nabokov's readers marvel at the cheerful indifference with which she
dismisses her sordid past: the years she endured, like one of Lekh's
doomed birds, the caged circle of Humbert's will and desire (*Lolita*
274). Against all odds, odds made even greater by her sordid experience with Quilty, Dolores Haze proves capable not only of love and
laughter but of compassion for the man who abused her. Moved to
pity by Humbert's tears, she even apologizes to him for her behavior:
"Stop crying, please," she pleads in their farewell scene. "Oh, don't cry,
I'm so sorry I cheated so much, but that's the way things are" (281).[7]

The radical contrast between Nabokov's "poor little girl" and
Kosinski's unregenerate boy—the role that each image of the child
plays in the writer's work and imagination—is conveniently high-
lighted by the way Nabokov formulated, for his own very different
purposes, the metaphor of the painted bird. In the early 1950s, the

period when Nabokov was composing *Lolita* and a decade before Kosinski's novel was published, he delivered the lecture on Dickens discussed in chapter 4. In *Bleak House,* Nabokov declared to his students at Cornell, Harold Skimpole "is a painted bird with a clockwork arrangement for mechanical song. His cage is an imitation, just as his childishness is an imitation." Skimpole, in other words, is only a *simulacrum* of the creature he purports to be. Adopting the role of a misunderstood child denied his true freedom, Skimpole is a fake. Pretending to be trapped by circumstance, he is, in Nabokov's words, "not really caged" at all (*Lectures on Literature* 89).

Now, a lecturer's passing reference does not carry the same implication or intensity as a novelist's extended metaphor. Still, the contrast between Nabokov's brief formulation of the painted bird and Kosinski's elaborate symbol helps to suggest the cultural and philosophical divide separating their art and thought. In relegating Skimpole to the category of a painted bird, Nabokov posits a universe in which the difference between truth and its imitation, reality and its simulation, is essential. In Jean Baudrillard's terms Nabokov clearly honors fiction, in this case Dickens's, that addresses "the real." Here "representation," says Baudrillard, "still attempt[s] to absorb simulation by interpreting it as a sham representation, [whereas postmodernist] simulation encompasses the whole field of representation itself and makes of it a simulacrum." Nabokov, for all the technical sophistication and narrative reflexivity of his fiction, here suggests that the difference between true childishness and its simulation is as fundamental to the writer and reader as that between a real bird and a painted imitation. Skimpole plays at being a victimized child, held captive by a harsh society imprisoning his spirit. The lie by which he preserves himself is, to Nabokov, a betrayal of the child's essential innocence and vulnerability.[8]

The distinctions to which Nabokov's metaphor of the painted bird draws attention—the polarities of nature and culture, spontaneity and artificiality, freedom and imprisonment—are systematically dismantled in *The Painted Bird*. Once Lekh, the bird catcher, paints the bird's feathers, the other members of the flock cannot distinguish between the bird's original identity and his painted one. Nor, as Kosinski's novel proceeds to illustrate, can human beings, either as a group or as individuals, distinguish between human identity as culturally constructed and that regarded as innate, authentic, or "real." For Kosinski, unlike Nabokov, childishness does not signify an original or essential state of being. (It should by now be clear that the words *essential* and *essence* are employed neutrally, as a way of discussing the impact of a literary text and the imaginative vision it conveys—and without the pejorative connotations that have lately been affixed to them in critical debates.) According to Kosinski's antiessentialist formulation, "Childishness is what we see in children": what, in other words, we as a collective make *of* them. Children, he admits, begin life with an imagination still "uncensored" in its "mental mobility"; but youthful flexibility only speeds up the inevitable process of "adaptation." As the boy proceeds, with amazing alacrity, to admire and imitate his Nazi oppressors, any notion of the child's essential innocence—that ancient "idyll of childhood," as Kosinski says—is permanently laid to rest (*Passing By* 211–12).[9]

Kosinski's image of the painted bird signals the individual's profound alienation from essence. It "manifests," as he says, "the author's awareness, perhaps unconscious, of his break with the wholeness of self" (*Passing By* 210). In Kosinski's universe every child is always, already a painted bird whose nature proves indiscernible from the colors that coat, or the society that constructs, it. In a way that recalls Michel Foucault's formulation in *Discipline and Punish* cited earlier, Kosinski's boy can claim no inborn, innate being or essence. Quite the opposite: his so-called human nature comprises all those outer trappings—all those layers of cultural paint, fabric, cloth—that in Foucault's words have been produced "around, on, within the body by the functioning of a power" exercised on it. These are the elements that constitute what Foucault, in his inversion of the Judeo-Christian paradigm discussed earlier, deems the child's soul: the construct that seals and imprisons the naked body. A painted bird in this sense as well as in others, Kosinski's boy is both product and prisoner of the collective. Unable to see, let alone fly, beyond the bars of his cage— the soul that constructs and contains him—he can only reiterate, in the language afforded him, the terms of his oppression.

The Child of Apocalypse

Golding's *Darkness Visible*

Commenting on the effects of World War II on his generation, William Golding attests to their shattering intensity: "The basic point my generation discovered about man was that there was more evil in him than could be accounted for simply by social pressures." Unlike Kosinski, Golding finds the power of the collective insufficient to account for the blinding cruelty, injustice, and tyranny of which humanity is capable. To Golding the human being must be "morally diseased." Among the global wreckage brought on by World War II, Golding includes the explosive demolition of Rousseauian faith in original goodness. Destroyed along with it was any belief in human progress or social perfectibility. Such idealism, Golding suggests in his novels, will not relieve but only abet the moral darkness in which we originate. As corollary, any hoped-for salvation from darkness depends, to begin with, on our accepting the "broken-down criminality" of human nature, "the curse brought from Eden."[1]

Few postwar novelists share Golding's broadly Christian vision, but those who do—among them Flannery O'Connor and Walker Percy —testify to the fact that spiritual vision may yield strange and bitter fruit when subjected to the elemental force of creative imagination. As readers of O'Connor well know, uncompromising insight into the contemporary human condition is more likely to shock than to console. The bitter fruit of O'Connor's texts bears no likeness to the processed pieties served up for mass consumption by the media's well-groomed prophets and pundits.

In its harsh and unflinching rendering of the human condition, the vision of a Golding, an O'Connor, a Percy at times resembles—and is often mistaken for—a bleak, even nihilistic expression of secular dread and despair. To those who perceive a world riddled with the powers of "darkness," Golding points out, darkness implies something more virulent than the scientist's "absence of light" (*Hot Gates* 172–73). To them evil is primal: rather than Nabokov's perceived absence of good, evil is a dynamic force manifestly (and tirelessly) at work in the world. Despite the telling contrast between Golding's spiritual vision of fallen humanity and Kosinski's deterministic one, Golding, like Kosinski, employs the image of childhood to explore the source and nature of human evil. Golding's first and most famous work of fiction, *Lord of the Flies* (1954), bears a distinct affinity with *The Painted Bird* in its straightforward narrative, overt symbols, and ritualistic events. The greater stylistic and thematic complexity of his later novel *Darkness Visible* (1979) gives rise to a richer, if more ambiguous, image of childhood: one that starkly contrasts with Kosinski's metaphor of the painted bird.

Structural and thematic parallels highlight the differences between *Darkness Visible* and *The Painted Bird.* In each novel, for example, a young male child orphaned by disaster emerges against the backdrop of World War II. Each child survives, against all odds, the violence inflicted on him by the machinery of war and the cruelty of his fellow human beings. Each is a social outcast whose origins, like the name he received at birth, remain unknown to those around him; each is marked by features that establish his difference from others, who perceive such difference as repulsive and threatening. Both outcasts—as Golding's narrator puts it in *Darkness Visible*—bear an "unusual relationship to language," which underscores their social alienation. Like Kosinski's boy, who takes years to recover the power of speech, Golding's Matty speaks only rarely and with tortuous difficulty: words "burst out of his twisted lips" like "jagged" objects, creating "awful passages of pain and struggle that made the other children laugh" (17–18, 71). Such structural parallels heighten the contrasts between each novel's rendering of the child theme, of fundamental human nature, and of a source of light—if, indeed, there is one—potent enough to alleviate the darkness in which human beings exist.

Making Darkness Visible

Wresting a biblical vision of fallen humanity from the sordid pan-
orama of modern warfare, social dissolution, and political terrorism,
Golding situates the child at the vortex of this violent force field. In
Darkness Visible the image of a deformed child serves as the emblem of
human nature, intrinsically maimed and "badly scarred" by original sin
and inevitable suffering (93). At the novel's opening, which takes place
during the London Blitz, a crew of firemen are amazed to discern the
blazing shape of a tiny child emerging, not at a run but "with a kind of
ritual gait," from the fires of a burning city. In the incendiary glare the
crew's captain notes how badly burned the child is, marveling at the
miracle of his survival. After bandaging the child's mutilated body and
calling for an ambulance, the captain suffers a "positive explosion of
human feeling": he is filled "with grief, not for the maimed child
but for himself, a maimed creature whose mind had touched for once
on the nature of things" (9, 14, 16). Sparked by enemy bombs raining
down on the city, the blazing fires evince the spiritual darkness that
ignited them. They recall John Milton's image of the lightless fires of
hell in lines from which the title of Golding's novel is taken: "from
those flames / No light, but rather darkness visible" (*Paradise Lost,*
book 1, ll. 62–63). In the "open stove" of this "melted end of the
world," the flames of apocalypse dissolve the "screen" of appearances.
To the captain the nature of things is revealed: he understands that he
and his fellow human beings have brought this terrible judgment on
themselves (11–13).

The deformed child, initially called number seven by the various
hospitals and care centers to which he is consigned, is eventually given
the name Matthew Septimus: a name that recalls one of Jesus' disciples, as it recalls the mystic number of the Apocalypse, or Revelation
(16–17). Known as Matty, the fire-scarred child grows up to become a
Pentecostal prophet whose vision of salvation is as deeply inspired and
profoundly irrational as any espoused by O'Connor's backwoods
prophets. At the novel's end Matty Septimus Windrove is reclaimed by
the fires whence he came.[2] While rescuing a wealthy Arab schoolboy
—a Middle Eastern prince whom he appears to regard as a possible
messiah—from the child's would-be kidnappers, Matty catches fire
for a second time. The blaze, this time sparked by a terrorist bomb,
once again transforms him into a "shape of flame" that jigs and whirls

before collapsing. Matty dies in the act of salvation, having fulfilled, it would seem, his earthly mission.

Issuing from no known origin other than the "sheer agony of a burning city," the mysterious child called Matty Windrove appears to carry a message of hope to humanity. His role as symbolic messenger differs dramatically, however, from that of Wordsworth's youthful emissary, "trailing clouds of glory" from his celestial realm. Far from embodying the primal innocence that some critics ascribe to him, Matty is marked—indeed, maimed—from the outset not only by his severe physical deformities but by his profound sense of guilt and sin. True, he walks into the world like a fiery spirit, recalling both the burning bush of the Bible and the eponymous burning babe of Robert Southwell's poem. Appearing to the poet on Christmas Day, the child is literally on fire with love, burning to redeem "men's defiléd souls" ("The Burning Babe," ll. 12–13). But if, as the novel's countless biblical allusions suggest, Matty acts as a divinely inspired messenger—fulfilling, in Don Crompton's words, the role of "prophet, priest, king, and suffering servant all at the same time"—he does so in mortal guise.[3] Whether pilgrim, prophet, or inspired madman, Matty embodies both the sign and the curse of humanity's condition: the congenital deformity of original sin.

Even in the hospital, as the wounds from his burns begin to heal and the bandages are removed, Matty strikes the "casual visitor" as looking singularly old. The left side of his skull, left permanently hairless by the fire, has the "appearance of baldness." His mouth, deformed and lopsided, lends a decidedly "unchildlike" effect to his "slow and painful" efforts to smile (19–20). While Matty's scars are visible to all from the outset, revelation of his "spiritual face," also "badly scarred," comes later—after he has been sufficiently healed, physically, to attend school (93). As soon as Matty is well enough to "limp from hospital into his first school," he manifests his scarred spiritual face by growing jealous of another child, a beautiful boy named Henderson. After Matty curses the boy for committing an "evil" actually caused by an adult, Henderson accidentally falls to his death. The adult, Sebastian Pedigree, is the boys' teacher at Foundlings School in Greenfield.

Pedigree, or Pedders, as his students call him, is a hopeless pederast, a lover of little boys who professes lofty reverence for the child—what he calls his "spiritual relationship" to a beautiful young boy—while secretly registering (and struggling to control) a much more visceral form of attraction (37, 22). Pedigree's "fantasy," like Humbert Humbert's in *Lolita,* fosters a dual image of the child. Just as Humbert must pretend that the nymphet is not really a child but a demon in disguise, Pedigree pretends to himself that he is the fond possessor—in his words, the "owner"—of two little boys: one, the embodiment "of pure beauty, the other, an earthly little man!" (21). By mentally dividing one aspect of the child's image (and the adult's psyche) from the other, the aesthete in Pedigree continues to extol the ideal of platonic beauty while the pederast pursues more concrete satisfactions.

As the professed devotee of pure beauty, Pedigree is grateful to nature for generously bestowing on him, "year after year," a "constant supply" of "handsome little fellows." So preoccupied is the schoolteacher with youthful beauty that in class it is "his custom and entertainment to arrange the boys in order of beauty so that the most beautiful occupied the front row." The "middle of the front row" is reserved for his favorite of the moment, the "exquisite" young creature named Henderson—"a child of bland and lyric beauty" (26–27). Pedigree's aesthetic obsession has, however, a malicious side. Delighting in the charming perfection of the boy on whom he fixes his attention at a given moment, Pedigree simultaneously falls prey to ugly resentment as "the beauty of the child beg[ins] to consume him, obsess him, madden him." Like Lekh in *The Painted Bird,* the pederast grows angry and ultimately sadistic toward the object of his desire. To punish his unwitting tormentor, he abruptly turns "cold and indifferent" toward the child who has so recently enjoyed his teacher's "wonderful" attention (22).

When Matty arrives at Foundlings School and is assigned to Pedigree's classroom, the schoolteacher, repulsed by the new boy's deformed face, assigns him a seat at the back of the room. When Pedigree sarcastically calls the "ugly boy" a "treasure," Matty is gratified by what he perceives to be his teacher's kindness (28). Naive and "literal-minded," he is privy to the discomfort Pedigree begins to exhibit in Henderson's presence. Pedigree, having been warned by the headmaster to stay away from Henderson, denies the boy entry to his office, and a stormy scene between the schoolteacher and his pupil follows. Matty, having "understood nothing" of Pedigree's passion for the beautiful youth, assumes that Henderson is to blame for his teacher's unhappiness (32).

Convinced that Henderson is evil, Matty apparently curses the boy, who, after wandering onto the fire escape in a fit of "furious passion," falls "fifty feet" to his death (35–36). Beside himself with grief, Pedigree,

unwilling to acknowledge his terrible guilt, blames Matty for the disaster: "You horrible, horrible boy!" he shouts. "It's all your fault!" (37).
Profoundly confused (a confusion that offers a considerable challenge
to Golding's readers, who must puzzle out events incomprehensible to
Matty, from whose point of view they are rendered), Matty is sum-
marily dismissed from school. After Pedigree loses his position and is
sent to jail, Matty falls "into a deep grief" and resolves to seek penance
for his sin. From the moment of his moral awakening, Matty remains
spiritually bound to Pedigree, whom he believes he has wronged and
from whom he seeks forgiveness. Matty's reconciliation with Pedigree,
which occurs nearly two decades later and is described in the third,
and final, section of the novel, takes place back in Greenfield, to which
both characters return after an absence of many years.

The Illusion of Innocence

Introduced in part 1 of the novel, which is titled "Matty" and devoted
to his story, the child theme is further developed (in a dramatically
different key) in part 2, titled "Sophy." Unlike Matty, Sophy Stanhope
is neither an orphan nor a solitary child. Her twin sister, Antonia
(nicknamed Toni), is fair-haired and extremely pale, whereas Sophy is
brunette, "with masses" of "dark curls all over" her head. Only ten
years old at the outset, both children are already accustomed to the
"magical" effect they have on grown-ups, who "go all soppy" in their
presence (105). To Matty, who first notices the "beautiful" little girls
standing outside Goodchild's Rare Books, they look so "like angels"
that he is "careful to turn [the] bad side [of his face] away" from them
(101). He would not sully their purity with the sight of his deformity.

Similarly transfixed by the pristine beauty of two heavenly looking
children, James's governess, we recall, soon discovers the duplicity of
appearances in a fallen world. What the governess can only dread may
be true—that the children's "more than earthly beauty" is a "fraud"—
proves unquestionably the case in *Darkness Visible*. At the tender age of
ten, Sophy and her sister appear, like Miles and Flora, the very picture
of "innocent wonder" (*Turn of the Screw* 48, 58). It soon becomes clear,
however, that the two little girls routinely perform "their 'remarkable
children' thing" to deflect attention from the seething rancor of
their inner lives (*Darkness Visible* 122). As Sophy's narrative in part 2

unambiguously reveals, this charming child not only detests her angelic-looking twin; she is enthralled by the powers of darkness (105).

Shortly after the day on which Matty first remarks the heavenly beauty of the children standing outside Goodchild's bookstore, Sophy discovers the thrilling extent of the darkness within her. The discovery occurs on an idyllic summer's day that only appears to embody the Rousseauian idyll of childhood. Bathed in sunlight, the cheerful landscape is rich with twittering birds, bright blossoms, and a babbling brook. (James's readers will recall that equally idyllic, equally deceptive June day on which the young governess arrives at Bly.) Under Sophy's intense gaze a "chirping brood of fluffies, a mother and her ten chicks," descend from the banks of the brook to the water. In a trance of pleasure "the small girl" seizes "a large pebble lying to hand among the grasses" and fits her little fingers "nicely over the smooth, oval shape." The child watches in "complete satisfaction" as the stone she has tossed hits a "scrap of fluff," the last of the tiny dabchicks trailing behind their mother. "Then," continues the narrative, registering Sophy's point of view, "there was the longer pleasure, the achieved contemplation of the scrap of fluff turning gently as the stream bore it out of sight" (107–9).

Out of reverence for the hidden powers that, in the child's view, have guided her inexperienced but "preordained hand"—helping her to launch the pebble in its perfect, and deadly, "preordained arc"—Sophy does not try to repeat the wonderful event. Still, recollection of "that arc, that stone, that fluff" intensifies the pleasure she takes in the rest of her summer vacation. The dabchick's vividly rendered death also undermines, for Golding's readers, any residual assumptions concerning the child's natural innocence. At the heart of young Sophy's "cheerful, buttercup-plastered enjoyments" lies the thrilling experience of the dabchick's death, its mother's "staccatissimo" cry of fear, and Sophy's power to inflict pain (109–10).

By the time the twins turn eleven, Sophy has become preternaturally conscious of what she later identifies as the "darkness inside her" (158). At eleven she already knows that her outward appearance, "the little girl with her smiling face," is false. The child "know[s] herself to be not Sophy but *This*"—this "Sophy-thing that sat inside the mouth" of a "dark tunnel." Like a dark thing staring out from "the back of her head," this evil presence manipulates the outward creature "like a

complicated doll, a child with all the arts and wiles and deliberate de-
lightfulness of a quite unself-conscious, oh a quite innocent, naive,
trusting little girl" (113, 123–24, 131). Here, through the voice and
viewpoint of the child, Golding offers dramatic confirmation of the
governess's disenchanted discovery in *The Turn of the Screw*: that the
child's innocence is a "game" and a "fraud" (*Turn of the Screw* 48). This
insight, for which James's governess has been roundly attacked and
even accused of insanity by critics, informs the world of Golding's
novel.

Not all children, *Darkness Visible* makes clear, are as powerfully
drawn to evil as Sophy, no matter how loveless or deprived their backgrounds. But all children—from Henderson, the beautiful youth with
his "furious" and fatal "passion," to Sophy, with her innate "thirst after
weirdness" and wickedness, to Matty, with his spiritual "grief" and
desire for redemption—contain the worst as well as the best in human
nature (132, 37). Childish acts of cruelty, anger, and revenge differ not
in kind but only in degree and extent from adult murderousness.
As the novels of Doris Lessing and Milan Kundera (discussed in the
next chapter) further attest, writers do not have to share Golding's
Christian outlook to register the darkness cast by the shadow of the
child's image.

The pleasure that killing the dabchick affords ten-year-old Sophy
is one she not only recalls but seeks to repeat as an adult. Later she stabs
her first boyfriend, Roland, when she tires of him. Her thrill at feeling
the blade of the "tin pearl-handled knife" penetrate his skin prompts
her first orgasm. Implicitly comparing this shiver of sadistic pleasure
with the one she experienced as a ten-year-old, Sophy mentally draws
a connection between the pebble she threw at the dabchick and the
knife she jabs into Roland's shoulder. Both objects, she reflects, come
magically "to hand" when she needs them (144–46). Both of these
events look forward, moreover, to Sophy's climactic scene in the novel,
when, having plotted to kidnap an Arab child to secure a huge ransom,
she fantasizes stabbing the "valuable" child to death instead (171). In
her fantasy she discovers the commando knife owned by her present
boyfriend, Gerry, lying conveniently "to hand"—just as she had once
discovered the "pebble lying to hand among the grasses" (108). Grab-
bing hold, in her hallucination, of the terrified child as she would a
"thumping" rabbit, Sophy "deliriously" thrusts the knife deep into the
boy's skin. As she feels her victim's body "explode with convulsions,"

her own body apparently convulses in orgasmic release. After a brief but indefinite spell Sophy comes "to herself with a terrible start"—still "trembling with the passion of the mock murder" (252).

The darkness that resides within Sophy and ultimately engulfs her identity holds constant from childhood through adulthood. It participates in that larger darkness in which human nature and history are shrouded: a darkness made palpable, Golding suggests, by the wasteland of contemporary culture. From the wartime destruction of London, with which *Darkness Visible* opens, to the chaotic 1970s, in which it closes, the novel depicts the increasing social disorder, noise, pollution, crime, and terrorism characterizing twentieth-century Western culture. If the droning airplanes over London no longer seem those harbingers of death evoked in T. S. Eliot's "Little Gidding" or in the wartime conflagration that opens *Darkness Visible,* they still serve as reminders of a fragmented society in thrall to technology and nihilistic despair. Lying immediately "to hand" are all the weapons of destruction that originate in, as they aid and abet, the darkness in human nature. So virulent are the contemporary forces of evil that even the loveliest and most innocent-seeming child can grow up to be a liar, a murderer, a terrorist. (Sophy's fair-haired sister, Toni, is even more adept than her twin at fulfilling this description.)

If, as Golding affirms, human beings are not "socially perfectible," they do not appear socially explicable either. Granted, Sophy and her sister do not enjoy an ideal childhood: their mother abandons the family to run off with another man, leaving the children's cynical father to raise them in an atmosphere of coldness and indifference. At the same time, they do not experience physical abuse or material deprivation; nor do they suffer from lack of attention. Unlike so many of Dickens's helpless orphans, they have a fond grandmother as well as teachers and nannies who look after them. What they clearly lack, however, is that primal gift, the potent moral force of original innocence, inherited from Rousseau by previous literary children—from Dickens's countless "poor" creatures to good-natured Huck Finn, from wise and true Maisie to resilient Dolly Haze.

In *Darkness Visible,* to be sure, the most cruelly used and abused child, the deeply scarred creature who emerges from the "howling wilderness" of a burning city to become Matty Windrove, evinces a profound capacity for love and self-sacrifice (28, 264). Unlike Dickens's and Nabokov's literary children, however, Matty cannot bring his own goodness to light until he recognizes, with a sense of profound internal grief, the sin and guilt that are also his: "For however ignorant a man is," Matty realizes, "he always knows his sins until he is [spiritually] lost" (93). Demonstrating the corollary of this Christian principle, Sophy, embracing the power of evil and rejecting the burden of conscience, ensures that she will be "lost" to the light—with "nothing visible but darkness" (253).

The Stanhope twins are not the only characters in the novel who serve the powers of darkness. That the children's beauty is readily mistaken for innocence attests to the moral confusion of those with whom they come in contact. One such avatar of childhood innocence, a man tellingly named Goodchild, gives voice to the confusion that, the novel suggests, underlies the cult of childhood: "There was no doubt about it," Sim Goodchild declares, "the Stanhope twins shone in Greenfield like a light!" (213). A self-confessed romantic, Goodchild nurtures a reverence for the child—most particularly, for the Stanhope twins—that is also a mask, like Pedigree's, for deeper and more suspect impulses (224). Committed, mentally and emotionally, to placing the little girls on "a pedestal," Goodchild secretly yearns to exploit these objects of "pure" worship (22).

Like the schoolteacher Sebastian Pedigree, Sim Goodchild is a literary man, the owner of the bookstore where Matty first catches sight of the angelic-looking twins. In contrast to Pedigree, however, Goodchild is not a social outcast but the married father of two grown-up children; whereas Pedigree's maddening passion for little boys provokes him to reckless action, Goodchild keeps his penchant for little girls carefully under wraps. Endeavoring to confine his admiration to the aesthetic realm, he couches his child worship in self-consciously "Wordsworthian" turns of phrase, some of which he borrows directly from the poet (195). Echoing a line from the immortality ode, he thinks to himself at one point: "Heaven lies round us in our infancy" (247; "Ode" l. 66). Tellingly, the allusion surfaces when, with "a quivering of salt lust," he mourns the inevitable loss of the little girls' "exquisite childhood." Determined to discover in the beauty that enchants him the essence of original innocence, Goodchild insists that the Stanhope children "exemplify in themselves all the pure, the beautiful and the good" (122). Repeating to himself and others (including his wife) how very "clean and sweet" the children are, he emphatically protests too much. (Possibly gleaning the truth, Mrs. Goodchild tends to interrupt her husband whenever he carries on for too long.)

Goodchild's lofty allusions to Wordsworth and Plato notwithstanding, his attraction to these "enchanting children" is far from high-minded (122). No matter how determinedly he tries "to turn his mind aside to things that were really clean and sweet," he cannot deny their erotic allure (213). In a way that recalls Humbert's sexually overt celebration of the nymphet's "fairytale" beauty, Goodchild finds himself bewitched by the "fairy delicacy" of the little girls: "no matter how wonderfully *nubile* they became" in later life, he thinks to himself, "they could never surpass that really fairy delicacy of childhood, a beauty that could make you weep" (213). In the dark depths of his fantasy life Sim fails to maintain the polite distance he preserves from the children in public. At these solitary moments he is moved by the children's fairy beauty in more ways than one. Summoned by his fantasizing imagination, their images are made to "perform the silly dance, the witless Arabian thing," for an audience of one: an audience made up of, as the narrator punningly puts it, one "unruly member" (223–26). In style as well as content Sim's sexual fantasy recalls Humbert's more obvious paeans to nymphet love—particularly the passage in which Humbert achieves climax, onanistically, as a "robust Turk" in his "self-made seraglio" (*Lolita* 62).

In *Darkness Visible* both Goodchild and Pedigree try (with varying degrees or shades of darkness) to convince themselves that their worship of children is an expression of "the pure, the beautiful and the good." Even as an old man who has suffered intolerable humiliations, including several stints in jail, Pedigree stubbornly insists on the "nobility" of his "condition": "it's a beautiful condition," he says of his love for little boys. "I don't *want* to be cured" (230). By clinging to his delusions, insisting on the "spiritual relationship" that his adoration of the child fosters, Pedigree attempts to deny both his guilt and his fallen condition. Similarly evasive is Goodchild's insistence on the innocence—James Kincaid's "sexless simplicity"—of the little girls who enchant him. Although he has but a passing social acquaintance with the Stanhope twins, Goodchild extols their purity as well as beauty. By rhetorically obliterating their sexual nature and allure, he would cleanse his obsession of any moral taint or suspicion. The myth of original innocence is spiritually degrading, the novel suggests, because those who purport to revere children are endeavoring to claim that (factitious) innocence for themselves. Still worse, they rely on that claim or pretense to further their exploitation of the child.

In *Darkness Visible* the romantic cult of childhood emerges as yet another manifestation of humanity's immemorial urge to deny its flawed nature and history. In Rousseau's celebration of the "natural man" one may even discover the seeds of nihilistic violence. Thus Gerry, a thief who becomes Sophy's lover and accomplice in crime, extols the "virtues" of his soldier friend, Bill. Bill, Sophy's lover tells her, is "the natural man": "He likes killing." "All those millions [killed in war]," Gerry adds, it "wouldn't be done if it wasn't natural to do it" (154–55). Romantic idealizations of human nature, *Darkness Visible* suggests, are partly responsible for the disintegration of the social order. Thus Sophy Stanhope, since childhood the object of adulation by Goodchild and others, employs her rosy and innocent appearance to gain the trust of the staff at Wandicott School, from which she plots to kidnap the little Arab prince for a "million" or a "billion" in ransom money (159). After visiting the school on parents' day and inspecting the layout, even Sophy is struck by how easily she gains entry: "On the way back to London it seemed to her more and more incredible that these valuable children should be so freely available to inspection" (171).

For Sophy, of course, the children are valuable in a strictly material sense; like jewels or other precious items, they can be stolen and then sold for cash. All her life, however, Sophy has traded on her own cherished, or valuable, appearance. With the exception of her father—who at one point shocks Goodchild by calling his daughter an "idle little bitch"—the world has been ready to share Goodchild's "generation-long folly" concerning the Stanhope girls (218, 223). Their father, a bitter man who has shown his daughters little love, obviously bears some responsibility for the way they have turned out; still, his reaction to Goodchild's idealistic commentary is telling. When Goodchild protests to Stanhope, "But she's so enchanting—they're both so enchanting," such paragons of "innocence" and "beauty"—Stanhope emits "a cackle of laughter" and tells him to grow up: "Be your age. That generation's not enchanting, any of it" (219). At this point in the novel it is already the 1970s; not only London but virtually every other metropolis in Britain, Europe, and America is reeling under the impact of a flourishing youth culture. With its noisy discos and dangerous drugs, that culture itself seems a carryover from the cult of childhood and its inherent contradictions.

Subjecting the myth of natural innocence to the blaze of apocalyptic revelation, Golding's novel brings human darkness to light. Even romantic Sim Goodchild must ultimately confront the truth about the "enchanting" creatures he has idealized for so long. That the innocence of the beautiful Stanhope girls is itself a trick of lighting—sheer illusion—is graphically suggested to Goodchild when, later in the novel, he and his friend Edwin Bell unintentionally surprise grown-up Sophy in her former home. As the two men and the young woman face one another in a room lit only by a lightbulb, Golding's narrator draws attention to the light's revealing effect: "The single, naked bulb made a black shadow under each nose. Even Sophy looked monstrous, huge, black eye-hollows and the Hitlerian moustache of shadow caught by the light under her nostrils" (243). The reference to Hitler is notable, its implications clarified by Paul Cantor's statement in an essay on Don DeLillo: "In a world where truth is now generally thought to be relative, Hitler often seems to stand as the lone remaining absolute: the incarnation of absolute evil."[4]

As Sophy hurries to hide from the two men her preparations for the kidnapping, she instinctively switches on "a table lamp with a pink and bobbled shade." With that telling gesture she substitutes the lamplight's sentimental pink glow for the harsh glare of the "single, naked bulb," which she promptly flicks off. The "hideous shadows" are magically "wiped from her face to be replaced by a rosy and upward glow." Shrouded once more in the deceptive radiance of her outward beauty, Sophy flashes a stunning smile at the two men. "Astonished," Sim "stare[s] at her face in its rosy glow and [can]not believe that the smile owe[s] everything to the lamp." Misinterpreting the source of Sophy's heightened complexion, Sim Goodchild assumes that the young woman's excitement betrays a forthcoming sexual "assignation" (243–44). Apprised of her true nature and purpose, readers know that Sophy's excitement stems from the crime she is about to commit. Soon afterward, as she hurries from the telephone booth where she has tried to alert her accomplices, the "glare from the street lighting" once again makes darkness visible, exposing Sophy's "white and ugly" face (249).

It is the maimed creature, Matty Windrove—and not some idealized image of youthful purity and innocence—who plays a vital role in dispelling both Goodchild's and Pedigree's romantic illusions. When

Goodchild, at the prompting of his friend Edwin, first meets the mysterious stranger in the "broad-brimmed black hat," he winces at the sight of Matty's scarred face, with its ugly "deformation": "With a sudden lurch of his stomach Sim saw that this thing was an ear, or what was left of it." Soon, however, Sim sees past Matty's deformity, discovering something altogether different in his appearance: "the man seemed outlined . . . against his background in a way that made him the point of it" (207). By the time Sim meets Matty again, he actually identifies with the deformed man. The transformation is prepared for when Sim and Edwin, as a result of the latter's efforts to arrange a kind of séance with Matty, find themselves in the little flat that Sophy and her sister used to occupy on their father's property.

When Goodchild enters these rooms that for so long he could only conjure in his fantasies, he is stunned: something in the "atmosphere" of the place, something beyond "the battered, second-hand furniture, the armchair . . . or the stained table," speaks to him not of idyllic beauty or innocence but of "what could only be called his grief." Trying to explain his overwhelming sadness, Sim says, "That's what it must be. Grief. Neglect." Accounting for his sudden gloom, he says to himself, "yes of course, yes, they weren't looked after and they . . . had no mother—poor things, poor things!" But the grief Goodchild experiences is—as indicated by the narrator's use of the possessive—*his*. Goodchild's sorrow is due not to social injustice or to the children's deprivation but to *his* own loss: "Inside Sim, the illusions of twenty years vanished like bubbles." Divested of his former ideals, Sim stands in a new relationship to reality as well as to the Stanhope twins. The "ancient staleness" of the room comprises more than stale "food," cheap "scent," and "sweat"; it speaks to him of things he has long known but refused to recognize: the ancient truth of flawed human nature (228–29).

Having earlier discovered, in his initial encounter with Matty, the "extraordinary grief" inscribed on the deformed man's face, Goodchild finally assumes his share of that mortal burden, the weight of human guilt and sin (207). Like the captain who, in the novel's opening chapter, registers the terrible impact of the child's maimed image, Sim grieves for the loss of that innocence in which he believed—*his* innocence as well as the child's. Thus, like the captain, he grieves "not for the maimed child but for himself, a maimed creature whose mind had touched for once on the nature of things." Almost immediately after this revelation Sim meets Matty for the second time and notes once again the two-toned "white and brown" face, the same "black hat," and the "only too visible" ear. "No longer," however, does he gaze at the deformed man with cold detachment. In Matty he beholds not "a forbidding monstrosity but only another man" (231).

As Sim extends his hand, Matty takes it "as if it were an object to be examined and not shaken." Under Matty's influence Sim is also moved to gaze at his hand, and suddenly he has an epiphany: "he fell through into an awareness of his own hand that stopped time in its revolution. The palm was ... made of light. It was precious and preciously inscribed with a sureness and delicacy beyond art and grounded somewhere else in absolute health. . . . Sim stared into the gigantic world of his own palm and saw that it was holy." In this fleeting moment Sim has a Blakean apprehension of eternity: he literally holds "[i]nfinity in the palm of [his] hand" and "[e]ternity in an hour" (Blake, "Auguries of Innocence" ll. 3–4). From Matty he has received "a word" that remains unidentified but originates in a single "radiant" note that sounds like *joy*—for it begins with a "consonant," quickly explodes into a "vowel lasting for an aeon," and closes with a "semi-vowel." It is a word that speaks to Sim of the "world of spirit" that lies beyond human darkness. Then, as quickly as it begins, the epiphany fades: "the man in black let[s] go of Sim's hand," and the hands become "nothing more than just hands again" (231–33).

Later, after the bomb goes off at Wandicott School and Matty dies in the process of rescuing the Arab child, it turns out that the meeting held by Sim, Edwin, and Matty in the Stanhope twins' former flat has been recorded on camera—the police having had Sophy and her sister, a political terrorist, under surveillance for some time. The recorded film is endlessly replayed on television, along with a protracted legal inquiry into the events. Scorned and ridiculed by strangers who now recognize (and suspect) him wherever he goes, Sim suffers the knowledge that he and Edwin are innocent of the kidnapping plot. "I had nothing to do with it," he assures himself. But then, with a degree of self-recognition and remorse never before experienced, he adds, "Nevertheless, I am guilty. My fruitless lust clotted the air and muffled the sounds of the real world" (257). Divested of his faith in "those lovely creatures," Sim is tempted to believe that he has lost the most valuable thing in his life, the "treasure" that was "not just for them but for all of us" (259).

The so-called treasure of cherished illusions has, as Sim admits, clouded his understanding, muffled or obscured his sense of reality. More than that, it has served as a veil or "partition" closing him off from other people, keeping him "in solitary confinement." Now he acknowledges both his lust and his guilt, recognizing that they are part of the human condition—that "the whole damned [human] race" is "wrapped in illusions, delusions, confusions" (234, 261). With that darkness now made visible to him, Goodchild assumes his burden of grief, the knowledge of his participation in humanity's waywardness and evil. But with the loss of those illusions in which he had wrapped himself, denying the worst in his nature, Sim arrives at the brink of possible enlightenment. It is here that Golding leaves Goodchild. With the news that the authorities have discovered dead Matty's journal, which promises to "throw some light" on the Wandicott case, Sim switches off the television. Heartened by Matty's memory, he feels "happy almost. . . . Before he knew what he was about he found himself staring intently into his own palm" (261).

In Sebastian Pedigree's case, on the other hand, revelation comes only at the brink of death—after Matty has been reclaimed by fire. In the novel's closing chapter Matty, having caught fire from the blaze ignited by the terrorists' bomb, fulfills his destiny. According to the narrator, "a strange thing happened in the fire. It seemed to organize itself into a shape of flame." Attaching itself to a "strange man" (one of the kidnappers) carrying "a blanket from the end of which small feet protruded and kicked," the fiery shape pursues the kidnapper until the "man dropped the bundle and a boy leapt out of it and ran away." The kidnapper also runs away, after which the "fire-monster jigged and whirled." Then, "after some more time," the narrator adds, "it lay still" (248). Matty Windrove dissolves back into the fires whence he came; and it is in this form, as a shape of flame, that he visits his old teacher, now released from jail, in a vision at the novel's end.

On the autumn day on which the novel closes, Pedigree—breathless from exertion and a weak heart but still in the grip of his pedophiliac "obsession"—has once more arrived at "the paradisal, dangerous, damned park where the sons of the morning ran and played." Once more he has carried a brilliantly colored ball to the park, using it, as Goodchild earlier says of the children's books Pedigree shoplifts, as "bait" for the young boys (262, 213).[5] Seated on a bench in the sunlight, waiting for the boys to approach, the old man closes his eyes.

Then, slowly becoming aware of a "sea of light" warming him, he opens them to find "without any surprise at all that Matty was coming. He knew this ought to surprise him because Matty was dead." Most unusual of all is Pedigree's reaction to the deformed, "ugly" creature he has despised for so long: now he finds Matty's approach "even agreeable." Dressed in his usual black, Matty is to Pedigree still a boy, still "ugly little Matty"; but now "the boy was not really as awful to look at as one might think." Indeed, in Pedigree's vision, the boy's image, as he wades "waist deep in gold," strikes him as positively "pleasant to look at!" Not only Matty but the surrounding world is transformed; now, Pedigree understands, "they were in a park of mutuality and closeness." Sensing that he must be dreaming, Pedigree tells Matty, "I don't want to wake up and find I'm inside [jail], you know" (263–64).

Pedigree may well be dreaming or hallucinating; in one sense, however, he has never been so awake. Suddenly he realizes "that it [was] you, ugly little Matty, who really loved me! I tried to throw it away you know, but it wouldn't go." And then Pedigree begs Matty to help him, for he is terrified that he will someday hurt a child—"just to keep a child quiet, keep it from telling." It "was at this point," the narrative ambiguously reads, "that Sebastian Pedigree found he was not dreaming." The "golden immediacy of the wind" swirls "upwards round Matty," and Pedigree watches "in terror as the man before him [is] consumed, melt[s], vanishe[s] like a guy in a bonfire." Matty's "face [is] no longer two-tone but gold as the fire," and the "smile round the lips [is] loving and terrible." Suddenly Pedigree understands that Matty, like a terrible angel of deliverance, is summoning him to the other side. In awe and terror he clutches the "brilliant ball" to his chest —the ball that has now assumed the pulsing rhythm of his own beating heart—as the fiery shape leans over the dying man, takes "the ball as it beat[s]," and removes it with Pedigree's last mortal breath (264–65).

Like the spirits who appear to Matty in part 2 of the novel, Pedigree's vision of Matty as an angel of deliverance is rendered subjectively, through the old man's eyes. *Darkness Visible*, like *The Turn of the Screw*, is fraught with ambiguities that do not add up to a concerted affirmation or denial of the "world of spirit" apprehended by individual characters in the text. Golding has singled out this novel as "the one of my books I have refused to talk about; and the more I have been pressed the more stubborn my refusal has become." Like James's ambiguous ghost story, *Darkness Visible* appears designed, in Philip Redpath's words, to leave its readers "worried, uncertain, puzzled." Noting the "tension between clarity and obscurity, precision and mystery" at "the heart of the text," Redpath adds, "Golding makes us shift the perspective from which we view the universe by opening [a] seam of doubt in our minds"; his "novel tells us more about the way we see than it tells us about the universe."[6]

Whether the reader interprets Matty's saving appearance at the end of the novel as Pedigree's revelation or his hallucination, the dying man discovers Matty's love for him. Here, at least, Pedigree breaks through the partitions that divide people from one another and contribute to their moral confusion. The extraordinary nature of this discovery is underscored by a swift return in the novel's closing lines to the world of human disorder and misunderstanding. Arriving at the other side of the park, unaware that Pedigree has just died, the "tired and irritated" park keeper notes "the brilliant ball lying a few yards from the old man's feet where it had rolled when he dropped it." Convinced that "the filthy old thing would never be cured," the park keeper begins, from a distance of "more than twenty yards," "talking at him bitterly" (265). On this phrase the novel ends, returning its readers to the familiar plane of flawed existence—with its bitter lack of understanding and love.

The darkness of human error, confusion, misunderstanding is brilliantly illuminated in *Darkness Visible*. At the same time the novel evokes a rare and saving beam of light: the suggestion of human possibility embodied in the child's image. Whether or not Matty truly is a spiritual messenger, he sacrifices his life—becomes a burnt offering—to save a child whom he regards as the source of messianic promise (238–39). The reader does not have to share Matty's spiritual vision to see that the kidnappers—by regarding the child as a valuable thing to be possessed and exploited—embody the forces of darkness that threaten humanity's hope for the future. Similarly, whether or not Goodchild can rationally explain his Blakean vision, this fleeting insight has an indelible effect on his consciousness. Before exiting the novel, Goodchild gazes, once again, "into the gigantic world of his own palm." Not just in grief but in recognition of life's beauty and promise, he contemplates the nature of things (231, 261).

Both darkness and the possibility of salvation from darkness are made visible in this novel. The vision of possible redemption is, however, more accessible to Golding's readers than to his characters, who are unaware of the panoramic structure of the novel—the totality of its narrative details and thematic effects. In the only reflexive commentary that the narrator is allowed, Golding's readers are alerted to the privileges they enjoy. The passage occurs near the end of the novel, as Sim and Edwin await Matty's arrival. They do not realize, as the reader learns immediately after this scene, that Matty has, in the words of the narrator, "the best of all reasons for not coming"—he is dead. Bitterly disappointed at Matty's failure to show up, Sim experiences an "overwhelming sense of futility": "He trie[s] to imagine some deep, significant spiritual drama, some contrivance, some plot that would include them both and be designed solely for the purpose of rescuing Pedigree from his hell" (247).

This passage obliquely comments on the novel's structure and effects. From his limited vantage Goodchild can only dream of participating in some plot or spiritual drama. Golding's readers, on the other hand, recognize that Sim's desire to participate in a larger pattern of meaning and value is ultimately fulfilled. Like Edwin, who also plays a role in the drama but who lapses into sleep at its climax (when Matty becomes a burnt offering), Sim cannot see past "the blank wall of his daily indifference and ignorance" (247). Only Golding's readers, by paying careful attention to each aspect of this elegant literary "contrivance," can gauge the impact and significance of the spiritual drama enacted by its characters.

Darkness Visible extends, and complicates, the "rigorous demolition of the Rousseauistic vision of children" that, as Reinhard Kuhn points out, began with *Lord of the Flies.* In deconstructing natural innocence, however, *Darkness Visible* does not promote, as Kuhn contends, the author's alleged vision of "the inherently evil nature of the human species." If, as Golding implies, the origin of human evil lies beyond rational or social explanation, *Darkness Visible* suggests that the redemptive power of love is also a mystery. Whereas *Lord of the Flies* announces in its closing lines "the end of innocence, the darkness of man's heart," this novel sheds a richer, more hopeful light on that darkness (248). *Darkness Visible* gives rise, as Don Crompton observes, to the "fruitful uncertainties" and "mysteries" characterizing Golding's later literary works.[7] The Arab child whom Matty rescues belongs to the world of such fruitful uncertainties. What he may become remains a mystery; but his salvation embodies the kind of miracle that can still be effected in a dark world by acts of love and sacrifice. In this sense the novel's break with tradition is less radical than Kosinski's. Rather than severing the literary child's tie to transcendence, *Darkness Visible* redefines it—by recalling that Christian vision, its texts and traditions, on which the Romantics drew for their secular myth of the child. If human darkness, not innocence, is the condition into which each human being is born, recognition of this bleak fact does not preclude but rather impels a more searching exploration of our shadowy existence. Reflected in the prisms of Golding's novel is an image of childhood that beckons readers to peer beneath the veil of appearances. Only after gleaning the dark truth of our flawed human nature—making that darkness visible—may we proceed as best we can toward the light.

CHAPTER

New Versions of the Idyll
Lessing's *The Fifth Child* and
Kundera's Infantocracy

From diametrically opposed vantages *Darkness Visible* and *The Painted Bird* shatter the idyll of childhood, exposing their child protagonists to the harsh elements of nature and culture. Under the searching light of Golding's apocalyptic vision or of Kosinski's grimly deterministic one, faith in the child's innocence is shown to foster dangerous as well as complacent illusions. To insist on humanity's innate goodness, both novels suggest, is not only to ignore but also to abet the forces of darkness. The process holds true whether these forces are defined metaphysically, as pure evil, or materially. Conveying the latter perspective, Kosinski's novel depicts the massive weight of history and culture—in all its codified prejudice and superstition, all its institutionalized power and fear—bearing down on the tiny individual, pressing the human subject into collectively identifiable shape.

In *The Fifth Child* (1988) Doris Lessing offers, from yet another perspective, an indictment of the romantic idyll and the dangerous illusions it fosters. More explicitly even than Golding's, her novel exposes the darkness at the heart of both nature and human nature and undermines the pastoral dream. In *Darkness Visible,* we recall, the darkness inside Sophy, the will to hurt and kill, exerts a tremendous power. Like a magnetic force, it draws her down, deeper and deeper into the "cone of black light" that "stretche[s] away infinitely," luring her from the world of light (134). In *The Fifth Child,* on the other hand, Lessing's "black cave that ha[s] no end" signifies the primordial abyss beneath the familiar world of appearances (10). Existing before time and history, the black cave recedes into the infinite heart of darkness: the primal wilderness whence the human race sprang, still present in the instincts of the species but no longer accessible to memory or consciousness. It is this amoral force of nature—the dark origin of our species—that belies and finally destroys the pastoral dream of Lessing's protagonists.

"Nature never did betray / The heart that loved her," Wordsworth declares in "Lines Composed a Few Miles above Tintern Abbey": she is the "nurse," the "guide, the guardian" of "all my moral being" (ll. 122–23, 109–11). Latter-day disciples of Wordsworth and Rousseau, Lessing's Harriet and David Lovatt rehearse in contemporary guise the Romantics' affirmation of faith in nature as humanity's nurse and guide. Withdrawing from the harsh realities of social life and historical circumstance, they take refuge in the idyll of hearth and home. Entrusting themselves to Mother Nature, they celebrate her benign fertility by assiduously cultivating their garden, rapidly producing a prodigious number of well-fed, rosy-cheeked children. With the birth of their fifth child, nature takes revenge on their romantic construction, laying waste the idyll.[1]

Centering on the conception and birth of an alien or monstrous offspring, Lessing's modern fable parodies as it pays tribute to its famous literary precursor *Frankenstein* and the "pervasive maternal anxiety" registered in that novel. As Anne Mellor points out, *Frankenstein* gives concrete form to the unspoken fears that each mother tries to quell as she contemplates childbearing: "even if I love and nurture my child," the prospective parent asks herself, "even if I provide the best education of which I am capable, I may still produce a monster—and who is responsible for that?"[2] This question comes to haunt Lessing's protagonist, although she hardly thinks to ask it before her fifth, and final, pregnancy. As different as Lessing's complacent young couple are from Shelley's obsessed scientist, they initially share his naive belief that any creature they bring into the world will be beautiful.

As their name, Lovatt (pronounced Love-it in the British manner), suggests, Lessing's young couple do not examine their capacity, anymore than Frankenstein does, to love it—the unknown being that nature will deliver to and through them.[3] Like those trusting souls mocked by Pär Lagerkvist's narrator in *The Dwarf,* the Lovatts believe that nature "is made for them, for their well-being and their happiness." But the dwarf, whose stunted frame eloquently belies such complacency, poses the question that the Lovatts fail to consider: "Who knows what nature carries in her womb? . . . She bides her time, and eventually we see the thing to which she has given birth" (*Dwarf* 42). As Peter Brooks says in regard to *Frankenstein,* "Nature is not one thing, and those who think it [is] are caught in a self-destructive blindness." Nature is "a monstrous potentiality so close to us—so close to home—that we have repressed its possibility." Every newborn, notes Ellen Moers, brings an aspect of the "monstrous" into this world from the "other."[4] In most cases, however, neither the newborn's homely features nor the gory details of its birth produce so stunning a demonstration of nature's monstrous potentiality as the Lovatts' fifth child. Only the birth of their own monster brings *home,* literally and figuratively, this terrible truth.

The "hideous progeny" born to Victor Frankenstein acts, as we have seen, like a judgment on his scientific hubris. Having assumed, as Mellor says, "that he can violate Nature and pursue her to her hiding places with impunity," Frankenstein becomes prey to those "elemental forces" of nature he so thoughtlessly unleashes. Nature thus demonstrates her power "to punish those who transgress her boundaries."[5] Like an avenging fury, Frankenstein's creature becomes his destroyer, wreaking havoc and vengeance on all those whom Victor loves. The Lovatts' hubris—their transgression against nature—arises from a different source. They mean not to usurp nature but to worship it. In this sense they resemble not Frankenstein, the monomaniacal scientist, but those more balanced, content individuals who are among the scientist's nearest and dearest—from his loyal friend, the Wordsworthian poet Henry Clerval, to his tranquil and loving fiancée, Elizabeth Lavenza.

In Shelley's novel, Mellor observes, characters "capable of deeply feeling the beauties of nature" are duly "rewarded" by nature.[6] In contrast to Frankenstein, they possess profound "physical and mental health" until the scientist disturbs the natural order and brings on their destruction. The fate of Lessing's young couple serves as an ironic comment on this romantic conception. The Lovatts' blind trust in nature—their complacent expectation of the physical and mental health with which nature presumably rewards its disciples—paradoxically unleashes nature's elemental forces and destroys their dream. An offspring of nature in a sense very different from Rousseau's, the fifth child is both product and harbinger of those elemental forces. An emissary from the primal dark, the alien wilderness from which life springs, he wreaks havoc first with the Lovatt family and then with the social order. Erupting into the domestic "kingdom" through his mother's body, he takes both body and domestic "fortress" by storm (22). Little is left intact.

Shattering the idyll of childhood and its romantic underpinnings, the darkness made visible by the fifth child brings other themes and relationships to light: most notably, the way the Lovatts' dream of withdrawing from society is both fostered and reflected by that society. This paradoxical analogy between the Lovatts' domestic circle and the political realm is more than hinted at by Lessing's repeated use of the word *kingdom,* which explicitly links the private and public spheres (8, 22). As Patricia Meyer Spacks points out, novelists have for centuries drawn on the "analogies between large and small bodies politic." Citing Henry Fielding, she notes how the "threat of a usurper disappears in *Tom Jones;* the kingdom's order restores itself, and the miniature kingdom of Paradise Hall also returns to serenity." In "the twentieth century, the political analogy no longer has such reassuring implications." If the "family . . . and society stubbornly survive, they do so under threat of devastation from within."[7] On this threat of devastation Lessing homes in; the elemental forces that ravage the Lovatts' domestic kingdom are dismantling the larger one as well.

To appreciate the implications of Lessing's social analogy, readers must first note the broad contrast on which such subtle resemblances are based. At the outset of the novel Lessing's narrator underscores the tension between her two protagonists, self-styled "freaks and oddballs," and their social environment (4). David Lovatt meets his future wife at a London office party in the turbulent 1960s. Leaning against a wall of the company's "solemn boardroom," now transfigured by a noisy, bibulous crowd, David spies Harriet's figure as a "pastel blur" in "an Impressionist picture." A "girl merged with her surroundings," she "stood near a great vase of dried grasses and leaves and her dress was something flowery." At this point the narrator's ironic voice takes over, offering the reader a more detached perspective: "The focussing eye then saw curly dark hair, which was unfashionable," "soft but thoughtful" blue eyes, and "lips rather too firmly closed." The narrator concludes, "A healthy young woman, but perhaps more at home in a garden?" (4).

The surroundings with which Harriet merges offer a striking contrast to the discordant social environment, the crush of noisy party goers frantically displaying themselves on the dance floor. Tranquil if indistinct, the pastel blur incorporates a pastoral image of benign vegetation: the vase of dried foliage and the pattern of flowers on Harriet's dress. In David's first glimpse of his future wife, Lessing provides a subtle arrangement of visual details that foreshadow the novel's action. Harriet and David will meet, marry, and dedicate themselves to the settled pleasures of domestic life. Unwitting at the outset, knowing only that they are alienated from "the spirit of the times," the young couple will seek refuge in an idyllic age (21). Nostalgic for the safe old world of legendary England—that flowering isle sheltered from the rude winds of change—they would shun the present and turn their backs on society. Elaine Tyler May's comments on twentieth-century family life provide a helpful gloss on the Lovatts' domestic idyll: "intense preoccupation with the family" as the "focus of hopes for the good life," she points out, "often rests upon a mythic vision of a golden age in which a timeless, stable domestic haven existed."[8]

Sequestering themselves in their private domain, or garden, Harriet and David Lovatt are convinced, for a while at least, that they have found refuge from society. Only gradually do they recognize that the public domain is profoundly implicated in their private one. Lessing, on the other hand, alerts her readers early to the parallels between the microcosmic and macrocosmic settings of her novel—between, that is, the Lovatts' private kingdom and the beleaguered social conditions of contemporary England.[9] Even in the most casual aside, Lessing's narrator establishes the analogy: David's "parents left the [Lovatts'] garden, and then England with relief" (14).

Let us return briefly to "the famous office party" at which the future progenitors of the fifth child embark on their domestic idyll. Only an instant after David glimpses Harriet, the couple exchange looks of recognition, glide toward each other, and withdraw from the noisy throng. Both know "at once that this was what they had been waiting for. Someone conservative, old-fashioned, not to say obsolescent" (3). Here once again a nodding reference to the couple's obsolescence hints at a profound irony that gradually becomes more pointed: in the attempt to elude history, Harriet and David are caught in its force field. Coming of age in the discordant 1960s, they are also, to recall the title of Lessing's five-novel series, children of violence.[10] The violence not only of history but of prehistory proves the Lovatts' unclaimed heritage. Children of nature and its violence, they unwittingly carry the genetic trace of their primeval ancestors. Ironically, these two "freaks," or "oddballs," misfits only in the social sense, are destined to

conceive a true aberration—a genetic throwback to the human race's
dark past (4, 6).

Trusting in nature to protect and guide them, Harriet and David
also trust in the rights and privileges that nature bestows on her creatures. Even the shared certainty that "they were made for each other"
is an affirmation of romantic faith: the belief that, as Peter Coveney
summarizes Rousseau, "virtue" is their "natural state" and "happiness"
their rightful "kingdom"—their "inheritance by nature."[11] It is this
faith that Lessing's narrator subtly mocks early in the novel. In the following passage, for example, repeated emphasis on the words *happiness*
and *happy* draws attention to the young couple's naive complacency:
"Happiness. A happy family. The Lovatts were a happy family. It was
what they had chosen and what they deserved" (21). So certain is
Harriet of her right to happiness that, long before she meets and mar-
ries David, she has come to regard domestic bliss as her "birthright."
Like a fairy-tale princess, she has only to wait for her prince, the "man
[who] would hand her the keys of her kingdom" (8).

The kingdom appears assured when, shortly after they marry, the
Lovatts acquire a large Victorian house with an "overgrown garden,"
located at a considerable distance from London and the pressures of
urban life. Eager to fill this enormous "three-storeyed house," the
young couple vow to have, by contemporary standards, an inordinate
and financially exorbitant number of offspring: "Six children at least,"
they agree, although "they could not say this to anyone else" (8–9). For
the Lovatts this outsize and old-fashioned house offers a dual refuge,
temporal as well as spatial, from contemporary life. Sheltered within
the sturdy walls of its Victorian frame, they hope to recapture the rituals and rewards of a bygone era.

In the nineteenth century, Mark Spilka points out, the Victorian
home was "conceived as a pastoral retreat," a source of "refuge and
sanctity," and a bulwark "against an increasingly commercial and urban
culture." Noting the Victorian tendency to "recoil from the City,"
Walter Houghton observes that "the home was irradiated by the light
of a pastoral imagination. It could seem a country of peace and innocence where life was kind and duty natural." Whether "urban or suburban," Spilka concludes, "the Victorian home continued the pastoral
and romantic tradition of the country refuge."[12] To its owners the
Lovatts' Victorian house holds out similar promise of nostalgic retreat.

The ironies in the Lovatts' attempt to recapture the age-old dream of the pastoral idyll are already discernible in its earlier, Victorian manifestation. One has only to recall Jaggers's law clerk, Mr. Wemmick, in *Great Expectations,* whose tiny home outside London is constructed like a miniature castle surrounded by a diminutive, highly symbolic moat. There in the suburb of Walworth, Pip notes, Wemmick miraculously recovers the humanity he appears to have sacrificed during the workday to the exigencies of urban life (224–28). But while Wemmick undergoes the transition in a relatively short time, his Walworth home lying within walking distance of central London, David Lovatt's "contribution to the dream" is more exacting: it will take him "nearly two hours twice a day to get to and from work" (15). As David assumes the egregious burden of a four-hour commute, the Lovatts' old-fashioned dream of domestic happiness acquires a distinctly modern cast.

The modern family, Philippe Ariès pointed out several decades ago, is the culmination of a tendency, which arose in the eighteenth century and intensified during the Victorian era, to define and confine human sociability within the family circle. "The history of modern manners," Ariès observes, "can be reduced in part to this long effort to break away from others, to escape from a society whose pressure had become unbearable."[13] The intensified pressures felt by members of industrial, and now postindustrial, society have thus given rise to new forms of pastoral longing, new idylls of retreat. Hence the paradox at the heart of Lessing's novel: the domestic kingdom to which the Lovatts nostalgically desire to retreat is at the same time a quintessentially modern phenomenon—the nuclear family envisioned as last refuge from worldly assault.

Yet as Rushdie comments in *Imaginary Homelands,* the modern world no longer countenances any "hiding places; the missiles have made sure of that." He adds, "we are all irradiated by history, we are all radioactive with history and politics." As the term *nuclear family* suggests, contemporary life is charged by awareness of the atom—whose power to invade our lives and bodies evinces, with dread finality, our inescapable exposure to outside forces. These are precisely the forces—"the unceasing storm" of contemporary history, in Rushdie's phrase—that the Lovatts seek to ignore (99–100). As they set about constructing their idyll, Harriet and David cannot always ignore that "outside this fortunate place, their family, beat and battered the storms of the world." They persist in believing, nonetheless, that their fortress is secure from attack (21–22).

While resolving not to tell anyone the full details of their exorbitant scheme, Harriet and David cannot conceal the financial toll that their dream house exacts.[14] Having little or no money of their own, the newlyweds are indebted to David's father, James. Divorced from David's mother and now married to a rich woman—of whose "flashy" lifestyle David disapproves but to whom he will henceforth "be beholden"—James kindly assumes responsibility for the thirty-year mortgage (14). Not only the outsize Victorian house but the dream that goes with it depends on social and economic conditions that the Lovatts otherwise ignore.

The newlyweds take possession of their dream house on an afternoon that seems resonantly idyllic: "they stood hand in hand in the little porch, birds singing all around them in the garden where boughs were still black and glistening with the chilly rain of early spring." Marveling at the vast kitchen and family room that "would be the heart of their kingdom," Harriet and David ascend the stairs to their bedroom and lie down on the large, old-fashioned bed. The harmony of their impressions again sounds a pastoral note: "Shadows from a lilac tree, a wet sun behind it, seemed to be enticingly sketching on the expanses of the ceiling the years they would live in this house" (9–10).

Abruptly, however, the note changes pitch; it becomes strident, insistent, even as the shadows in the bedroom deepen. With "deliberate, concentrated intensity" David recklessly and repeatedly makes love to his wife. Although she attempts to remind him of their plans "to put off having children for two years," Harriet cannot restrain her husband. As he laughs "a loud, reckless, unscrupulous laugh, quite unlike modest, humorous, judicious David," the pastoral setting darkens to a different landscape: "Now the room was quite dark, it looked vast, like a black cave that had no end. A branch scraped across a wall somewhere close." Discovering herself in a new and threatening world, Harriet senses that "she [does] not know" her husband at all (10). Carried beyond, or beneath, his familiar daytime self, David yields to primal instinct—the procreative urge that forges all kingdoms, even the most domestic ones. All of a sudden, nature appears neither benign nor trustworthy; its furious energy is the driving force behind David's reckless actions and unscrupulous laugh. The idyll descends into the black cave of the primordial past—a world so apparently alien to

Harriet that she believes herself caught in a "spell." Then, as David's energy is spent and the spell subsides, "ordinariness slowly" reasserts itself. To Harriet's relief her husband returns to his familiar self, and they exchange "small reassuring daytime kisses" (11).

Conceived on this reckless afternoon, the Lovatts' first child, Luke, is born right after Christmas of 1966. When Luke is only three months old, Harriet finds, with some dismay, that she is pregnant again. When David hears the news, he laughingly comments, "There's something progenitive about this room, I swear" (18). Playfully ascribing to their bedroom his own procreative energies, David shuns knowledge of his primal nature, formed in the black cave of prehistory. Literally entrusting themselves to nature, whose "processes" they are loath to "tamper with," the Lovatts reject "the Pill" (92). With a rapidity that Harriet finds startling (though to Lessing's readers it seems predictable, given their reluctance to tamper with nature), the Lovatts conceive "four children in six years." Despite Harriet's mounting fatigue, and the financial burden of so large a family, the domestic idyll still appears, for a while, intact.

Their domestic duties notwithstanding, the Lovatts occasionally make "themselves read the papers, and watch the News on television, though their instinct [is] to do neither. At least they ought to know," they remind each other, "what [goes] on outside their fortress, their kingdom" of "safety, comfort, kindness" (22). By the early 1970s life in the suburbs has taken a decidedly nasty turn: "Brutal incidents and crimes, once shocking everyone, were now commonplace. Gangs of youth hung around certain cafés and street-ends and owed respect to no one. The house next door had been burgled three times: the Lovatts' not yet, but then there were always people about.... There was an ugly edge on events: more and more it seemed that two peoples lived in England, not one—enemies, hating each other, who could not hear what the other said" (22). Ironically, while the Lovatts are busy securing their fortress against these hostile outside forces, the enemy —the very "processes of Nature" they have "relied upon"—invades from within (92).

Soon after the birth of her fourth child, Harriet discovers, with dismay bordering on despair, that she is pregnant for the fifth time. Listless and unwell from the first week, she begins to feel that the fetus is poisoning her (32). In the fifth month it seems to be "trying to tear its way out of her stomach." The "ceaseless battering and striving" make her "cry out in pain" (38–39). Isolated by her incomprehensible suffering, Harriet cannot help but regard "the savage thing inside her" as the "enemy": "Sometimes she believed hooves were cutting her tender inside flesh, sometimes claws" (40–41). As she struggles for survival against the alien creature attacking her from within, the world outside—which has formerly seemed so remote from their little kingdom—mirrors this savage conflict. The evening news broadcasts accounts of brutal crimes and murders in the Lovatts' immediate vicinity.

Relaying such information in a "professionally cool voice," the television newscaster detaches himself, as he has been trained to do, from its terrible import (44). Yet the message is clear: in present-day England the hostility of a divided population—consisting of "two peoples," or "enemies"—has reached the stage of murder. Not only the Lovatts' private kingdom but the social order is being ravaged from within. As this theme develops, the full irony of the Lovatts' attempted retreat from history (and prehistory) begins to emerge. The demise of their dream is an eloquent comment on the society from which they have sought to escape. Tearing down both kingdoms, the Lovatts' domestic stronghold and the public domain, are the chthonic forces of nature: not the domesticated nature of the pastoral idyll but the primordial wilderness, the black cave from which the human race has evolved and to which it may yet revert.

These forces literally erupt in the Lovatt household with the arrival of their fifth child. When this ugly creature is born, it hardly looks like a baby at all: "He had a heavy-shouldered hunched look, as if he were crouching there as he lay." His "yellowish" hair forms a "wedge" that comes low on the forehead; his hands are "thick and heavy, with pads of muscle in the palms." With "greeny-yellow eyes, like lumps of soapstone," the fifth child looks alarmingly predatory (48–49). (Significantly, the features of the troglodytic newborn, whose hair is blond and whose eyes are "greeny-yellow," carry no hint of a racial stereotype.) On this formidable creature Harriet bestows the ordinary name Ben; but nothing about the fifth child is ordinary (50, 56). At nine months he does not crawl but walks; when left alone in the garden to play, he tears up flowers and stalks birds. At one year he strangles a pet dog and three months later the family cat. By the time Ben is eighteen months old, he has "to be watched every second. He slept very little. He spent most of the night standing on his window-sill, staring into the garden, and if Harriet looked in on him, he would turn and give her a long stare, alien, chilling" (62–63). Terrified by their ferocious sibling, the other four Lovatt children begin locking their bedroom doors at night. In Ben's alien presence the garden reverts to wilderness.

Emerging from the wilderness of prehistory, the fifth child is, Harriet soon realizes, a genetic "throwback" to a prehuman species— a savage race that may have "rape[d] the females of humanity's fore- bears" and "left their seeds in the human matrix, here and there, to appear again" (75, 130). As Harriet eventually confides to her mother, Dorothy, "Ben makes you think . . . all those different people who lived on the earth once—they must be in us somewhere." "Perhaps," her mother answers, "we simply don't notice them when they do" appear among us. We do not notice, Harriet replies, "because we don't want to" (114, ellipses in original). Shattering the Lovatts' domestic harmony, the fifth child opens Harriet's eyes to a dark truth, an alien sphere of reality—one that she may have glimpsed but did not acknowledge on that reckless day when her first child was conceived.

Not only the fifth child's parents but also his siblings are implicated in his alien nature and past. Underscoring the link between the alien and human spheres, between prehistory and history, is an evocative scene midway through the novel. The scene opens as the two older Lovatt children, Luke and Helen, emerge from the "dark winter gar- den" in which they have been playing. Stripped of its spring foliage and twittering birds, the "starkling black" garden hints openly at the primordial black cave beneath the familiar "shapes of tree and shrub." As the two children emerge from the garden, the narrator describes their "two small figures" as issuing "from the black." Then, after they do a quick "stamping dance around and around," Luke and Helen dash indoors—to "the warm, lit family room," where their parents await these "two slight, elegant little creatures, with . . . eyes full of the excitements of the dark wilderness they had been part of. . . . For a moment it was the meeting of two alien forms of life: the children had been part of some old savagery, and their blood still pounded with it; but now they had to let their wild selves go away while they rejoined their family. Harriet and David . . . could see themselves clearly, two adults, sitting there, tame, domestic, even pitiable in their distance from wildness and freedom" (74–75). A striking contrast to Ben's squat and ugly frame, these "elegant little creatures" are linked, nonetheless, to the alien. Conceived in the black cave of their parents' "progenitive" bedroom, they readily descend, like the garden, into wildness and savagery. At the origin of life lies the dark wilderness from which, generation after generation, children emerge—abandoning (though never entirely) their wild selves as they join the charmed circle of domestic life.

Immediately after this scene that implicates the Lovatt children, and by extension all of humankind, in Ben's alien nature, a "small black van" arrives to carry Ben away. With the reluctant consent of his wife, David has arranged to send him to an unnamed institution in the North. There, Harriet gleans, the fifth child "is not expected to live long" (74–75). Ben's removal abruptly restores the household to harmony and peace. The "high spirits" and shining eyes of the four Lovatt children express their profound sense of liberation and joy. Watching them, Harriet understands anew "what a burden Ben had been, how he had oppressed them all, how much the children had suffered." Yet she is tormented by "guilt and horror" at his possible fate. No longer willing or able to retreat from disturbing reality, she resolves to find out "what they are doing to Ben" (76–77). Infuriating David, Harriet departs for the North, where she finds Ben, drugged and straitjacketed, in a virtual dungeon, dying of starvation in a padded cell. In the cell "everything—walls, the floor, and Ben—was smeared with excrement. A pool of dark yellow urine oozed from the pallet, which was soaked" (82). Within this remote institution British "officialdom" is quietly dispensing with those alien elements, genetic "freaks and oddballs," that society is loath to recognize (112).[15]

By bringing Ben back with her, Harriet incurs the wrath of her husband and children, who cannot forgive her for ruining their happiness. The alien is now even more difficult to control; filled with rage and panic from his treatment at the institution, he lashes out in a "storm of terror" (89). Enduring the family's resentment, Harriet defends herself by explaining that the institution was "murdering" Ben. When she tells David that he did not see the brutal conditions there, he replies: "I was careful *not* to see" (87). David's statement underscores the theme of willful ignorance, of rejection of knowledge, developed throughout Lessing's fable. Like Frankenstein's creature, the fifth child forces what Mellor calls a "confrontation of the human mind with an unknowable nature." Each of these monsters functions as "the sign of the unfamiliar, the unknown."[16] Like Victor Frankenstein,

David Lovatt refuses to acknowledge his offspring. In refusing to *see* Ben—that is, to register the sign of the alien—he joins all those who deny the other or unknown. That human beings are willing to carry denial to the point of violence is made clear by the unnamed institution: one that calls to mind countless asylums, prisons, concentration camps, and torture chambers around the world. *The Fifth Child* illustrates, among other things, the way denial of the alien—in nature and human nature and in the world they together create—may perpetuate the most lethal forms of inhumanity.

With Ben's return the Lovatt household, riven by fear, hostility, and resentment, gradually falls apart. One by one, the other children drift away, preferring to attend boarding school or to stay with relatives and friends while Harriet struggles to cope with the fifth child. Seeking counsel from a series of teachers, doctors, and other professionals, she longs for a sign or word confirming her recognition of the alien. Yet expert after expert refuses to admit that Ben is abnormal. According to the liberal institutions of learning, medicine, and social welfare, everything is explicable, a mere problem of "adjustment" (100). One psychologist even chides Harriet, "The problem is not with Ben, but with you. You don't like him very much" (103). Hiding behind the paraphernalia of science, the social "Authorities" shun reality and evade responsibility (97). The experts Harriet encounters exhibit the same "psychologism," the same "technical consciousness" that Valerie Suransky detects in many trained professionals. With "technological precision," she observes, these experts methodically chart, measure, and demarcate every stage of childhood from infancy to adolescence. Reducing the "child to a set of isolated functions," they "cement" more blocks in the social "edifice of anomie."[17]

Much the same can be said of the child experts whom Harriet consults about Ben—from the unnamed doctor who signs Ben into the institution without examining him to the child psychologist Dr. Gilly and Harriet's obstetrician, Dr. Brett, both of whom are equally reluctant to "see" Ben. Just as Dr. Brett declares Ben "physically normal for eighteen months," "all of them," Harriet begins to realize, "*wouldn't* see how different [Ben] was" (63, 48). "No schoolteacher, or doctor, or specialist," she concludes, would "take responsibility" and say, "That is what [Ben] is" (132).[18]

Occasionally Harriet glimpses, behind the experts' professional manner, "horror of the alien, rejection by the normal for what was

outside the human limit." But this "moment of truth" is never articu-
lated; nature's "monstrous potentiality," to recall Brooks's phrase, is
again "repressed." Here Lessing's reader is reminded of the kindly
magistrate in Shelley's *Frankenstein* to whom Victor recounts a portion
of his "hideous" tale. "Shudder[ing] with horror," the magistrate inadvertently reveals the narrative's impact on him; when, however, he is
"called upon" by Frankenstein "to act officially in consequence, the
whole tide of his incredulity returned" (169). Similarly, the authorities
to whom Harriet pleads her case sometimes betray their horror of
Ben. As experts, however, they must act professionally; denying the
alien, they erect a fortress of facts and statistics to shield themselves
from its sight. Bureaucratic officialdom, it would seem, has constructed its own version of retreat.

Seeking refuge from the harsh world of contemporary culture, Harriet
and David Lovatt serve, paradoxically, as its unwitting accomplices.
Harriet's recognition near the end of the novel of Ben's devastating
effect on their household is particularly suggestive. To David she says,
"We are being punished" for "presuming. For thinking we could be
happy. Happy because *we* decided we would be" (117). The idyll they
sought to create was built, she implies, on blindness and denial; their
private kingdom, on a shaky and meretricious foundation. That the
entire social establishment is in retreat from reality gradually becomes
clear to Harriet. By the time Ben goes to school, she has "given up
trying to read to him, play with him, teach him anything: he could not
learn. But she knew the Authorities would never recognize this, or
acknowledge that they did" (97). Even Harriet is surprised, however,
when at the age of eleven Ben, far from being ostracized by the other
youngsters at school, becomes a respected leader (120). "Ben Lovatt's
gang," she learns, is "the most envied in school, and a lot of boys, not
only the truants and drop-outs, wanted to be part of it" (122).

By this time the "barbarous eighties" have set in; local newspapers
feature endless stories of "muggings, hold-ups, break-ins," and "rapes"
(107, 122–23). When Ben and his gang disappear for several days at a
time, Harriet wonders which of these reported crimes they have now
committed. Meanwhile, society appears to conspire in its own victimization, the media producing endless images of violence for mass consumption. Not surprisingly, Ben and his gang are avid consumers as
well as producers of violence. When not out on a rampage, they sprawl
around the television set to get their kicks. Downing take-out food

from greasy packages, they take in the "shootings and killings and tortures" flickering past on the screen. Harriet, in the next room, listens to their "moans of excited participation as the bullets poured into a body, as blood spurted, as the tortured victim screamed" (122).

The fifth child appears the only genetic throwback in the novel, but the other members of Ben's gang have clearly reverted to a comparable state. Their eyes turn on Harriet with the same icy stare, and in their hulking gestures and movements she reads evidence of naked aggression (122–23). Ben, the alien, is virtually indistinguishable from the rest of this "alienated, non-comprehending, hostile tribe" (129). The answer to Harriet's question—"Would people always refuse to see [Ben], to recognise what he was?"—seems obvious (131). People cannot distinguish the alien from the human because the very image or ideal of the human is being eroded, drowned in a sea of "television noises" and electronic violence (133, 129). In the vision of contemporary society that Lessing evokes, the human being, human culture, is losing definition—reverting to a condition that, for all its technological complexity, recalls the dark wilderness of our alien past.

Alerting readers to this lack of definition, to the vanishing border between the human and the nonhuman in contemporary culture, Lessing again reworks and subverts the themes of *Frankenstein*. In Shelley's novel both Frankenstein and the strangers who encounter his creature immediately misconstrue the latter's abnormal, or alien, appearance. To all those who see him, the creature is not only grotesque but evil, a wicked fiend or hateful demon. By constructing the creature as evil, the novel's characters—and Frankenstein most particularly—force him to become evil. The creature turns into, as Mellor says, the monster he is semiotically construed to be: Frankenstein and the other characters "use language, their visual and verbal constructions of reality, to name or image the human and the nonhuman and thus to fix the boundaries between us and them." Relying on Michel Foucault's observations, she notes that society employs this border or site between the normal and abnormal to "discipline and punish" the latter.[19]

In *The Fifth Child,* on the other hand, Lessing suggests that the lack of such culturally defined borders—society's failure to identify what is acceptably human and what is not—fosters horrors beyond Foucault's repressive prisons, hospitals, and schools. The society that cannot name or notice "Ben, the alien, the destroyer," is responsible both for the unnamed institution to which the fifth child is surreptitiously sent to die and for countless other edifices of anomie, to recall Suransky's phrase. Lessing calls attention, for example, to the secondary school at which Ben's gang is the most powerful and envied among the boys. Hardly an institution of learning, the school is a repository for increasing numbers of "the uneducable, the unassimilable, the hopeless"—all shuffled "from class to class," all "waiting for the happy moment when they can leave" (120). Finally, there are those "half-derelict buildings, the caves and caverns and shelters of the big cities," where the homeless and helpless remain hidden. Here, Harriet imagines, Ben and his gang will eventually wind up—still "overlooked" by those "in authority" who "had *not* been seeing Ben ever since he was born" (131).

At the novel's end Harriet asks herself whether rescuing Ben from the institution was right or wrong. If she had allowed him to stay there, her children would have remained at home; they could have been a family again. She admits that "if I had let him die, then all of us, so many people, would have been happy, but I could not do it." To Ben, "after all, she had given birth," had "carried him for eight months, though it nearly killed her" (131). To let him be killed was not humanly possible, whatever the sacrifice—and Harriet's sacrifice could hardly be greater or more lonely. When she turns to her husband for forgiveness or to the social authorities for help, she finds that no one will testify to the terrible truth that has shattered her dream. Harriet alone strives to see, driven by her "need, her *passion* to know more" about this alien child and the "far-away past" from which he arrived (131, 116).

Such profound curiosity, such passion to know, has radically transformed Harriet from the happy "innocent" she once was (130). Virtually abandoned by her husband and children, she sacrifices comfort and happiness for knowledge, the idyll for engagement with reality. Although she hopes one day to find "an amateur of the human condition, perhaps an anthropologist of an unusual kind," who would acknowledge the "truth" about Ben, Harriet is presently the only one to bear witness. For the sake of truth she has lost nearly everything: "It was as if the strain of her life had stripped off her a layer of flesh—not real flesh, but perhaps metaphysical substance" (112). The loss of this "invisible substance" sets Harriet apart from her family at the end of the novel. Enervated and elderly looking at the age of forty-five, she has been "drained of some ingredient that everyone took for granted, which was like a layer of fat but was not material" (129). By tearing from her that protective layer—those comfortable illusions shielding her from reality—the fifth child, nature's child, has robbed Harriet of everything she once claimed as her birthright. But Ben has also forced open her eyes. In the painful process of awakening she has gained something more reliable than dreams, more lasting than happiness. Alone among the characters in the novel, she is willing to confront the alien, within and without.

As Harriet gradually assumes her burden of knowledge, her fall from innocence appears necessary, no matter how unfortunate. In contrast to this painful but necessary awakening, contemporary culture, with its bureaucratic methods, reliance on scientific data, and faith in technology, appears blindly, perhaps fatally in retreat. The images Lessing uses to portray the dangerous spectacle of cultural retreat recall, rather unexpectedly, those that Jacques Derrida employs when discussing the crisis of interpretation in contemporary philosophy and the social sciences. Drawing on images of childbirth, he announces "a kind of question, let us still call it historical, whose *conception, formation, gestation,* and *labor* we are only catching a glimpse of today." Invoking "the operations of childbearing" as he signals—with a kind of mental spasm or contraction—his premonitions of a new, as yet unnameable cultural or "historical" development, Derrida characterizes a society on the verge of a new historical stage as one in which people "turn their eyes away." Any culture—including that "society from which," he says, "I do not exclude myself"—is bound to turn away, to beat a hasty retreat "when faced by the as yet unnamable." But it is this unknown or unnameable next stage that, he adds, "is proclaiming itself and [that] can do so, as is necessary whenever a birth is in the offing, only under the species of the nonspecies, in the formless, mute, infant, and terrifying form of monstrosity."[20]

Beneath the slippery syntax and wordplay (for example, "the species of the nonspecies") Derrida sounds optimistic, even reassuring about the state of Western culture. He suggests that the future, like Yeats's "rough beast," is always monstrous; it is always, already alien to those who try to conceive of it. The terrifying form of the formless, so to speak, only seems a monstrosity because it is other—because it is nameless and as yet unnameable. Lessing, whose novel vividly renders the arrival of the alien—its "conception, formation, gestation, and labor," to repeat Derrida's words—appears less sanguine. The fifth child, this unnameable alien conceived in the present, signals a stage in modern history that Derrida's formulation fails to take into account.

Far from terrifying others with his monstrousness, as Frankenstein's creature does with such tragic consequences, Ben "the alien, the destroyer," comes and goes without remark. Who can say that his nature is other, alien or nonhuman, when his actions, speech, and conduct are indistinguishable from those of his cohorts, who merge with the undifferentiated mass. From Berlin to Buenos Aires, Madrid to Los Angeles, Lessing's narrator warns, contemporary culture has become increasingly distracted and indifferent to its own besieged humanity. Failing to define for themselves and society an image or standard of the human—and to differentiate what is human from what is not—members of Western culture may be collectively embarked on a new version of the idyll, a lethal form of retreat.

Savaging the Idyll: Kundera's *Book of Laughter and Forgetting*

The idyll is never free from political implications and consequences, *The Fifth Child* provocatively suggests, no matter how insistent the idealist's efforts to retreat. The Lovatts' desire to turn their backs on society mirrors, as it contributes to, social breakdown and disorder. The connection between the private kingdom and the public domain is inextricable. As Milan Kundera, a novelist whose fiction centers on this theme, said in an interview, "The metaphysics of man is the same in the private sphere as in the public one."[21] To Kundera, an exile from the former Czech communist regime, the age-old dream of pastoral retreat has dangerous political implications. As his narrator comments in *The Book of Laughter and Forgetting* (1978), "People have always aspired to an idyll, a garden where nightingales sing, a realm of harmony where the world does not rise up as a stranger against man nor man against other men, where the world and all its people are molded from a single stock, . . . where every man is a note in a magnificent Bach fugue and anyone who refuses his note is a mere black dot, useless and meaningless, easily caught and squashed between the fingers like an insect" (8). The way this serpentine sentence glides from the pastoral garden (where nightingales sing) to the political jungle (where men get squashed like insects) suggests the seamless connection not only between the private and public spheres but between nature and society, art and politics. There is no clear border, Kundera suggests, between the dream of idyllic harmony and a world of political tyranny, where the dead body of a previously revered revolutionary swings "back and forth like a bell ringing in the new dawn of mankind" (9).

In the poet's romantic longing or the composer's celestial harmonies Kundera discovers the same totalizing urge, the same desire to transform reality in toto, that fuels faith in a cosmic order or in sundry ideologies promising to create paradise on earth. The same impulse that compels the poet to seek immortality in song, or Bach to celebrate divinity in a fugue, leads others to seek perfection—utopia— in grandiose political schemes. The quest for total harmony, the desire for retreat may end, as with the Lovatts, in communal disaster. Drawing on his personal history as a dissident in and ultimately an exile from cold-war Czechoslovakia, Kundera establishes as the premise for his narrative one of the more suggestive implications of Lessing's novel: that an entire society can be lured by the pastoral idyll. In *The Book of Laughter and Forgetting* he boldly characterizes the modern totalitarian state as simply another version of that ancient idyll. Lulled by the dream of pastoral harmony, individuals allow "the flowers of forgetting" to spread and "grow like weeds on ruins" as collective memory is swept clean of the imperfect past (158). Significantly, the image of childhood proves every bit as important to the totalitarian idyll as to its romantic precursor. Once more, the child serves as emissary of a more perfect world—in this case, the transcendent future, where all stains and blots on human history are miraculously wiped clean.

Toward the end of *The Book of Laughter and Forgetting* Kundera's narrator identifies the "joyful" tune sung by "children's voices" on the day his father died as the "Internationale": "Everywhere east of the Elbe," he explains, "children are banded together in what are called Pioneer organizations" that teach them to become good communists. On the day that the narrator's father dies, Gustav Husák—brought to power by the Russians in 1969 and later installed as the seventh president of Czechoslovakia—receives an award from these children's groups. At a "festive ceremony in the Prague Castle," the narrator tells us, Husák, "*the president of forgetting*," is "being named an Honorary Pioneer." At the end of the ceremony the president's words, amplified over the loudspeaker, drift in through the window of the room where the narrator's father lies dying: "Children! You are the future!" Husák proclaims. "Children! Never look back!" (158, 173–74). Because, as the narrator later points out, children "have no past whatsoever," they bear no "burden of memory"; hence "childhood is the image of the future" (186–87). Through children the totalitarian regime fosters its dogmatic faith in the future, the "new dawn of mankind," and attempts to blot out the bloodshed, betrayal, and failures of both present and past.

In Kundera's antiromantic vision children serve as emblems of the mindless "infantocracy" overtaking contemporary culture in both the democratic West and the formerly Soviet East. In Western technocracy's enslavement to the mass media, as well as in Eastern Europe's seventy-year subjugation to communist rule, he detects the same mindless faith in the future. Wooed by the urge to escape history and its burdens, contemporary culture risks losing not only its collective memory but the source of individual identity. Memory of the past, recorded as history, keeps alive our sense of differentiation and identity; it prevents us from slipping into the "nameless infinity" of "undifferentiated reality." As one of the novel's characters comes to realize, the "sum total of her being is no more than what she sees in the distance, behind her. And as her past begins to shrink, disappear, fall apart," she begins "shrinking and blurring" as well (86).

Such shrinking and blurring, Kundera suggests, befall each of us as we age, lose our faculties, and slowly surrender to the obliviousness of a second childhood. The aging mother in part 2 of *The Book of Laughter and Forgetting* begins to lose not only her sight but also her memory— and with it her relation to history. "One night," the narrator explains, "the tanks of a huge neighboring country came and occupied their country. The shock was so great, so terrible, that for a long time no one could think about anything else. It was August, and the pears in their garden were nearly ripe. The week before, Mother had invited the local pharmacist to come and pick them. He never came, never even apologized. The fact that Mother refused to forgive him drove [her son] Karel and [his wife] Marketa crazy. Everybody's thinking about tanks, and all you can think about is pears, they yelled" (29). Karel's old mother, the narrator suggests, has "moved on to a different world" of a second childhood. She has joined "a different order of creature: smaller, lighter, more easily blown away" (30).

While an old woman's second childhood serves as a source of laughter in the novel, notwithstanding the death knell it sounds, the erosion of memory suffered by Kundera's central character, a young Czech woman named Tamina, is far more tragic. In exile from her country and all that she loves, Tamina prematurely dies when she is brought to an island wilderness populated by children. Here, surrounded by these tiny beings who have no past, no memory, no history, she is literally consigned to oblivion (166). On this remote "children's island" Tamina confronts a world hostile to personal as well as collective history. "We're all children here!" the island's inhabitants gleefully shout (170). Held captive like Gulliver among the Lilliputians, Tamina tries to escape from her tiny captors. Making a run for shore, she spies the children dancing together in a clearing and takes refuge "behind the thick trunk of a plane tree." From this hiding place she watches the children jerk and gyrate to the rhythms of rock music, the din of amplified guitars blaring from a tape recorder set down in the middle of the clearing. "The lewdness of the motions superimposed on their children's bodies," says the narrator, "destroys the dichotomy between obscenity and innocence, purity and corruption. Sensuality loses all its meaning, innocence loses all its meaning, words fall apart" (188).

Linking the forces of forgetting with the death of difference, Kundera's narrator suggests for his purposes what Lessing's novel makes clear in its own way: culture, like language or the meaningful construction of childhood, depends on the recognition of dichotomies, whether between human and nonhuman, child and adult, or innocence and experience. The image of childhood—emptied of vital significance by late-Victorian culture's insistence on the child's monolithic sexlessness—now suffers a comparable fate from the opposite extreme. Under the influence of the mass media children learn to mime adult sexuality before they are ready to experience it. If history, the effort to retrieve and preserve experience, dissolves into virtual reality, both individual and cultural identity are bound to disappear.

A world without history or memory is a child's world, but an infantocracy is no Rousseauian idyll. In the artificial paradise of the modern infantocracy, the "flowers of forgetting" are not the spontaneous expression of innocence; they spring, instead, from humanity's dangerous longing for oblivion. The ancient song of the sirens, promising escape from memory, sounds even louder today in its technologically amplified forms. Political propaganda, media advertising, celebrity hype—each calls to us in its own irresistible way, promising refuge from the vicissitudes, and consequences, of daily existence and accumulated history. In the closing scenes of *The Book of Laughter and Forgetting* Kundera treats his readers to yet another version of the idyll, which serves as a telling counterpoint to the symbolic wilderness of the children's island.

Here, at the private beach of an abandoned island somewhere in the Adriatic, a small resort hotel caters to vacationers. Supplanting the symbolic circle of identical children encountered by Tamina before her death is a population of vacationing nudists equally uniform in their nakedness: "They went naked down the steps to the beach, where other naked people were sitting in groups, taking walks, and swimming—naked mothers and naked children, naked grandmothers and naked grandchildren, the naked young and the naked elderly" (226). Surrounded by this anonymous population, Kundera's protagonists, a young man named Jan and his girlfriend, Edwige, befriend a small group of naked people, all of whom have come to this "natural paradise" hoping to rid themselves of "the hypocrisy of a society that cripples body and soul." By casting off their clothing, the group embraces the ideal of natural freedom, of living "at one with nature." A theory advanced by one member of the group, "a man with an extraordinary paunch," formulates their collective ideal and goal: to "be freed once and for all from the bonds of Judeo-Christian thought." The idyll of "perfect harmony," perfect freedom, "perfect solidarity" requires that the accumulated legacy of the past—the traditions, norms, structures, and systems of a civilization, the cultural language by which its members identify themselves to one another and themselves—be not altered or improved but erased (227–28). As the narrator earlier remarks, "Eternal values exist outside history" (187). Hence the futility, and danger, of the dream—particularly in a world where, to recall Rushdie's observation, "we are all irradiated by history."

In the nudists' shared dream of a natural paradise Kundera exposes the "collective lyrical delirium" governing all utopias, all dreams of heaven—giving rise, in turn, to the hell latent in each artificial paradise that humanity seeks to create on earth. As Jan gazes at the naked bodies scattered along the shore, he has a dark inkling of the connection between the various versions of heaven on earth and the forms of hell to which they give rise. Made "melancholy" by the spectacle of so much undifferentiated, "meaningless" flesh, he is suddenly "overwhelmed by a strange feeling of affliction, and from that haze of affliction came an even stranger thought: that the Jews had filed into Hitler's gas chambers naked and en masse." Jan then considers the possibility that nudity itself is a kind of "uniform." Jolted by "the sight of all those naked bodies on the beach," he arrives at the startling revelation "that nudity is a shroud" (226).

Bewitched by a virulent strain of "totalitarian poesy," the German nation participated in the dream of an Aryan paradise—and stoked the hellish fires of the gas chambers. "Once the dream of paradise starts to turn into reality," Kundera remarked in an interview, "people begin to crop up who stand in its way, and the rulers of paradise must build a little gulag on the side of Eden. In the course of time this gulag grows ever bigger and more perfect, while the adjoining paradise gets ever smaller and poorer."[22] The structure is maintained through violence; elements that cannot or will not join the happy circle must be cast out—consigned, if not to prisons and torture chambers, then to more subtle forms of social elimination. Like Lessing's institution, plenty of asylums, nursing homes, juvenile detention centers, orphanages, and reservations exist for the removal of social undesirables. Once removed by the authorities, the undesirables are conveniently forgotten by the rest of the populace. In this way a local hell gradually subsumes the earthly paradise dreamed up by social engineers. Genocide is only the most malignant outgrowth of the totalizing impulse, or collective lyrical delirium, that impels the nude bathers to free themselves from the fetters of the past. Mass murder, mass extinction, is, Kundera paradoxically suggests, the darkest fulfillment of humanity's dream of utopia.

Kundera's vision of the contemporary idyll is as foreboding as Lessing's. Even the sunlight that shines on the closing scene of his novel is tinged with dark irony. Like so many overgrown infants, the nudists standing in a circle on the sand look harmless enough as they congratulate themselves on their temporary release from the "civilization" that "imprisons" them. But then the aforementioned individual whose paunch offers a gross caricature of the toddler's distended belly begins to extol the future and its promised liberation from the strictures of the past. As the group attends to what the fat man is saying, the narrator draws the scene and the novel to a close: "On and on the man talked. The others listened with interest, their naked genitals staring dully, sadly, listlessly at the yellow sand." More eloquent than any words the nudists can muster is the limp expression of their exposed genitals.

Like domestic pets turned loose from their leashes, these naked organs appear bewildered by their sudden release from bondage; something more than mere clothing has been discarded.

Exposed to the harsh glare of daylight, the nudists' bodies inadvertently register the oblivion into which they have been cast: the hell of undifferentiated reality. The pride and vigor of their once private parts have mysteriously (and ominously) vanished with the clothing that constrained them. The body's sudden liberation from social bonds—from all the trappings of civilization or, to recall Foucault's subversive formulation, from the fetters of the imprisoning "soul"—consigns these sad appendages to the same flaccid and impotent condition, Kundera wittily suggests, that the mind's longed-for deliverance from history and culture inevitably entails. The so-called natural paradise is no fertile garden, after all, but a desert, a vast wasteland.

In *The Fifth Child* Lessing similarly hints at the abyss—the "dark cave without end" hidden beneath the idyllic garden, ready, like Kundera's gulag, to spring up and overtake it. As long as those in charge, the social and intellectual authorities, are allowed to pursue adjustment rather than reality, accommodation rather than truth, the lure of the idyll, with all its dire implications, will persist. Deluged by images of violence and disorder, by endless news of riot, rape, and war, an infantocratic culture retreats ever further from the exigencies of history. Not only the image of childhood but the crucial identity of the human threatens to fade into undifferentiated reality. In the process, both novelists warn, not only a political kingdom but the entire social order may be dismantled—consigning history to oblivion, the garden to wilderness.

History's Offspring

Rushdie's *Midnight's Children*

Like Kundera, Salman Rushdie stresses the role of memory not only in the writer's art but in the individual's personal and political life. The fragile umbilical cord that links each of us to the elusive past, memory is the precious, if always partial and fallible, source of individual and collective identity. That both Kundera and Rushdie are, in the latter's phrase, literary migrants—seeking to re-create in their work "imaginary homelands" from which they have long been exiled—may help to account for this striking affinity between two such culturally disparate authors (*Imaginary Homelands* 10). Rushdie, like Kundera, has immediate knowledge of political oppression. (The death sentence issued against him in 1989 by Ayatollah Khomeini of Iran was technically revoked in 1999, but its legacy continues to hamper Rushdie's freedom.) Born a few months before India's declared independence, to a Muslim family living in Bombay and later immigrating to Pakistan, the novelist can speak personally of India's divisive history.

Discussing the political implications of *Midnight's Children* (1980), his "novel of memory and about memory," Rushdie enlists Kundera's novel *The Book of Laughter and Forgetting* to celebrate the resistance memory can stage against the forces of oppression: "particularly at times when the State takes reality into its own hands, and sets about distorting it, altering the past to fit its present needs, then the making of the alternative realities of art, including the novel of memory, becomes politicized. 'The struggle of man against power,' Milan Kundera has written, 'is the struggle of memory against forgetting.'" Rushdie adds, "the novel is one way of denying the official, politicians' versions of truth" (*Imaginary Homelands* 14). Just as memory in Kundera's novel challenges the programmatic lies and erasures perpetrated by the totalitarian state, the memory of Saleem Sinai, the narrator in *Midnight's Children,* opposes official versions of India's history by appropriating that history—in all its ambiguous plurality and overwhelming multiplicity—as his own.

Episodic in form, encyclopedic in scope, *Midnight's Children* is narrated by a protagonist whose birth and history are simultaneous, and virtually synonymous, with India's. Both Saleem Sinai and the newly independent nation of India are born at the stroke of midnight on 15 August 1947. As ontogeny is said to recapitulate phylogeny, Saleem's autobiography encapsulates the birth and life of his nation; the two stories, as Saleem demonstrates, are "inextricably entwined" (286).[1] Interweaving personal and political narrative, autobiography and national history, *Midnight's Children* explores the literary and cultural construction of childhood against the larger construct of history. If, as I have suggested, the image of childhood cannot be separated from the culture in which it is clothed, the same may be said of a nation's collective image or identity. As *Midnight's Children* eloquently suggests, the history of a nation—the record of its birth, growth, and development—is also a cultural construct, dependent on its culture's inhabitants, or children, for form and meaning.

History, it is often observed, is inevitably someone's, her or his story. Hayden White maintains that what we call "history—the real world as it evolves in time—is made sense of in the same way that the poet or novelist tries to make sense of it. . . . It does not matter whether the world is conceived to be real or only imagined, the manner of making sense of it is the same." Historians, in other words, discover or create meaning through the same linguistic and symbolic patterns that characterize narrative fiction. (The word *fiction* derives from the Latin *fingere,* meaning to shape, mold, or model. To shape or make a story is also, inevitably, to make it up.) In fictional and historical narratives, White points out, "we recognize the forms by which consciousness both constitutes and colonizes the world it seeks to inhabit."[2]

White's description of the mind or the consciousness as colonizing its universe invokes an epistemological process implicit in political acts of colonization—a process whose implications, however, extend far beyond finite actions and events. Here the occupying force comprises

the elusive processes of thought and perception, while the colony—
no longer confined to a specific geographical location—becomes the
whole of perceived reality. Subverting common usage, White calls
attention to the intangible forces of culture, which always precede and
exceed its material manifestations of authority and power—namely,
governments that make war on other governments, subjugate other
peoples, and occupy their lands. The epistemological implications of
colonization do not gainsay but instead help to illuminate the tremendous impact of the British presence in India for three centuries. As
Midnight's Children demonstrates, the effects of that massive invasion,
culminating in a century of British rule, could hardly vanish at the
stroke of declared independence. "Decades following the death of the
Raj," Una Chaudhuri observes, "a class of Indians continues to
collude, unwittingly, in a spectral colonization of India." *Midnight's
Children,* she maintains, demonstrates the enduring legacy of this spectral form of colonization; the British raj's "psychological structures,
its institutions, its habits of mind, its language" are reflected, not least
of all, in Saleem's "blue eyes."[3] India's experience under British rule
proves as lasting a "burden of history," Saleem discovers, as its turbulent
precolonial past (*Midnight's Children* 457).

The colonizing power of consciousness and its relationship to culture, which shapes and is shaped by human perception, occupy both
foreground and background in *Midnight's Children.* Faced with the
task of recording his own history as well as India's, Rushdie's thirty-
year-old narrator soberly contemplates the naive optimism with which
the birth of his nation and his own illustrious beginnings were initially
celebrated. At the time it seemed "as though history, arriving at a point
of the highest significance and promise, had chosen to sow . . . the
seeds of a future which would genuinely differ from anything the
world had seen up to that time" (234–35). Attending each birth was
the "democratic-romantic" notion that a child or a nation is free to
choose its identity. In the words of the popular ditty that Saleem later
parodies, "anything you want to be you kin be" (552). The governing
myth in both cases, Saleem comes to realize, is the potent but ultimately false "myth of freedom." Like Kundera, Rushdie reveals how
misguided and potentially dangerous is one's faith in an idyllic future
freed from the constraints, hostilities, bloodshed, and oppression of the
past (546). As Philip Weinstein observes in another context, the image

of the child "innocently awaiting" a "destiny" that belongs to the future does not survive recognition of the past as "a medium soaked in time and human suffering."[4]

Midnight's Children illustrates from the outset that the past is inescapable for both the narrator and his vast, troubled nation. A history of foreign invasion and internal conflicts, ancient ethnic and religious hatreds, widespread economic and political injustice—all tear at India's newly minted image and identity. The first fatal crack in that hopeful facade occurs at the instant of the nation's birth: with the advent of India's postcolonial independence, the subcontinent partitions into the Muslim states of East and West Pakistan. (The riots between Muslims and Hindus that took place before, during, and after partition eventually culminated in the bloody Indo-Pakistani war of 1965; six years later a war between East and West Pakistan led to Indian intervention and the establishment of Bangladesh, formerly East Pakistan, as an independent state.)

The past is inescapable; the newborn nation is, as Saleem says of his nascent self, "handcuffed to history" (3). Even as he playfully narrates an account of his prenatal existence, Saleem describes himself as a fetus "floating in the amniotic fluid of the past." The umbilical cord that serves as a lifeline to the mother's body also signifies the intangible ties that bind human beings, as individuals or as groups, to the vast body of the past. Unlike the physical cord, these bonds—this inescapable inheritance bestowed on one and all—cannot be severed at birth. "How many things people notions we bring with us into the world, how many possibilities and also restrictions of possibility," Saleem exclaims as he prepares to render an account of his birth (124–26). Later in his story, as India's auspicious beginnings are quickly overshadowed by strife and disillusionment, Saleem draws the connection between the birth and the demise of hope more boldly. With the "thousand and one possibilities" ushered in at India's birth, "a thousand and one dead ends" also come to light (240).

That India's political independence cannot liberate its peoples from the weight of the past is symbolized by the fate of those thousand and one children—midnight's children—who, by Saleem's account, are born at the hour of India's political independence. A mere thirty years later, in January 1977, the surviving children of midnight (including the narrator) are subjected to a program of enforced sterilization that mirrors the one carried out by Indira Gandhi's regime on legions

of citizens. Narrating his story, and India's history, after these catastrophic events, Saleem speaks as a man deprived of the capacity not
only to procreate but to hope. More lethal than any medical proce-
dures are the fatal operations of consciousness induced by such a hor-
rendous experience. The lives of Saleem and the other "metaphorical"
children of midnight testify to the death of the idyll. Their story, the
history of a newborn nation, evinces the process by which "the true
hope of freedom" is "forever extinguished" (240).

As the narrator tries to make sense of chaotic events, the colonizing force of his own consciousness, inextricably entwined with India's
turbulent history, occupies center stage. Identified from the instant of
his birth as India's "chosen child"—whose life, as Prime Minister
Jawaharlal Nehru writes to Saleem in a letter, is "the mirror" of the
nation's "own"—Saleem cannot extricate his developing consciousness
from the massive "matter" of India (143). His existence is permeated,
invaded, colonized by this elephantine nation in ways that dramatize,
by their excess, the onerous burden of history and culture on every
child's existence. At the same time Saleem's efforts to tell the story of
his nation, to narrate its growth and meaning in order to discover his
own, construct a version of India's history formed, and flawed, by his
own. If Saleem's birth, childhood, and growth prove, as Nehru tells
him, a mirror of the nation's, it is at best a "broken mirror"—reflecting
the narrator's partial, fallible memory. The history that Saleem narrates,
as Rushdie says elsewhere, is fraught with "mistakes of a fallible memory
compounded by quirks of character and of circumstance." That Saleem
is "suspect in his narration" is a given, which neither the author nor
the narrator seeks to hide (*Imaginary Homelands* 11). Employing the
devices of metafiction to explore metahistory, Rushdie's narrator
reveals the extent to which postcolonial India is in turn colonized,
in Hayden White's sense, by the subjective processes of consciousness
in which the novel's author, narrator, and reader are all engaged.

The cultural immersion and colonization revealed throughout
Saleem's narration give the lie to Rousseau's idyll of childhood while
undermining notions of Indian independence. As M. Keith Booker
points out, Rushdie's fiction undermines the "stable unified" notion
of both history and the self, revealing each to be a problematic construct: "the Romantic notion of the self as a basis of authority or
source of truth must be a fiction."[5] Viewed from this vantage, all of us
share "the privilege and the curse" of Rushdie's "midnight's children,"

who, from the instant of birth, are "both masters and victims of their times" (*Midnight's Children* 552). As Saleem's narrative exposes and undermines what he calls, in the novel's concluding lines, "the greatest lie of all"—that "anything you want to be you kin be"—it deconstructs the notion of unmediated history or reality. As witnesses as well as participants, even the most abject victims of history become its unlikely masters—constructing (or colonizing) reality through memory and experience, perception and imagination.

Challenging the premises on which so much history is recorded and reported, the narrator juxtaposes the so-called objective rendering of political events—radio announcements, eyewitness accounts, and written documents—with Indian myth and legend. Sometimes, he suggests, the most outrageous, blatantly fantastic accounts of human events prove more illuminating than the so-called facts. The effect, in Linda Hutcheon's view, is to foreground and thereby subvert "the totalizing impulse of western—imperialistic—modes of history-writing by confronting it with indigenous Indian models of history."[6] By the same token, Saleem exposes much of India's official history as fiction in the worst sense: as deliberate falsification of evidence. Wielding self-consciousness as both strategy and defense, he celebrates the fictional status of both his and the nation's history. The narrative design of *Midnight's Children* undermines the temptation, shared by novelists, historians, and readers, to mistake the structure of any narrative for "the multitudinous realities" of a protean world beyond words (*Midnight's Children* 207).

If, as Margaret Doody observes, "the Novel represents the union between history and myth," *Midnight's Children* is a model of the genre. In contrast to the "totalizing" claims of literary realism and so-called objective history, the novel's structure and discourse, says Doody, allow "history to be seen with some detachment, and playfully." Each novel, she adds, creates "a world where many persons exist and the final or definitive is not plausible. Hierarchies disappear, frontiers of separation become blurred. . . . The line between what is real and what is imaginary always gets blurred within the Novel, even destroyed." Full "of mixture and variety, of boundary-crossing and changing," the novel "rejoices in a rich muddy messiness."[7] The messiness of the novel's hybrid form, Doody implies—the numerous open-ended, endlessly various shapes it takes—announces its paradoxical fidelity to human experience in all its complexities and contradictions.

Drawing attention throughout *Midnight's Children* to the daunting nature of his task—to contain or capture within the narrative the enormity of India—Rushdie's narrator begins by detailing the "mixture and variety" of elements constituting India's complex and contradictory history: "there are so many stories to tell, too many, such an excess of intertwined lives events miracles places rumours, so dense a commingling of the improbable and mundane!" (4). At every turn the narrator's quest for order and meaning threatens to devolve into chaos as multitudes of contending voices, facts, legends, languages, and cultural myths jockey for position and priority in his narrative. Inevitably, as Doody says, "hierarchies disappear," and "frontiers of separation become blurred," including the "line between what is real and what is imaginary."

Careful to distinguish his version of history writing from those traditional forms that claim objectivity, Saleem deliberately injects his facts with fiction, paying indirect tribute to the freedoms of the novel's narrative form, which allows for the union of history and myth. Rushdie, Uma Parameswaran points out, "spoofs the traditional form of histories. He takes liberties with dates, undermining chronometric exactitude that is one of the cornerstones of traditional historical writing. Saleem changes the date of Gandhi's death and of the 1957 election, but he does not retract when he realizes his error." This blurring of borders reflects, in Aruna Srivastava's view, the divided cultural identity imposed on India by British colonialism. Saleem tries to balance "a chronological view of history, passed on by the ruling British and now part of the Indian national consciousness," with a "Gandhian, mythical view of history—properly and traditionally Indian, but suppressed by more 'progressive' ideas about history and its relation to time."[8]

Calling attention to the devices by which history is both made and made up, Saleem nonetheless declares himself in pursuit of truth and meaning. To make sense of the matter of India, a world "teeming" with "multitudes" of peoples, races, and religions, the narrator must rely on its myriad, often jarring literary and cultural traditions, both ancient and modern (126). Informed by, and ironizing, the traditions of Islam, Hinduism, and Buddhism, Saleem's narrative also incorporates references to a plethora of political ideologies and events—from Mahatma Gandhi's doctrine of nonviolence to General Ayub Khan's declaration of martial law and Indira Gandhi's declared state of emergency. In addition, *Midnight's Children* registers a dizzying range of old and new Western influences, including authors and philosophers from Laurence Sterne and Rousseau to George Bernard Shaw, the commercial glitter of Hollywood, and the blandishments of Madison Avenue, whose version of consumer heaven blares from countless Bombay billboards. Juxtaposing the images of capitalism with those of ancient religion, Rushdie's narrative simultaneously pays homage to the pantheon of Hindu gods and the saints of biblical lore. So richly allusive and inclusive is the text that it continually parodies, as it foregrounds, the narrator's futile attempts to contain or "swallow the world" he is depicting (126).

Recalling an Indian painter who aspired to become a miniaturist but whose paintings grew larger and larger until he fell ill with elephantiasis, Saleem wonders if the "urge to encapsulate the whole of reality" is a distinctively "Indian disease" (50, 84). If so, India's chosen child—the mirror of his nation—is appropriately infected from infancy with those germs. As soon as he is born, Saleem embarks on a "heroic program of self-enlargement." Graced with an insatiable appetite as well as a "monstrous" nose, the burgeoning baby manages, by the time he is a month old, to drain his "mother's not inconsiderable breasts" (145). A wet nurse hired by the family is "dried-out as a desert after only a fortnight," and she accuses "Baby Saleem of trying to bite off her nipples with his toothless gums" (145).

Monstrous as baby Saleem's nose and appetite appear, they carry no hint of the child's alien nature. Unlike Lessing's Ben Lovatt, "good baby Saleem" is "a quiet child" who "laugh[s] often" and responds to human affection. True, it is through a "freak of biology" that he and the other "one thousand and one children" of midnight acquire "features, talents or faculties which can only be described as miraculous." But as that symbolic literary number—explicitly recalling the 1,001 tales told by Scheherazade in *The Arabian Nights*—suggests, the children's larger-than-life qualities signify not freakish difference but symbolic stature. They mirror and magnify the condition in which all children exist. As Saleem points out, his story contains India's history, just as India's contains his: "I am the sum total of everything that went before me, of all I have been seen done, of everything done-to-me." He adds, "everyone of the now-six-hundred-million-plus of us" contains "a similar multitude" (457–58).

Of the 1,001 children born during the first hour of the new nation's existence, only Saleem and his rival, Shiva, arrive exactly on the stroke of midnight (234, 239). Like the other children of midnight, Saleem and Shiva are "only partially the offspring of their parents"; they are also "fathered," as Saleem puts it, "by history." That Shiva and Saleem are changelings, having secretly been switched at birth by Mary Pereira, the Sinai family's ayah, or nurse, further underscores their symbolic role as "children *of the time*" (137). Like his alter ego, Saleem possesses powers more prodigious than those granted the other children of midnight. Noting this "remarkable fact," he explains that "the closer to midnight [the children's] birth-times," the greater their "gifts." Whereas Shiva, to whom "the hour had given the gifts of war," acquires formidable powers of destruction, Saleem receives "the greatest talent of all—the ability to look into the hearts and minds of men" (238–39).

Early in his childhood Saleem—like the hero of Sterne's *Tristram Shandy,* whose theme of noses echoes throughout *Midnight's Children*—suffers a disastrous accident involving his nose.[9] As a result, his peculiar proboscis becomes a kind of radio receiver picking up and transmitting voices from all over the subcontinent. Describing the results of the accident that befalls him before the age of nine, Saleem says, "the inner monologues of all the so-called teeming millions, of masses and classes alike, jostled for space within my head." Most startling of all is the moment when the nine-year-old discovers, "beneath the polyglot frenzy in [his] head," those "precious signals" broadcast from all corners of the new nation by the children of midnight (200). By means of this bizarre "telepathy," India's chosen child tunes his inner ear to the throng of India's voices—a chorus that includes the inner voices of his family, friends, classmates, and teachers—and registers their experience as well as his own. Through the first-person singular, "I," Saleem endeavors to voice the multilingual, multicultural experience of a multitudinous "we."

Having succeeded, in this sense at least, in swallowing the world, Saleem gradually realizes that he cannot contain his own or his nation's history for long. It is only a matter of time before the fragile microcosm of self—that temporary vessel of consciousness—collapses under the weight of its "macrocosmic" burden (130). Just as the partitioning of India and Pakistan, its cracking into pieces, is announced at the nation's birth, every newborn, most particularly India's chosen child, is subject from birth to fragmentation and disintegration. Now

in his thirtieth year, the narrator is "racing the cracks" appearing in his
"fissured body" as surely as they are splitting "the fissuring earth" (325,
38–39). Like Sterne's Shandy, Proust's Marcel, and Nabokov's Humbert,
Saleem pits his narrative as a rescue operation against the forces of
time. "I am falling apart," he announces at the outset: "I am not speaking metaphorically. . . . I have begun to crack all over like an old jug."
Buffeted by "too much history," says Saleem, "my poor body" "has
started coming apart at the seams. In short, I am literally disintegrating,
slowly for the moment, although there are signs of an acceleration. . . .
This is why I have resolved to confide in paper, before I forget. (We are
a nation of forgetters.)" (37). Echoing Kundera's narrator in *The Book
of Laughter and Forgetting,* Saleem asks himself how long memory can
hold against forgetting, the body against time. How long, he wonders,
before history—his own and India's—"pours out of my fissured body"
and is lost forever by this "amnesiac nation" (38, 549).

  If history is a bulwark against time, the opposite is also true: history
is the record of disintegration. Time leaves its imprint on everything,
carving out "cracks in the earth" that are, says Saleem, "reborn in
my skin" (124–25). History does not, in other words, escape the "unchanging twoness of things" that pervades Rushdie's contradictory,
indeterminate universe and its profoundly ambiguous reality (167).
Everything contains its opposite; nothing is purely fact or fiction,
appearance or reality, love or hate, hope or despair, creation or destruction. The promise of childhood—the freedom of "being other, by
being new"—is doomed to begin with, "because children are the
vessels into which adults pour their poison." The child is born under
sentence; childhood must "die" or be "murdered," because children
are not *essentially* or only what they momentarily appear. They are at
the same time children and incipient adults (306–8). The unchanging
twoness of things gives the lie to India's dream of an innocent new
future as well to the idyll of childhood.

  Evincing this twoness, or duality, Saleem's changeling status casts an
ambiguous light on his origins and identity. As he eventually discovers,
he is not the biological son of the prosperous couple Amina and
Ahmed Sinai, who are his acknowledged parents; nor, as it turns out,
has he been fathered by the husband of his biological mother, Vanita.
Unbeknownst to her poor, penniless husband, Vanita was seduced by a
British colonialist named William Methwold. It is Methwold's child
whom she delivers at the same stroke of midnight that announces the

birth of Amina Sinai's biological son. Unlike Amina, Vanita fails to survive childbirth; shortly after delivering her child, Vanita hemorrhages
and dies. In an impulsive attempt to stage a "revolutionary act," the
nurse Mary Pereira changes the babies' name tags—"giving the poor
baby a life of privilege and condemning the rich-born child . . . to
poverty" (135–36).

Pointing to his birth and origins as examples, Saleem informs his
audience—both the reader and his immediate interlocutor, or "necessary ear," Padma—that nothing is what it seems (177). Acting the role
of a (female) Sancho Panza in Saleem's quixotic history, down-to-earth
Padma is outraged by his belated presentation of the facts.[10] Indig-
nantly she queries, "What are you telling me? You are an Anglo-Indian?
Your name is not your own?" (136). Adding insult to injury, Saleem
introduces a further note of ambiguity. It was Methwold's "Samson-
like" hair, particularly its elegant "centre-parting," that wielded irresistible power over Vanita's weak flesh. What Vanita failed to notice,
however, was the deception that Saleem reveals to his audience:
Methwold's notorious, "brilliantined black hair" was a "hairpiece"; this
would-be Samson, as Padma bluntly puts it, was a "baldie" (130–32).
Like the nation whose history he seeks to recount, Saleem's birth
and genealogy are fraught with ambiguity, contradiction, deception.
Far from attempting to hide these "inevitable distortions," Saleem
draws attention to them. Pointing out the distance he has traveled
from optimistic youth, the narrator says of himself, "Saleem is no
longer obsessed with purity" (549). Accepting his "impure," half-
British identity, Saleem is ready to make peace, as Padma is not, with
the ineradicable past. In contrast to Shiva, whose bellicosity speaks for
all the warring factions tearing at the national fabric, Saleem embraces
India's heterogeneous nature. India's "multiplicity, pluralism, hybrid-
ity," Rushdie suggests elsewhere, constitutes its only viable cultural
and political identity (*Imaginary Homelands* 32).

While underscoring the impurities or distortions of narrative,
whether public or personal, Saleem unequivocally affirms the significance of memory and the past. It is not biology but history that
identifies him as the son of Amina and Ahmed Sinai. When Padma
accuses him of trickery for having falsely claimed to be Amina's child
and the grandson of Aadam Aziz, Saleem tells her, "there's something
more important than [biology]. It's this: when we eventually discovered the crime of Mary Pereira, we all found that *it made no difference!*

I was still their son: they remained my parents." He adds, "we simply could not think our way out of our pasts" (136–37). By the time Mary Pereira confesses her "crime," in other words, Saleem has shared eleven years of history with his family. The weight of their collective past cannot be removed any more than India's remote or recent past can be separated from its current identity.

Saleem's ambiguous origins demonstrate that he has been mothered as well as fathered by history. Although she is not his biological mother, Amina Sinai makes it clear to Saleem that he is her son. Just as Amina never doubted the newborn's "authenticity" at birth—when she recognized "his grandfather's nose" on the face of baby Saleem—she affirms his authenticity again, eleven years later, after learning of Mary Pereira's audacious act. Thus she tells Saleem, "Love, my child, is a thing that every mother learns; it is not born with a baby, but made; and for eleven years, I have learned to love you as my son" (344). With the full force of motherly love, Amina accepts the paradoxical nature of Saleem's origins: it is nurture rather than nature, history rather than blood, that binds him irrevocably to the Sinai family and determines their kinship. Through the changeling theme the image of the child as a creature clothed in culture is doubly exposed.

Just as Saleem and his parents cannot renounce their mutual past, Saleem cannot renounce his bond with the Sinais' biological son, Shiva. Shiva, who is reared in abject poverty and never acknowledged by his biological parents or apprised of his changeling status, haunts Saleem's consciousness. Informed, along with the rest of the family, of Mary Pereira's crime, Saleem feels guilty for having "denied [Shiva] his birthright." That buried secret gradually becomes for Saleem, as he says, "a stabbing twinge of guilt; then an obsession; and finally, . . . a sort of principle." This principle bespeaks not only dread—what would the vengeful Shiva do if he should find out?—but uncertainty. It hints at the duplicity of appearances. The secret crime that, as Saleem ironically puts it, robbed him of his "true inheritance of poverty and destitution" also deprives the world he perceives of stability and logic (358, 472). The pillars (and polarities) of the social hierarchy—the honored distinctions between privilege and poverty, education and deprivation, the cultivated few and the great unwashed—are shown to rest on the shakiest of foundations (358, 472). The rule of chance and accident threatens, moreover, to undermine whatever meaning Saleem hopes to discover in the history he is attempting to construct. As he confesses at the outset, "above all things, I fear absurdity" (4).

It is not through binary oppositions that Saleem ultimately discovers meaning in and gives shape to history. As M. Keith Booker points out, "Rushdie's overall assault on polar logic"—the "deconstruction of dualities"—creates the possibility for meaning in the tragic tale that Saleem tells.[11] To deconstruct these polarities, of course, the narrator must first introduce them, which is one function of the changeling theme. Bred on "vengefulness and violence," Shiva inspires fear and dread in all who encounter him (358). His prodigious talent for destruction is buoyed by a vicious cynicism that values only material power. When Saleem voices his optimistic faith in the creative promise of childhood, Shiva can only scoff at his silly idealism. "The world," Shiva scornfully tells him, "is not ideas, rich boy; the world is no place for dreamers or their dreams; the world, little Snotnose, is things. Things and their makers rule the world. . . . Little rich boy, that's all just wind. All that importance-of-the-individual. All that possibility-of-humanity. Today, what people are is just another kind of thing" (307).

In many ways Shiva's nihilistic vision appears triumphantly confirmed; by the novel's close this vengeful child has proved himself an invincible warrior. A major in the Indian army, he is a tyrant who thrives on the endless cycles of bloodshed that punctuate each phase of the new nation's war-torn history. On the other side of the coin is Saleem, whose suffering mirrors that of myriads of Indians and Pakistanis alike, victims of all this slaughter and violence. (Saleem, for example, loses his entire family in the Indo-Pakistani war of 1965 and suffers a prolonged period of amnesia from a blow he receives in the bombing. Six years later, in the war between East and West Pakistan, his childhood friends are reduced to unidentifiable bloody stumps on the killing fields.) Drawing an analogy between the story of his rivalry with Shiva and the history of India as well as the modern age, Saleem implies that each narrative evinces the triumph of cynicism over idealism and hope: "Shiva and Saleem, victor and victim; understand our rivalry, and you will gain an understanding of the age in which you live" (515). Adding to Saleem's sense of despair and defeat is his responsibility for the destruction of hope in the other children of midnight. Like so many "'political' prisoners taken during the Emergency" declared by "the Widow," Prime Minister Indira Gandhi, Saleem is arrested by Major Shiva and tortured by the war hero's uniformed henchmen. To

Saleem's undying grief and shame, he surrenders the "names addresses physical descriptions" of the surviving children of midnight, who are promptly rounded up and imprisoned (516–17).

The shattering events that signal the death of hope for Saleem and his nation culminate, as mentioned above, in the regime's program of enforced sterilization. Still more lethal are the operations devised for the children of midnight. "Not for us," comments Saleem, were "the simple vas- and tubectomies performed on the teeming masses; because there was a chance, just a chance that such operations could be reversed . . . ectomies were performed, but irreversibly: testicles were removed from sacs, and wombs vanished for ever." Denied "the possibility of reproducing themselves," the children of midnight suffer a still more fatal loss—signified by the word Saleem coins for this disaster: "Sperectomy: the draining-out of hope." Saleem's history thus records "the tale of [the midnight children's] undoing." Buried by the "tormented cry of children who had lost their magic" is the optimistic idyll of childhood (521–23, ellipses in original). Deprived of the capacity to procreate, the children are also robbed of their capacity to hope and dream. Reduced to literal and figurative impotence, they can no longer imagine themselves fulfilling "the promise of [their] birth" and—"by being other, by being new"—creating a future different from the sorrowful past (306).

In keeping, however, with the novel's "assault on polar logic," the children's crushing defeat is complicated by a "paradoxical observation" Saleem makes shortly after his sperectomy. This "most precious of discoveries" undermines the logical opposition between victor and vanquished, destroyer and creator (506). The revelation occurs to Saleem while he is standing in his "sightless cell," registering the terrible impact of the "drainage" induced by the hundreds of ectomies— and the collective sperectomy—carried out on midnight's children. Even his enemy, Shiva, has undergone, out of loyalty to the Widow, "voluntary vasectomy." Yet in Shiva's case, Saleem belatedly realizes, the operation has come far too late. Gleefully, Saleem recalls all "the legendary tales of the war hero's philandering, of the legions of bastards swelling in the unectomied bellies of great ladies and whores." Yes, indeed, "every cloud has a silver lining." "Shiva, destroyer of the midnight children," is also their savior; "midnight's darkest child" is at the same time "Shiva-the-procreator." With an exhilarating sense of irony Saleem understands that his arch rival has fathered a whole new generation of children, who "at this very moment" are "being raised towards the future" (524–25, 506). Shiva, the harbinger of destruction, is also "a principle of life" (364).

The point of this paradoxical observation is driven home by the birth of one of Shiva's many anonymous, illegitimate children: the one Saleem ultimately claims as "my son Aadam Sinai" (531). Born to Parvati the witch, another child of midnight, Aadam Sinai gains his legal name when Saleem agrees to marry the pregnant Parvati and save her honor. (Shiva, by contrast, is "a notorious seducer" who promptly deserts the bedroom of "anyone who [becomes] pregnant" [487–88].) The inextricable destinies of "Saleem-and-Shiva," these "changeling-rivals" and prodigious children of midnight, achieve their ultimate "synthesis," as Saleem says, in their mutual "son, Aadam" (529, 507). Named after Saleem's legal (not biological) grandfather Dr. Aadam Aziz, baby Aadam embodies the same saving illogic by which Saleem has inherited Aziz's most prominent feature, his nose. Like Saleem, Aadam is "the child of a father who [is] not his father." And although he fails to inherit his biological great-grandfather's enormous proboscis, Aadam is born with gigantic ears that make his head look like that of a "tiny elephant." Heir to the generation of midnight's children, Aadam is marked at birth by India's elephantiasis (500–501).

Later, after the death of Parvati and his release from prison, Saleem gazes into the eyes of this child, now almost two years old, "who [is] simultaneously not-my-son and also more my heir than any child of my flesh could have been." Here, in the limpid gaze of a child who both is and is not his son, Saleem rediscovers a hopeful image of the future. "I understood," he says, "that Aadam was a member of a second generation of magical children who would grow up far tougher than the first." True to the paradoxical nature of reality, however, this image is quickly countered by another, glimpsed in what Saleem calls the "mirror of humility" (534).

In a bus depot in Shadipur, Saleem, Aadam, and the child's wet nurse sit waiting for a bus to Bombay. Suspended above them is an angled mirror in which Saleem spies the reflection of a dwarf's "young-old face": "Looking upwards into the mirror, I saw myself transformed into a big-headed, top-heavy dwarf; in the humblingly foreshortened reflection of myself I saw that the hair on my head was now as grey as rainclouds; the dwarf in the mirror, with his lined face and tired eyes, reminded me of my grandfather Aadam Aziz. . . .

Castrated, and now prematurely aged, I saw in the mirror of humility a human being to whom history could do no more" (533–34). No longer the hopeful child of midnight, Saleem is a creature drastically diminished, or dwarfed, by history. Here the tribute that *Midnight's Children* pays throughout to Günter Grass's epic novel *The Tin Drum,* and its dwarfish protagonist, is made explicit.[12] More specifically, in this image of himself as dwarf, Saleem gleans "intimations of mortality" announcing his "approaching demise." The image reflected in the station's angled mirror contrasts markedly with the one Saleem detects in the infant's "empty, limpid pupils"; yet each compels Saleem to gaze into the "mirror of humility" (533–34).

Limning the dualities in these contrasting images—one a gray-haired dwarf battered by history, the other a wide-eyed infant lacking virtually any history—Saleem reads the same message in both: his own redundancy. It is not his generation but the next, a new "tribe of fearsomely potent kiddies," who are ready to forge the future (534–35). Yet there is something still more telling in Saleem's superimposing these images. All the promise embodied in the traditional myth of childhood—those limpid pupils so empty of history and its disappointments, so fearsomely potent with future possibilities—is, he implies, already subject to the "effects of a lifetime's battering" (550).

Saleem's point is not, of course, that the future has already transpired. To the contrary: in the novel's closing pages he explicitly states that in attempting to preserve a version of India's history, as though he were pickling the past, "one jar must remain empty." The "future cannot be preserved," because "it has not yet taken place" (550). But while the future remains empty of history, like the infant's eyes, both the future and the infant remain burdened, or handcuffed to history, in much the way Saleem's generation proved to be. The relationship between the child and the dwarf is reflected in their smallness: the infant's diminutive size, while it signals the child's potential for growth and apparent freedom from the weighty past, contains and foreshadows the diminished strength and stature of the "redundant oldster" (534).

Just as the birth of India is synchronous with its cracking and partition, "the disintegrating effects of drainage"—the gradual disillusionment that has carved itself in Saleem's "hapless, pulverized body" —begin practically at birth (550). The death knell that *Midnight's Children* sounds for the idyll of childhood springs from the inevitable twoness of things that underscores the novel's ambivalent, indeterminate vision of reality. Just as polar opposites are paradoxically, and inextricably, bound up in each other, our optimistic faith in the future, our deepest intimations of immortality, are inevitably shadowed by their opposite: what Saleem calls, in his challenge to Wordsworth, "intimations of mortality."

Like the narrator of Proust's *A la recherche du temps perdu,* Saleem resolves, at the end of *Midnight's Children,* to compose a history that constitutes the narrative being read. By the time he arrives at that decision, he is a changed man. No longer a quixotic dreamer who places his faith in the future, Saleem has forsaken the Rousseauian idyll. In three short decades the eager child—with all his prodigious talents, curiosity, and unrelenting hunger for experience—has become a wizened oldster. The narrator's battered body, scarred and reduced by experience, is the image and emblem of the story he resolves to write: the history of midnight's children. Inscribed by "the effects of a lifetime's battering," Saleem's body is "parched," cracked, and exhausted. As he studies "the cracks on the backs of [his] hands, cracks along [his] hair line and between [his] toes," Saleem asks himself, "Why do I not bleed?" Then he adds, "Am I already the mummy of myself?" (550). The suggestion is not as far-fetched as it sounds. When Saleem, earlier in the novel, spies his reflection in the bus-depot mirror, it is a living mummy that he perceives: "a human being to whom history could do no more." History can do no more to Saleem because it has already done so much. His skin, like the mummy's, is a kind of parchment on which history has been inscribed. No tidy polar logic distinguishes this human text or parchment from the history engraved on it.[13]

If Saleem is, in the end, drained of his youthful optimism—and of his faith in the idyll of innocence—he is more certain than ever of the importance of memory. Initially, he places his trust in the illusory freedom of the future, seeking his destiny "in prophecy or the stars" (534). But the "empty jar" of the future contains no assurances or promises; like the newborn's empty eyes, the future awaits fulfillment in time. It is the past, not the future, that offers a lifeline to the next generation. And it is history—or more precisely, history that announces itself in the shape of a novel—that preserves the past, however partially and impurely. In the novel's openness to contradictory experience, its salutary messiness, Saleem finds the freedom that, to recall Margaret Doody's words, "allows history to be seen with some detachment, and playfully." The history of the children of midnight is the only real legacy—the only source of order and insight, of shape and form—that the narrator can offer his son. Making way for the next generation, Saleem hopes that his narrative will help Aadam to "cope with the world [he is] leaving him" (550, 547). That is why the preservation of the past becomes for Saleem both an urgent task and a profound "act of love," not only for his child but for his "amnesiac nation."

Having spent years as an amnesiac, Saleem knows firsthand the forces of oblivion wreaking havoc on his nation. "Wiped clean" of memory by an exploded bomb that "wipes out" his family, Saleem wakes up in a military hospital not knowing who he is (413). With the loss of memory, that "glue of personality," come other dire losses. Deserted by any "awareness of [himself] as a homogeneous entity in time, a blend of past and present," the amnesiac is unmoored from history and released from the grip of human emotions. Brained, it would seem, by too many blows to the head and heart, Saleem wakes up to find himself "anaesthetized against feelings as well as memories" (420, 422). During this period of his life, still in his twenties, Saleem becomes an unnamed "tracker"—known only as the "buddha" (which in Urdu means old man)—in the West Pakistan army (418). Here once again Rushdie's narrator undermines the notion of a "stable unified" self: the young amnesiac not only becomes "old before his time"; he becomes "not I," or "not-Saleem." Until not-Saleem recovers his memory, the narrator insists, it is "not I" but "he, the buddha," whose actions the narrative relays (418, 431). Embarking on a mission, the buddha and three other soldiers soon lose their way, literally and figuratively, in a vast primordial jungle called the Sundarbans. So thick is this jungle, Saleem comments, "that history has hardly ever found the way in" (429).

Indulging "a miasmic longing for flight into the safety of dreams," the memoryless man "separated from his past" withdraws into "the historyless anonymity of the rain-forests" (431–32). Like the primordial jungle vividly described in Gabriel García Márquez's *One Hundred Years of Solitude,* a novel whose combination of history and myth is often compared with that of *Midnight's Children,* this "livid green world" is historyless in two senses. It embodies both a stage of human consciousness, or preconsciousness—a "miasmic state of mind"—and a prelapsarian universe before human time and history. As Saleem, or not-Saleem, and the other soldiers "surrender themselves" to the oblivion of this "dream-forest" of "phantasms," they are described as "regressing towards infancy" (434–35). In a symbolic rebirth the men are first carried back by "the magical jungle" to a miasmic state of consciousness, and then carried forward "towards a new adulthood" (436).

In a parodic reversal of the Edenic myth Saleem is bitten in the jungle by a "blind, translucent serpent," whose "venom," instead of instilling evil or despair, restores his memory and identity: "I was rejoined to the past, jolted into unity by snake-poison." Miraculously, Saleem is able to reclaim "everything, all of it, all lost histories, all the myriad complex processes that go to make a man" (436–37). In keeping with paradoxical reality, the snake's poison acts as a medicine. Like the magical jungle, this venom also rids Saleem of the "soul-chewing maggots of pessimism futility shame" that have "infected" him (431). Given the burdens imposed by history—the suffering brought on by endless waves of cruelty, injustice, and violence—the temporary loss or surrender of memory may prove necessary for survival. By regressing to infancy, the miasmic state before memory, Saleem discovers a lifeline to the primordial past. (In *Beloved,* as we shall see, the recovery of memory through a return to the primordial is the novel's overriding theme.) When Saleem recounts how he and the other men "turned their mouths up to the roof of the jungle and drank," it seems they are drinking from the fount of creation itself, replenishing their exhausted spirits as well as their parched bodies (434).

By novel's end Saleem has literally and figuratively recaptured his past: through a magical set of coincidences he is reunited with his beloved ayah, Mary Pereira, and takes a job as the manager of her pickling factory. With a renewed sense of the importance of memory, he dedicates himself to preserving the past. Drawing on his immediate present as well, Saleem compares "the great work of preserving" the past in narrative form with "chutnification": "My chutneys and kasaundies are . . . connected to my nocturnal scribblings." Through them "[m]emory, as well as fruit, is being saved from . . . corruption" (38). "To pickle," he later avows, "is to give immortality" (549). The playful yoking of the mundane and the eternal reflects the wisdom as well as humility Saleem has acquired. To preserve the past, its raw materials must be transformed, or reconstituted, in a process as painstaking and laborious as that of pickling the raw ingredients of a chutney. There is an art to preserving the past, whether in pickles or in words, and Saleem draws his metaphors from both endeavors: through the constant "process of revision," the "endless" effort to distill and intensify the final effect, the "chutnification of history" is achieved. "The art," Saleem concludes, "is to change the flavour in degree, but not in kind"; the finished product should "possess the authentic taste of truth" (549–50).

For all its playful reflexivity and postmodern ambivalence, its blurring of fiction and fact, *Midnight's Children* ends on a distinctly modernist note. Like those artist-heroes created by novelists early in the twentieth century—Proust's Marcel, Joyce's Stephen Dedalus, Woolf's Lily Briscoe—Saleem takes refuge in art. Here, as in those seminal works of modernism, the ability to wrest order and meaning from chaos affirms hope. Undermining distinctions between modernism and postmodernism—as it blurs the borders between fact and fiction, history and story, East and West, India and Pakistan, Hindu and Muslim—Rushdie's novel sustains its assault on polar logic. Embodying a vision of self and reality that transcends such dualities, Saleem concludes his narrative as a "young-old" man, a creature both ravaged by history and dedicated to seeking its meaning and truth. Having suffered the pain of sperectomy and been drained of all hope, Saleem conveys hope through his art. The paradoxes mount, the deconstruction of dualities continues as Saleem prepares, in the novel's closing paragraph, for his own end—which is also a beginning. The (circular rather than progressive) march of the generations will continue as the "son who is not my son, and his son who will not be his, and his who will not be his" assume the burden of history. That is the "privilege and the curse of midnight's children," whose paradoxical experience, Rushdie suggests, ultimately mirrors our own. Like the children of midnight, each of us comes into the world at once naked and handcuffed to history. However new to the present, we are already shrouded in the past. In the dense accumulations of history and culture we discover the medium that both clothes and confines, dwarfs and defines us.

9

Memory's Child
Morrison's *Beloved*

If Rushdie's characters bear the burden of history, Toni Morrison's are bludgeoned by it. The "Sixty Million and more" to whom the novel is dedicated—the estimated number of Africans who did not survive passage to the New World during centuries of slave trade—offer only a partial count of slavery's victims.[1] The phrase "and more" must stand, Morrison suggests, for countless others, including those who survived but lived out their lives in bondage. It is fitting, therefore, that the novel's central figure, the eponymous Beloved, appears suspended between the land of the living and the realm of the dead. At once child and grown-up, spirit and creature, Beloved sustains a dual identity throughout the novel. Recognized as the ghost of a murdered child who returns to her mother in the body of a nineteen-year-old woman, she also acts as the survivor of a slave ship on the Middle Passage.

The ambiguities of history and identity that undermine Saleem Sinai's claim to a stable or unified self in *Midnight's Children* are raised to a cataclysmic power in *Beloved* (1987). For Rushdie's characters the dream of a new Indian nation is belied by thousands of years of divisive history. The future of the subcontinent, and of baby Saleem, is inextricably tied to the troubled past. Giving the lie to the idyll of innocence, the infant nation, like its chosen child, begins life already formed and deformed by the past. For Morrison's characters the recent abolition of slavery also creates a false dream of freedom. Like the chokecherry tree carved on Sethe's back by her former masters, the dark history of slavery has left its psychic as well as physical scars.[2] So wracking has that experience been, so crushing to body, mind, and spirit, the survivors can muster little hope for the future. As Sethe later thinks to herself, "the future was a matter of keeping the past at bay." To her a "better life" means "simply not that other one" led as a slave (42).

Small wonder, then, that *Beloved* casts the child not as an innocent babe full of wonder but as an injured ghost bearing the scars of the past. Beloved's "lineless" skin notwithstanding, she embodies a history of grief and suffering (50). Her estrangement from the world of the living symbolizes, moreover, the tenuous hold that the novel's characters have on self and identity. Whereas Saleem can endeavor to give shape and meaning to history, Morrison's emblematic child speaks the traumatized language of an infant torn from her mother's side. If Beloved were suddenly graced with rhetorical eloquence, however, she might well say with Saleem: "I am the sum total of everything that went before me" (*Midnight's Children* 457). Beloved's story, like Saleem's, embraces the collective history of a people. Hers is the story of millions of black men, women, and children born or sold into slavery, living at the mercy of their white masters, dispossessed of their families and friends, abused if not raped and murdered. As Philip Weinstein observes, Beloved "incarnates at every level the tragedy that was American slavery. In her the unspeakable speaks, unspeakably."[3] At the same time she plays a pivotal role in the novel's drama: the story of the runaway slave named Sethe, her only surviving daughter, Denver, and the man who arrives to claim Sethe's affection eighteen years after his escape from a Kentucky farm.

Beloved opens in 1873, in the aftermath of the Civil War; but its central action takes place before the abolition of slavery. These crucial events, which begin in the 1850s, lie buried in the memory of those living in the postwar period. As the novel's characters start to recall their experience, the past comes alive and acts on the present, influencing its direction and outcome. The dark history of slavery suggests why, even before the brutal details of the protagonists' experience are fully disclosed, they are so resistant to the process of remembering. To remember—or, as the characters more often put it, to "rememory"— is to relive a past so full of pain, misery, humiliation, and horror that it threatens to destroy their sanity. The circular structure of the narrative reflects both the powerful current of memory and the human longing to repress it.

By 1873 Sethe has spent most of her adult life struggling to keep "the past at bay" (42). Ultimately, however, she must come to terms

with the painful past in order to recover from it. As another young
runaway comments to her early in the novel, "Can't nothing heal
without pain, you know." She also says, "Anything dead coming back
to life hurts" (78, 35). The runaway, a white girl named Amy Denver,
helps Sethe give birth to her fourth child in 1855, when Sethe, barely
out of her teens, is attempting to cross the Ohio River and escape
to freedom. As Morrison's narrative reveals, however, the course of
Sethe's ultimate release from bondage follows a circular rather than
direct route: many years after she crosses that river, she must return to
the past and relive its pain and grief in order to recover herself in and
for the present.

Setting this painful process in motion is the mysterious figure of
Beloved, who embodies Amy Denver's "dead coming back to life."
Whether the reader identifies Beloved as the grown-up ghost of
Sethe's slaughtered child or the survivor of a slave ship, she serves as
emissary from a world beyond the other characters' experience. Her
"traumatized language," as Morrison said in an interview, belongs to
the realm of death. This holds true, she added, whether Beloved is
"what Sethe thinks she is, her child returned to her from the dead," or
a "survivor from the true factualized slave ship. . . . Both things are
possible, and there's evidence in the text [to support both] . . . , because
the language of both experiences—death and the Middle Passage—
is the same."[4] If Morrison's ghostly child has anything in common
with Wordsworth's celestial one, it is this connection to the otherworld. Like the child who enters this world "trailing clouds of glory,"
Beloved arrives from "the other side," as Sethe puts it, of death (241).
But the message Morrison's child brings with her has less to do
with immortality than with mortal need, suffering, and loss. Beloved's
arrival wreaks havoc in the land of the living; her presence compels
Morrison's characters (and her readers) to remember and relive some
of history's darkest hours.

When as "a fully dressed woman" Beloved "walk[s] out of the
water" and into the characters' lives, the narrator offers no explanation
for her sudden appearance: "She barely gained the dry bank of the
stream before she sat down and leaned against a mulberry tree. . . .
Nobody saw her emerge or came accidentally by." Without further
ado, this "sopping wet" creature—a nineteen-year-old beauty with the
skin of a newborn—turns up in Sethe's front yard. Remarking that the
stranger's head looks "too heavy for [her] neck," Sethe notes that her

"feet were like her hands, soft and new" (50, 56). Such features, Karen Carmean points out, link the stranger to "certain river spirits" in African lore; "primarily identified by something strange about their hands and feet," they are believed to "have contact with the unseen world."[5] In further reference to the unseen world, the stranger announces herself as Beloved, the same name that appears on the headstone marking the grave of Sethe's dead child. To Sethe and Denver the young woman quickly assumes the haunting presence of that dead baby girl, now fully grown. With her arrival in the here and now Beloved sets new "wave[s] of grief" in motion (9). Slowly Sethe and her loved ones approach, in order to relive, the central, shattering event of Sethe's life: the murder she committed to liberate her children from the humiliations of slavery.

The "dragon" of racial hatred, as Morrison puts it, is a monster ever "thirsty for black blood"; before the abolition of slavery, this insatiable monster "swam the Ohio at will," tracking down runaway slaves (66). In 1855 the dragon goes after Sethe, who has crossed the river weeks earlier in search of freedom. Within a month of her arrival in the free state of Ohio, her former master and his slave catchers turn up at the house where she is staying; they mean to take her and her four children back to the Kentucky farm from which they fled. In a desperate act of defiance Sethe rushes to defend her children by killing them— by, as she says, putting "my babies where they'd be safe" (164).[6] By slaying her beloved children, Sethe would spare them the humiliations she has suffered—and spare herself the inevitable torment of not knowing whether some "headless" torso spied "hanging in [a] tree" was her own offspring, left there by "a gang of whites" on the rampage (251).

The ferocity of Sethe's maternal love identifies her, as more than one critic has observed, with the African archetype of the great mother, giver of life. Sethe possesses *nommo,* the creative power of women, and defines herself in terms of this power. Within her flows the river of life, of primordial creation—a river as "thick" with blood as Sethe's "too thick" love (164). The torrent of mother love is truly awesome, as unrelenting as the blood that flows through the umbilical cord binding the child to its mother. For Sethe this somatic connection cannot be severed; her children are part of herself, the best part: "Whites might dirty *her* all right, but not her best thing, her beautiful, magical best thing—the part of her that was clean" (251). Desperate to protect the only part of her she can love, her beautiful children, Sethe can think of only one way to keep them "safe"—and that is to kill them.[7] But before she can complete the bloody slaughter, she is discovered, and three of her children are rescued. Only her one-year-old daughter, whose throat she has slit with a handsaw, dies; the three surviving children are, nonetheless, psychically scarred by the murder. The two boys, Howard and Buglar, grow up fearing their mother and eventually run away; the youngest child, Denver, lives with Sethe in isolation, suffering the shame her mother has brought on them both.

Eighteen years after this bloody event, and shortly before Beloved reenters her mother's life, an old acquaintance arrives on Sethe's doorstep. A friend of her vanished husband, Paul D has been wandering the country since he too escaped, eighteen years earlier, from the Kentucky farm to which they all had been bound. As their mutual affection begins to grow, Sethe and Paul D are wary of their feelings, wary of any hope for future happiness. Since her release from jail, Sethe has buried herself in a round of cooking, cleaning, and caring for Denver. These tasks, like the daily kneading of bread, are for Sethe the means to a single end, aspects of one effort: "beating back the past" (73).

Soon after Paul D's arrival on Sethe's doorstep, the grown-up ghost, or "familiar," of Sethe's child arrives to claim life from the mother who killed her. Emerging from "the dark" into the sunlight of her mother's front yard, Beloved literally unearths the buried past. She startles Sethe and Paul D into new life by leading them, paradoxically, back into the past. At the furthest reach of consciousness, Morrison suggests, memory discovers not history but prehistory: the primal depths or wellsprings of life that predate by aeons the white man's brief reign on earth. The process of healing, or rebirth, that these characters undergo recalls the cycle by which the river flows into the sea and renews itself at the mountaintop. Beloved arrives from the dark water to deliver Sethe and Paul D to the sea of the past; in the depths of primordial memory and instinct, regeneration begins.

Permeating—indeed, saturating—the experience of Morrison's characters is the crucial link, biological as well as metaphorical, between the river and life, water and birth or rebirth. The waters of the Ohio River, the boundary between the North and the South that Sethe crosses in 1855, are identified not only with the sea of primordial existence but with the amniotic fluid sustaining life in the mother's womb. As though propitiating the river god—or in this case, goddess—that will carry her to freedom, Sethe, six months' pregnant, prematurely gives birth to her fourth child on the banks of the Ohio before crossing over. "As soon as Sethe got close to the river," the reader is told, "her own water broke loose to join it." As the passage continues, the river water merges with Sethe's own. Lying on the bottom of a stolen canoe to deliver her baby, she feels the "river water seeping through" the holes of the boat and "spreading over [her] hips. . . . When a foot rose from the river bed and kicked the bottom of the boat and Sethe's behind, she knew it was done and permitted herself a short faint" (83–84). Here, the riverbed from which Sethe feels her baby's foot rising is actually the bed of the boat, in which her waters merge with the river's.

Aiding Sethe throughout this ordeal is the other young runaway Amy Denver, who has encountered Sethe, hours earlier, fleeing through "a ridge of pine near the Ohio." Dreading that she has been "discovered by a whiteboy" with "mossy teeth" and "an appetite," Sethe is surprised, and relieved, to find a girl. As she later tells her daughter Denver, "It wasn't no whiteboy at all. Was a girl. The raggediest-looking trash you ever saw saying, 'Look there. A nigger. If that don't beat all'" (31–32). Like her literary precursor Huckleberry Finn, Amy Denver acts out of instinctive good nature rather than socially constructed hostility. With her "good hands" the white girl tends Sethe's body and keeps her alive, wrapping the newborn in rags as she has already wrapped the mother's bare and bloody feet (82).

This moment of unself-conscious humanity—of sudden community between two isolated and outlawed creatures, one black and one white—explicitly recalls the central image and theme of *Huckleberry Finn*. "A pateroller would have sniggered," Morrison writes, "to see two throw-away people, two lawless outlaws—a slave and a barefoot whitewoman with unpinned hair—wrapping a ten-minute-old baby in the rags they wore. But no pateroller came. . . . The water sucked and swallowed itself beneath them. There was nothing to disturb them at their work." After Amy Denver's work is done, she bids good-bye to Sethe in a frank and unsentimental manner also worthy of Huck Finn. She knows better, she tells Sethe, than to "be caught dead in daylight on a busy river with a runaway" slave (84–85). Registering her gratitude to the white girl, Sethe names her newborn Denver before sinking back into sleep.

Recasting Twain's two runaways, the white boy and the black slave seeking freedom from oppression, Morrison shifts the focus from male to female, white to black, as she shifts the narrative perspective from present to past. The linear plot of Twain's picaresque tale of adventure gives way to a modernist narrative that relentlessly circles back on events, as the currents of memory and rememory unearth layers of buried history. (Here the contrast between Twain's nineteenth-century classic and Morrison's contemporary masterpiece owes as much to a century of narrative experimentation as to differences of race and gender.) Most important for this discussion is the way Morrison rewrites, and renews, Twain's great theme of the river.

Because Morrison's handling of the theme proves crucial to the effects of her novel, I will briefly compare it with Twain's. The comparison should help to clarify her evocation of the river not only as the characters' means of escape to freedom but as their link to primordial creation. In Morrison's novel as in Twain's, the river's untamed current is celebrated for its creative as well as destructive power. By contrast, in a novel such as Lessing's *The Fifth Child,* the destructive force of the primordial—and the child who issues from it—poses a threat to the fragile order of civilization. Focusing on the increasing disintegration of late-twentieth-century culture, Lessing warns of a new technological wilderness overtaking the West. In the urban jungle the prehistoric "black cave that ha[s] no end" has resurfaced in the form of countless "caves and caverns," the habitat of the homeless and hopeless, lining the depths of anonymous big cities (*Fifth Child* 10, 131). As the distinction between human and subhuman is increasingly eroded, Ben, the alien, becomes the leader of a gang of alienated youths who emulate his predatory behavior.

Beloved and *Huckleberry Finn,* on the other hand, depict societies whose iron order, far from disintegrating, is tightly organized around a perniciously constructed distinction between human and subhuman —categories assigned the white and black races, respectively, by a slaveholding society. One disciple of this vicious dogma, Sethe and Paul D's former master called "schoolteacher," instructs his nephews to note the "animal" versus "human characteristics" of each slave (193). Such calculations, he suggests, will help them to understand how slaves must be treated—no better or worse than the master's "own horse" and "hounds" (149). Denied their rightful claim to self and humanity by slavery, Morrison's characters discover not a threat but a possible source of regeneration in the primordial depths of creation. Delivered by water into the land of the living, the spirit of the dead child Beloved helps them to make this discovery.

The body of water that serves as both natural setting and supernatural presence in *Beloved* is not, of course, Twain's mighty Mississippi but that lesser tributary, the Ohio River. Yet as the narrator points out, the current of the Ohio is "dedicated to the Mississippi hundreds of miles away" (83). In *Huckleberry Finn* the juncture of the Ohio and the Mississippi is crucial to the story. Misled by the Mississippi's strong current and a thick fog, Huck and Jim unwittingly drift past Cairo, Illinois, learning of their mistake only when it is too late (*Huckleberry Finn* 77).[8] Having overshot their original destination, the two runaways surrender their fate to the river that bears them farther and farther away from the North into the dangerous depths of the slaveholding South.

Like an omnipotent god, Twain's Mississippi dictates the course of human fate, catching up white men as well as black, masters as well as slaves, in its overpowering current. "*Huckleberry Finn* is a great book," Lionel Trilling commented nearly half a century ago, "because it is about a god—about, that is, a power which seems to have a mind and will of its own, and which to men of moral imagination, appears to embody a great moral idea." Such moral imagination, Trilling's statement makes clear, has little to do with Christian doctrine or dogma. (Huck has heard plenty of preaching from the grownups around him.) Huck's "very intense moral life," Trilling adds, "may be said to derive almost wholly from his love of the river. He lives in a perpetual adoration of the Mississippi's power and charm": its "noble grandeur in contrast with the pettiness of men." As a critic, Morrison polemicizes against such traditional—white male—readings of *Huckleberry Finn* based on what she calls "sentimental nostrums about lighting out to the territory, river gods," and American "innocence." As a novelist, her creative engagement with and rewriting of these themes is, as we shall see, richly suggestive.[9]

The river does more than dwarf with its grandeur and mystery the petty interests of human beings in Huck's eyes. It places him on a new footing with his fellow creatures—most particularly Jim, with whom he confronts many life-threatening dangers and develops a strong bond of trust. On the river, isolated from a society with which he is at odds, Huck imagines another, greater reality: a universe that calls for a standard different from society's by which to judge one's fellow creatures. The discovery that Huck makes on the river—his realization that Jim, a runaway slave, is not only a human being but a noble, exemplary one—flies in the face of everything he has been taught. The revelation is a shock to his system: to the whole system of values and ideas that society has engraved on the consciousness of the Southern white boy.

Huck's discovery of Jim's humanity thus implies, as Trilling suggests, his recovery of or contact with a world that lies beyond socially constructed law and order. By delivering Huck to this primal vision, Twain's Mississippi fulfills its mythic promise. More than a means of physical escape, the river suggests the possibility for psychic freedom. In *Beloved* the river also serves as a liberating image, charged with the energies of a boundless universe extending back before human time and history. Issuing from those unseen depths, the mysterious figure of Beloved "walks out of the water" that flows in a stream behind Sethe's house and empties into the Ohio River six miles away. Just as the current of the Ohio eventually finds its way to the Mississippi, the great waters of the Mississippi reach their ultimate destination in the vast ocean. At the farthest temporal and geographical reach lies the primordial sea, the watery cradle of life. Forcing open the floodgates of memory, Beloved's arrival in Sethe's world creates a channel to that remote source, the dark origins of existence, where renewal and regeneration become possible.

When, on that summer afternoon in 1873, Sethe encounters the mysterious stranger sitting in her front yard, she does not consciously recognize her beloved dead daughter. Subliminally, however, Sethe's body registers a maternal response. The moment she gets "close enough to see" the young woman's face, Sethe's "bladder fill[s] to capacity." The "water she voided was endless," says the narrator, who underscores the connection between this breaking of waters and that announcing Denver's birth. Recalling that scene on the riverbank, Sethe thinks to herself: "There was no stopping water breaking from a breaking womb and there was no stopping now." Just as Sethe, in response to Denver's birth, drank endless quantities of "the Ohio" from a jar, so the mysterious stranger now drinks "cup after cup of water" in response to her apparent rebirth (51, 90).

Like a newborn eager for its mother's milk, Beloved quickly demonstrates an insatiable "thirst for hearing" what Sethe can tell her about the past. As she listens to the stories, Beloved "fill[s] herself with water from the bucket." "Storytelling," Sethe realizes, "became a way to feed her"; and Sethe gladly provides this nourishment, even though "every mention of her past life hurt" (58, 60). As a consequence, Sethe begins to recollect and relive suppressed details from the past, including the childhood loss of her mother. Along with the painful memory of her mother's death comes the buried recollection that Sethe's "Ma'am" spoke another language, a language Sethe once understood, and that she was brought to North America on a slave ship from across "the sea." Forced to couple with members of the ship's crew, Sethe's mother "threw away" with disgust the baby she bore, as she later discarded others forced on her. Sethe was the only child she kept, naming her after the baby's father, a black man on the ship whom her mother loved (62).

In recollecting and sharing her past with Beloved, Sethe manifests new signs of life—and a vital hunger for life that she has stifled. Now, when her need to know about the past gets the better of her, she reproaches her "rebellious brain" for being "a greedy child"; like Beloved, Sethe's "greedy" brain "snatche[s] up everything" and does not know when to say it "can't hold another bite." Beloved's craving for the past, for the stories and memories that shape and define human identity, expresses the vital energy by which children attach themselves to life and begin to develop a self. Thus, when Beloved begs Denver to tell her a story about the past, Beloved's "alert and hungry face"—her "downright craving to know"—makes "Denver begin to see what she is saying and not just to hear it." As Denver recounts the story of her birth, a story Sethe has often told her, she understands for the first time "how it must have felt to her mother. See[s] how it must have looked." By "nursing" Beloved's hunger, in other words, Denver also nourishes herself, intensely reliving the experience of her beginnings and claiming that experience for herself (70, 77–78).

As for Sethe, Beloved's arrival turns the tide of her life, overwhelming her with memories she has tried for years to hold at bay. Extending beyond the personal to the primal, the river from which Beloved emerges proves a monumental force. Like Twain's Mississippi—that primordial presence Trilling identifies as neither "ethical" nor "good" —the river can destroy as well as restore those who come into contact with it. Emerging from the dark water like a shiny "silver fish," this uncanny "water sprite," as Karen Carmean calls her, manifests the river's preternatural power (65).[10] Wreaking havoc on the lives she touches, Beloved even drives Paul D from Sethe's bed. Observing a pair of turtles coupling at the edge of the stream behind Sethe's house, she learns all she needs to know of nature's secrets (105). One night, in imitation of the turtles, Beloved entices Paul D to couple with her; although violently ashamed, he cannot resist her power (116). Overwhelmed by a force that is "more like a brainless urge to stay alive, a life hunger," than any personal attraction, Paul D joins Beloved in her element. In this primordial state he struggles like a turtle to reach "clear air at the top of the sea.... And afterward, beached and gobbling air, in the midst of repulsion and personal shame, he was thankful too for having been escorted to some ocean-deep place he once belonged to" (264).

Driven by shame from Sethe's house, Paul D is nonetheless changed, and ultimately restored, by his contact with the primordial. When he first arrives on Sethe's doorstep, he is determined, like Sethe, to "beat back" memory and feeling. To keep memory at bay has been his life-long method of survival. During his years as a slave he was caged like a wild beast, chained to a work gang, and harnessed like a dray horse with a bit in his mouth. Paul D has survived all this by sealing his memories in "that tobacco tin buried in his chest where a red heart used to be. Its lid rusted shut" (72–73). By the time he arrives at Sethe's house, he is convinced that "nothing in this world could pry" open "the tobacco tin lodged in his chest" (113). Nor, in the days following, does his growing affection for Sethe substantially change his mind. "For if," he tells himself, "she got a whiff of the contents [of that box] it would ... hurt her to know that there was no red heart ... beating in him" (73). Like Sethe, Paul D has survived by destroying the best part of himself—by cutting himself off from memory and feeling.

When Paul D mates with Beloved, the experience cuts through his temporary resolve as though that resolve were a flimsy tobacco tin. Their coupling is described in language that insists on this theme: Beloved "moved closer with a footfall [Paul D] didn't hear and he didn't hear the whisper that the flakes of rust made either as they fell away from the seams of his tobacco tin. So when the lid gave he didn't know it. What he knew was that . . . he was saying, 'Red heart. Red heart,' over and over again" (117). The life force that engulfs Paul D like "a brainless urge" does not stop for mortal shame or sorrow. As insistent as the swift current of blood pulsing through his red heart, this surge of the primordial awakens him to his own vital existence: "His tobacco tin, blown open, spilled contents that floated freely and made him their play and prey" (219). Nothing short of contact with primal creation, Morrison suggests, can restore Paul D to himself. The fluid force of instinct, the elemental craving for life, blows him wide open. But exposure is also release. Now for the first time, he can reclaim and begin to reintegrate all the bits and pieces of himself that have been chewed up, ground down, consumed, and spit out by the monstrous dragon of slavery.[11]

The fragmentation of self, the *dismembering* of identity that makes *remembering* so painful, is the ultimate inhumanity that slavery inflicts on its victims. When the relatively decent Kentucky master Mr. Garner died and was replaced by a man whose cruelty eventually drove Sethe and the other slaves to escape, they discovered the full extent of their deprivation. As Paul D later thinks to himself, "Everything rested on Garner being alive. Without his life each of theirs fell to pieces." That lack of wholeness, that dismemberment, those pieces are, he concludes, what slavery *is* (220). Haunted by visions of the dismembered bodies she has seen hanging from trees or burned to the ground, Sethe similarly wonders whether the "parts" of her will hold (272). Slavery has taught her "that anybody white could take your whole self for anything that came to mind. Not just work, kill, or maim you, but dirty you. Dirty you so bad you couldn't like yourself anymore. Dirty you so bad you forgot who you were and couldn't think it up." From this ghastly loss of self, a deprivation more dire than any physical torment, Sethe attempted to spare her children. Through violence she sought to save both them and "the part of her that was clean" (251). But the slaughter only dismembered her further, cutting off the life of one child and estranging her from the other three and from the surrounding community of women, who henceforth regard her as an outcast.

The haunting presence of Beloved embodies this fatal fragmentation. Her fate, Arnold Weinstein notes, is "defined in terms of human dismemberment. The body is pieced apart, the family is divided, the subject is cut off from its past."[12] A creature whose life has already been broken, Beloved struggles to gain a name and identity for herself before disintegration claims her—before she dissolves into nonbeing or breaks, once again, into pieces. In her monstrous craving for life she feeds on the lives of those around her, trying to usurp Sethe's identity. In her mother's face Beloved sees "the face [she] lost" and tries to reclaim it. Seeking to fill her emptiness, her lack of self, she consumes everything in sight. As she grows larger and larger, her stomach swells to "basket-fat" proportions that signify, on one level, her pregnancy by Paul D, on another, her insatiable hunger to exist (212, 242–43, 261).

But no matter how large Beloved grows, no matter how swollen her belly, she cannot deliver herself permanently into the world of the living.

As Beloved waxes, Sethe wanes—literally wasting away in her efforts to placate the spirit of her dead daughter: "The bigger Beloved got, the smaller Sethe became. . . . Sethe no longer combed her hair or splashed her face with water. She sat in the chair licking her lips like a chastised child while Beloved ate up her life, took it, swelled up with it, grew taller on it. And the older woman yielded it up without a murmur. . . . Sethe was trying to make up for the handsaw; Beloved was making her pay for it." In this grotesque inversion of the mother-child relationship, Sethe seeks to atone for her crime. At last, taking matters into their own hands, the neighborhood women arrive to exorcise this "devil-child" from Sethe's house (250–51, 261).[13] "Whatever Sethe had done" in the past, they do not "like the idea of past errors taking possession of the present" (256).

As the women begin to chant and sing, their voices mount, building "a wave of sound wide enough," Morrison writes, "to sound deep water and knock the pods off chestnut trees. It broke over Sethe and she trembled like the baptized in its wash" (261). Reasserting the "mother's voice," as Karla Holloway puts it, these black women are the guardians as well as the progenitors of the community (26, 39).[14] Imbued with the power of *nommo,* they arrive to rescue Sethe from self-destruction. The wave of sound launched by their mingled voices cleanses Sethe of her paralyzing guilt, baptizing her in its wash. In a final sequence of events Sethe relives the haunting episode of her past, imagining that the slave catchers have arrived anew to take her child. This time, however, she turns her fury outward, dashing into the yard to attack, with an ice pick, a white man she mistakes for her former master (262). (The man she attacks, Edward Bodwin, is by a twist of irony the abolitionist who saved Sethe, years earlier, from the gallows [265].)

Startled by Sethe's behavior, Beloved sees only that her mother has abandoned her for the others; in her view Sethe has joined "the people out there" and left her "alone" once "again." As though recognizing, in this series of confused actions and mistaken identities, her destiny, Beloved vanishes amid the chaos. "The girl who waited to be loved," says the narrator, "erupts into her separate parts," dissolving back into the stream from which she emerged (262, 274). These separate parts, Eusebio Rodrigues observes, represent pieces not only of Sethe's dead daughter but of racial history and memory. In her ultimate guise Beloved "becomes the embodiment of all slave daughters."[15]

At the end of the novel even Denver acknowledges that Beloved embodies not only the spirit of her dead sister but something "more" (266). The fusion of Beloved's personal and collective identity, at which Denver hints, is expressly rendered in four short sections of the novel (200–217). Here the narrative proper breaks off, replaced by a series of internal monologues—by Sethe, Denver, and Beloved—that finally mingle and swell into one choric voice. In the interior monologue devoted to Beloved's traumatized language and memories, the boundary between her immediate identity, as the ghost of Sethe's murdered baby, and her wider experience of suffering and death dissolves in the sea of collective memory. In her monologue—whose fragmented syntax simultaneously suggests the fragmented or pre-oedipal speech of infancy and the psychic disintegration of one who has witnessed unspeakable horrors—Beloved evokes the experience of millions of Africans on the Middle Passage.

Recounting her journey on a slave ship crossing the turbulent waters of the Atlantic, Beloved remembers crouching among countless other captives as the white crew, "men without skin," shove the dead and the dying overboard. The murdered child's ghostly memories of abandonment and separation, of crossing a river to "the other side" of existence, thus acquire universal significance (214–15). The stream of Beloved's fractured, unspoken language articulates the untold story of those sixty million and more to whom Morrison's novel is dedicated. The woman whose face "is there with the face I want" becomes, in Beloved's elemental consciousness, both Sethe and an African woman who sits picking flowers in her native land before being hauled onto the slave ship: "Sethe is the one that picked flowers, yellow flowers in the place before the crouching. . . . Now I have found her in this house. I will not lose her again. She is mine" (214). Dissolving the boundary between individual and collective memory, the narrative achieves Morrison's stated aim: to bridge the epistemological "gap" between "Africa and Afro-America," the "living and the dead," the "past and the present."[16] Just as the waters of the Ohio merge with Sethe's water when she gives birth to Denver, the "ocean-deep place" from which Beloved issues (and to which she returns) becomes the geographical ocean that, over three centuries, swallowed countless African lives.

Sometime after Beloved disappears into the dark waters from which she emerged, Paul D retraces his steps to Sethe's house and finds her mourning Beloved's loss. "She was my best thing," Sethe laments. But now Paul D corrects her, saying, "You your best thing, Sethe. You are." Quickened to life and the beating of his "red heart," Paul D would heal Sethe with his newfound vitality. Having opened himself to the past, he finds it possible to imagine the future. To Sethe he says, "me and you, we got more yesterday than anybody. We need some kind of tomorrow" (272–73). Eventually the memory of Beloved begins to fade, as Sethe, Paul D, and Denver focus on creating a future. Having rediscovered in themselves that ocean-deep place from which Beloved issued and to which she restored them, Morrison's characters can finally let go of the past. Something in it appears to have been set right, and further "remembering" seems "unwise." To whom, at any rate, could they entrust this painful history of suffering, death, and rebirth? To no one, apparently: as the narrator says in a refrain that signals the end of the novel, this is "not a story to pass on" (274–75). And yet Morrison has done just that: she has passed *on* this story to her readers. The story of slavery, and of the sixty million and more who died on the Middle Passage, should not be forgotten. It must not, as Sethe says earlier, be among the "things" that "pass on" and vanish from memory (35–36).[17]

Passing *on,* or delivering this story that must not be *passed* on, Morrison's narrator underscores the paradox: only by telling the story will the haunting cease, the past be put to rest. In telling, hearing, and reading stories, Margaret Doody observes, we encounter "our own desire *to be.*" The "love of story" expresses, in other words, "the love of being." In Morrison's novel, Doody points out, Beloved "is an extreme representation of the sacred love of being." By insisting that others tell her their life stories, Beloved "insists on having her being." Although she becomes a "menace" at the novel's end, threatening "to over-whelm the lives of her family," she is at the same time "a promise and a liberating force." Because of Beloved, Sethe is able to reconnect "parts of her terribly painful life"; "through the art of telling" she makes "that life conscious and bearable."[18]

Disruptive and demanding, as greedy for life as she is for stories, Beloved is the unruly spirit that drives the novel's action as she literally moves Paul D out of Sethe's bed and into her own. Beloved's desire for life, for being, compels Sethe and Paul D to recover their pasts and

themselves. Once the past has been confronted and laid to rest, the
future lies open to them. Memory's ghost, the dead child, has no further function in the land of the living. The mysterious creature, last
glimpsed by a child who sees "a naked woman with fish for hair" running through the woods, disappears into the stream behind Sethe's
house (267). "By and by," as the narrator says, "all trace" of her dissolves;
the "footprints" left "down by the stream" disappear. And finally, "what
is forgotten is not only the footprints but the water too and what it
is down there" (275). Yet while all trace of Beloved vanishes, *Beloved*
remains. Memory has rescued the story of the anonymous multitudes
who drowned in the lethean waters of the Middle Passage. And it has
rescued the stories of those who, like Sethe, Paul D, and Denver, survived to cross the river into freedom. Beloved's sacred love of being is
requited, in a larger sense, by the story that *Beloved* is and tells. Just as
Sethe and Denver nourish the child eager for stories, the novel nourishes us. The vivid life of its language and characters quickens the
imagination, stirs us to see "what it is down there" in the depths of our
collective past. Confronting the nation's dark history may constitute
the first step toward securing a better future for all its citizens. By telling the story of *Beloved,* Morrison moves her audience—both black
and white, the children of slaves and slave owners alike—a little closer
to that elusive goal.

10

Reclaiming the Lost Child

McEwan's *The Child in Time*

Ian McEwan's *The Child in Time* (1987) overtly draws the connection, implicit in the novels thus far examined, between the child's image and the culture that constructs it. Like Rushdie's *Midnight's Children,* McEwan's novel points to the significance of the child's image at every level of the text—making explicit reference, as well, to studies of child-hood that influenced its composition.[1] *The Child in Time,* it should be noted, offers a striking contrast to much of this British writer's work, which deals with incest, perversion, and murder and builds on gothic or grotesque effects. McEwan's first novel, *The Cement Garden,* published a decade earlier, also centers on childhood but constructs a dramatically different image of the child's nature and significance. Like Golding's *Lord of the Flies,* which McEwan has cited as an influence on his early work, *The Cement Garden* describes the primitive anarchy that results when children are released from the constraints of society and the adults' "civilized" order.

Whereas Golding's children, stranded on a desert island, succumb to acts of savage cruelty, the orphans in *The Cement Garden,* as Jack Slay Jr. remarks, "succumb not to savagery but to the stagnation of modern society." At first reveling in their freedom, the youngsters quickly slide into lethargy.[2] *The Child in Time* offers a picture of modern society no less monotonous but far more threatened by social disintegration. Composed by McEwan during the mid-1980s, the novel takes place in England a decade into the (decidedly bleak) future. On the most obvious level, the eponymous child of the title belongs to the novel's protagonist, Stephen Lewis, a successful author of children's books, and his wife, Julie. More precisely, that child *belonged* to the Lewises until, two years prior to the novel's opening, she, a three-year-old named Kate, disappeared, kidnapped in a crowded London supermarket. Permeating the novel's narrative and thematic structure is the image of an absent—missing or lost—child.

In *Beloved,* as we have seen, the image of a lost or absent child signals the moral and material contradictions created by a slaveholding society. So inhuman are the conditions into which the children of slaves are born that Sethe, a slave mother, believes she can protect her offspring only by killing them. Stephen Lewis's inability to protect his daughter from an anonymous kidnapper also exposes, albeit in a very different key, problematic elements in Britain's social order at century's end. Readers on both sides of the Atlantic, however, are likely to recognize the familiar phenomenon of missing children, whose published photographs turn up every day in the mail. The faces of all these absent children testify to the ease with which predators, particularly in urban centers like London, go unnoticed and undetected. Thus, one chilly winter morning in a south London supermarket, Stephen Lewis has only to glance away from his three-year-old daughter for an instant as he finishes unloading a grocery cart, and she vanishes forever into the crowd. (In the kidnapping case mentioned in chapter 1, it took about four minutes for the Liverpool toddler James Bulger to wander away from his mother's side, encounter two ten-year-old strangers outside the store, and leave the shopping center hand in hand with one of his kidnappers.)[3]

Despite the efforts made to find the lost child—Stephen's numerous interviews with the police, the newspaper advertisements promising a generous reward for information, the countless enlargements of Kate's photograph pasted on bus shelters and walls all over London—the days and months that follow lead nowhere. "During that time," Stephen recalls, he and Julie "had clung to one another, sharing dazed rhetorical questions, awake in bed all night, theorizing hopefully one moment, despairing the next. But that was before time, the heartless accumulation of days, had clarified the absolute, bitter truth" (21). The terrible truth is that their child is gone, lost to them in time and space. Now a mere entry on the authorities' long lists of missing children, Kate gradually becomes an abstraction: a sign without its referent, a ghastly emptiness, a tremendous void. So deep is the rupture left by her absence that her grieving parents find it impossible to maintain their

normal activities or even to continue living together. Just as Stephen is
unable to write, Julie, a professional violinist and teacher, stops practicing and performing. As she explains much later in the novel, playing
her instrument begins to seem like "an evasion," an attempt "to stop
thinking" about Kate's loss (255). The silence brought on by their child's
disappearance hints at an underlying theme that recalls the Romantics'
paradigm: the adult's creative vitality originates in the child, whose
imagination is animated by wonder and curiosity. Dispossessed of their
daughter, Stephen and Julie cannot maintain, literally or figuratively,
their creative connection to the child. The marriage in pieces, Julie
retreats to a country cottage to deal with her loss, while Stephen stays
alone in their London apartment.

In London, a metropolis gripped by heat wave and a drought that
has lasted for months, Stephen dwells in a state of torpor and isolation,
"avoiding friends and work" and "unable to read more than twenty
lines of print" (36–37). The self-declared "father of an invisible child,"
he does little beyond watching game shows on television, drinking
scotch, and continuing his futile search for his daughter (2). As months
turn into years, he remains on watch—surveilling throngs of children
on school playgrounds, scouring city streets and subway stations with
an avid gaze. The only scheduled activity in which he participates is
designed to address the significance of childhood and its social constructions. Appointed to serve on the government's Official Commission
on Child Care, Stephen attends weekly meetings of the Subcommittee on Reading and Writing, one of fourteen committees charged
with making recommendations to the commission. Two years after
Kate's disappearance, he makes his way, once a week, across London to
"a gloomy room in Whitewall" where the meetings are held. Here,
keeping "half an ear on the proceedings," he rehearses memories of
his missing daughter, his estranged wife, and that fateful morning in a
south London supermarket. As Stephen notes, "since loss was his
subject," even recollections of his own distant childhood take the form
of "a lost time and a lost landscape" (5, 8).

As Stephen's consciousness, lost in daydreams, drifts in and out of
the committee's debate on child development and methods of child
rearing, the image of the absent or "invisible" child takes on increasing
significance for McEwan's readers. Stephen's kidnapped daughter is
not the only lost child who becomes, in her father's paradoxical
phrase, "everyone's property" (15). The more the child is discussed in

committee and debated in theory, the more absent—lost or missing from the scene—the child seems. To McEwan's readers it becomes increasingly obvious, moreover, that the government's pronounced interest in children and their welfare is largely a sham: that the social authorities engaged in analyzing and studying the child are bent on repressing, controlling, and even removing children from view. Among the "opinion-forming classes," from whose ranks the commission's membership is drawn, "it was generally agreed that the country was full of the wrong sort of people. There were strong opinions about what constituted a desirable citizenry and what *should be done to children* to procure one for the future" (4, emphasis added). Meanwhile, during the lengthy period of meetings at Whitehall, Stephen encounters a growing number of children who are homeless or indigent, begging for money or peddling their bodies on the street.

The theme of lost childhood—buried or forgotten by a society increasingly indifferent to human creativity and individuality—is reflected not only in Stephen's personal and professional life and in the culture at large but in England's climate at century's end. The "parched months" described at the novel's opening signal, in the narrator's words, "what was to be the last decent summer of the twentieth century" (5). (The drought later terminates in apocalyptic rainstorms that strip the trees "bare in a week"; recalling the biblical deluge, "it rained every day for fifty days" [142].) In McEwan's dystopian vision the weather plaguing England in the 1990s is mirrored by a cultural and spiritual wasteland, of which Stephen's "own parched emotional state" is an emblem (91). That his daughter may have been "stolen to replace a lost child" points to the universal significance of her absence (21). The image of the lost child reflects a society steadily divesting itself of the creative vitality and freedom that the Romantics identified with the child's curiosity and wonder. A kind of wholesale robbery, the narrative suggests, is taking place in "advanced" Western culture: ever more competitive in its drive for markets and profit margins, capitalist society has grown increasingly hostile to the individual, particularly that nascent creative self embodied in the child. Putting an entire culture at risk are forces as anonymous and powerful as those that robbed Stephen and Julie of their daughter.

Presiding over the cultural wasteland of *The Child in Time* is a harsh, post-Thatcherite government interested in fostering ruthless competition and its own authoritarian control. The regime is engaged, Ryan

Kiernan observes, in "sharpening the nation's social and economic divisions, running down the welfare state, and disguising the rise of a police state ruled by the market as a return to law and order and traditional family values." Under the guise of concern for family values and the child's welfare, the government has authorized the creation of an official child-care handbook.[4] Members of the commission's fourteen subcommittees, including the one on which Stephen serves, have been told that the production of this handbook is the goal of their weekly meetings. As it turns out, however, these yearlong meetings and the Official Commission on Child Care's proposed final report are completely superfluous.

Four months before the commission's subcommittees are scheduled to complete their work, a "middle-level civil servant" working in "government publications" smuggles out a copy of the government's handbook on child care, completed independently of the commission's work (189–90). Secretly circulating proof copies "among the civil service elite and three or four Cabinet ministers," the government has intended all along to publish its handbook "a month or two after the commission had completed its own report, and to claim that the handbook drew from the commission's work" (191). Only after this disclosure, which causes a brief scandal in the newspapers before the handbook wins public acceptance, can McEwan's readers grasp the full irony of the excerpts—identified as quotations from *The Authorized Child-Care Handbook*—at the head of each chapter of the novel. Along with Stephen and the other members of the commission, McEwan's readers discover that they have been duped: the duly cited "authorized" handbook is the product not of the commission's collective efforts but of a solitary author secretly working "under his leader's [the prime minister's] supervision" (239).

Once Stephen recognizes the nature and success of the government's secret manipulations, he, too, feels like a lost child. Marveling "at his own innocence," he remarks to himself, "This was one of those times when he felt he had not quite grown up, he knew so little about how things really worked" (214). Living in a media-saturated world, whose events are largely stage-managed by those in power, McEwan's readers are likely to recognize this feeling of childish gullibility, just as they recognize the political implications of the child-parent paradigm that the government is attempting to foster. After the disclosure Stephen remarks to a colleague on his committee, "I don't see why [the government officials] couldn't trust the commission to come up with the kind of book they wanted. They appointed its chairman, and all the chairmen of the subcommittees." His colleague replies, "They couldn't leave it to . . . the experts and celebrities . . . to come up with exactly the right book. The grown-ups know best" (191). As Stephen's colleague ironically implies, the citizens of a democratic state should be treated not as children but as constituents, to be served by their government. If, as Stephen conjectures, England's prime minister occupies the role of "the nation's parent" in the "collective fantasy," Britain's citizens are well on their way to fulfilling the government's authoritarian ambitions (93).

The post-Thatcherite government depicted in McEwan's novel seeks not only to extend the child-parent paradigm into political life but, by "reform[ing] child-care practice," to construct that paradigm along lines that seamlessly transform the obedient child into the compliant citizen. As one excerpt from the government's handbook states, "Those who find it naturally hard to wield authority over their children should seriously consider the systematic use of treats and rewards. . . . In the past, too much has been demanded of parents, who have been exhorted to inculcate altruism in their children at all costs. Incentives, after all, form the basis of our economic structure and necessarily shape our morality; there is no reason on earth why a well-behaved child should not have an ulterior motive" (142). Explicitly identifying the source of moral conduct as economic, the handbook ultimately lays the question of ethics at the door of Darwinian theory. "Child-care writers of the postwar era," another excerpt states, "sentimentally ignored the fact that children are at heart selfish, and reasonably so, for they are programmed for survival" (182).

Under the guise of its concern for family values, the government designs its child-care handbook to foster social competitiveness and political obedience in the next generation of citizens. That this government is secretly at war with human creativity and freedom is more than hinted at when, in one of the last cited excerpts, the handbook establishes an "analogy between childhood and disease." The vital link that the Romantics perceived between the freedoms of childhood and those of a democratic state suggests why, in the government's authoritarian view, childhood should be regarded as a "disease" or aberration: "a physically and mentally incapacitating condition, distorting emotions, perceptions, and reason, from which growing up is the slow and difficult recovery" (211). The government's hostility to the disease of childhood is symptomatic of its growing opposition to, and attempt to eradicate, the freedoms honored by a democratic state.

Of the many ironies exposed by *The Child in Time* one would undoubtedly strike Michel Foucault, and even Philippe Ariès, as inevitable: a society in which the child becomes a primary object of study is keenly interested in controlling, repressing, and even eradicating children. As it turns out, the author of the government's secret handbook proves well acquainted with the work of these and other cultural critics. Sounding very much like Ariès in *Centuries of Childhood,* the handbook states: "There was a time when children were treated like small adults. Childhood is an invention, a social construct, made possible by society as it increased in sophistication and resource." Quickly, however, the tone shifts to one more in keeping with the government's political agenda: "Above all, childhood is a privilege. No child as it grows older should be allowed to forget that its parents, as embodiments of society, are the ones who grant this privilege, and do so at their own expense" (105). The child must be taught gratitude not only to his or her parents but to that society of which the parents are embodiments. Inculcating gratitude, in other words, sows the seeds of compliance, not dissent: instructed as children to be grateful to those in authority, adults are unlikely to question that authority or to insist on their freedom from it.

As both Ariès and Foucault suggest, a culture's most hostile or repressive elements tend (except in times of social crisis) to operate beneath the surface. To assess their impact on the individual, one must delve beneath appearances to find out what is happening, so to speak, in the dark. A similar theme arises from the novel's patterning of events, particularly those in the subplot that centers on the character Charles Darke. A highly successful businessman and politician, Darke is Stephen's former publisher as well as his good friend. Only after Darke commits suicide, at the end of the novel, does Stephen discover him to be the secret author of the government's "shadow child–care manual" (239). In keeping with the novel's other ironic twists, the handbook that Darke authors radically contradicts the deeply romantic vision of childhood he harbors in his private life and fantasies. The alleged sentimentality toward children that Darke derides in the handbook is, as Stephen discovers, outlandishly expressed in his friend's pathetic attempt to relive his own boyhood.

The intensity of Darke's longing for his lost childhood—and for the child lost to his adult self—violently conflicts with his adult ambitions and notions of success. Many years earlier, when Stephen and Darke first meet, the latter impresses Stephen as being the quintessential "grown-up." Yet for all his "worldly confidence, dark suit," and authoritative manner, Darke is only six years older than Stephen. In the two decades of their friendship Darke sustains his outward posture of "lively maturity," delivering "lessons in worldliness" to Stephen "as though to a child" (216, 30). Already looking "like a scaled down version of his father" at the age of eight, Darke quickly took on the "self-important posture" of his elders, advertising his reverence for discipline, restraint, and material progress. Successful at an early age, he cannot reconcile his adult ambitions and persona with a profoundly disturbing sense that "he had missed out on" a real childhood (239–40). The greater his success and the more money he makes, the more "trapped" and "depressed" he secretly feels (241, 238). The powerful conflict between Darke's worldly ambitions and his nostalgia for childhood gradually brings on mental collapse; by the time he resigns his post as a junior government minister, he has already made a "half-hearted" attempt at suicide (239).

At this point Darke's wife, Thelma, takes her ailing husband to live in the Suffolk countryside in order, as she later says, "to let him be a little boy." Here he enacts a grotesque parody of the romantic idyll (239–40). Clothed in "baggy short pants" and armed with a slingshot, the "forty-nine-year-old schoolboy" fills his pockets with all the paraphernalia of childhood: bits of peppermint candy, a dried newt, and marbles (123, 130–31). This outlandishly staged regression strikes Stephen as a bizarrely academic affair, as though "his friend had combed libraries" in pursuit of the proper rituals and objects with which to furnish his boyhood idyll. "It was too correct to be convincing"; the effect is "fraudulent" (130). Echoing a line from Wordsworth's short poem "My Heart Leaps Up"—"The Child is father of the Man"— Darke often pleads with Stephen on behalf of "the forgotten child within the adult" (31). Still, the psychic integration of the adult and child self contemplated by the poet of *The Prelude* is not available to Darke. His desperate efforts to recapture his lost youth exhibit the same single-mindedness that drove him to become a businessman and politician. That same compulsive energy now fuels his histrionic imitation of a "successful prepubescent" (125).

Later, after Darke kills himself, Thelma again summons Stephen to their country retreat. Here she reveals that her late husband was the author of the government's handbook on child care. When Stephen voices surprise that Darke, the child idolater, could have endorsed such a harsh and repressive approach to childhood, Thelma points to the contradiction as "a perfect illustration of Charles's problem": "It was his fantasy life that drew him to the work [of writing the handbook], and it was his desire to please the boss [the prime minister] that made him write it the way he did. . . . He could never bring his qualities as a child . . . into his public life. Instead it was all frenetic compensation for what he took to be an excess of vulnerability. All this striving and shouting, cornering of markets, winning arguments to keep his weakness at bay" (242). The fatal rift between Darke's qualities as a child and his adult persona is, we gradually realize, a hidden (or dark) analogue of the rupture created in Stephen's and Julie's lives by the loss of their child.

Charles's case, Thelma goes on to explain, is "just an extreme form of a general problem." A physicist by training, she compares her husband's malaise with the one she detects in the "scientific establishment and the men who run it," as well as in "science itself" (242). The rupture between Darke's "forgotten child" and his adult persona, between his intuitive and analytic faculties, is symptomatic of a general problem afflicting postindustrial society. In a culture based on grinding competition, marketplace values, and scientific objectivity, the definition of adulthood has become too narrow—stripping whole areas of thought, feeling, and perception from adult life. As the character Professor Brody says in his address to Stephen's subcommittee, "we are divided, deeply divided from ourselves, from nature and its myriad processes, from our universe" (85). The polarized mentality that ultimately destroys Darke is emblematic of an unhealthy rift in the way that adults in Western culture have been trained, or conditioned, to think about themselves and reality. Having discredited what Joseph Chilton Pearce deems "magical thinking," they are divided against themselves; the rift can only be healed by an effective "reintegration of self and child."[5] This is the rift that Stephen must begin to heal if he hopes to reintegrate his shattered life and be reunited with his estranged wife. Clearly his resources for accomplishing this task must be discovered outside the governing ideas or principles of a culture founded on, and fostering, such internal division.

Stephen's road to recovery, which involves reclaiming the lost child while accepting Kate's loss, is based on a reawakened sense of continuity between his adult self and his child self. Undergoing experiences that take him beyond the conventional boundaries of time and space, Stephen rediscovers the child's gift of perception. To see the world as a whole, to exist not as an observer but as a participant, McEwan suggests, is the only way to reclaim the lost child. Darke's pathetic act of regression is, by contrast, based on a static notion of childhood, steeped in nostalgia and the impossible longing to "escape from time" and the responsibilities of adulthood (238). The idyll of childhood that Darke temporarily enacts in his Suffolk retreat proves as fragile as that constructed by Harriet and David Lovatt in *The Fifth Child*. In each case desire for escape is a trap, not a refuge from but a symptom of foundering social conditions and cultural malaise. Stephen's startling discovery not of a nostalgic escape from time but of the child *in* time—and of time as a fluid, fertile medium for growth—ultimately grants him the "sense of a fresh beginning" (107).

For much of the novel, however, Stephen remains, like his friend Darke, "trapped in the dark, enfolded with his loss" (151). Sitting in front of the television, "suck[ing]" like a baby on a "tilted" bottle of scotch, he is the very picture of regressive behavior (144). Meanwhile, his lost child, Kate, is "getting harder to recall. She was fading, and all the time his useless love was swelling, encumbering and disfiguring him like a goiter" (151). Like Beloved's swelling stomach, which cannot deliver her permanently into existence, Stephen's swelling love becomes increasingly futile, not fertile. Filled with remorse, encumbered by regret, he can only look back at what he has lost; cut off from the present, he cannot imagine a future. At this point, nearly three years after Kate's disappearance, mourning is more than a habit. It is a "deep disposition" that has become a form of fixation akin to Darke's (2). If "Charles's case" is, as Thelma contends, "an extreme form of a general problem," Stephen also fits that general category. "Floundering" in his misery, transfixed by loss, he has ceased to participate in life; he has retreated, in Thelma's words, to a state of "catatonia" (242–43).

While Thelma's admonishments strike home, they are not entirely fair to Stephen at the time she delivers them. During the proceeding few months he has made a concerted effort to get back into life and can recognize some progress. Having cut his drinking "down to a single shot of spirits a day," he has even resumed writing (186, 179). To break his inertia, he has subjected himself to the rigors of learning classical Arabic and improving his tennis game. It is Stephen's tennis coach, in fact, who has roundly criticized him for the inertia and passivity also noted by Thelma: "You're passive. You're mentally enfeebled. You wait for things to happen, you stand there hoping they're going to go your way.... You're inert, spineless, you're half asleep.... You're not all here. Even as I'm speaking to you now you're not all here.... Wake up!" (185). As the novel gradually reveals, Stephen's need to wake up derives from a passive "disposition" that has characterized his life since long before Kate's disappearance. The torpor brought on by her loss is only an "extreme case" of his "general problem."

Indicative of Stephen's lifelong passivity is his career as a children's author, which is the result of a fluke: "That Stephen Lewis had a lot of money and was famous among schoolchildren was the consequence of a clerical error, a moment's inattention in the operation of the internal post at Gott's," a prominent London publishing house headed by Darke (25). After graduating from University College, London, and making a standard 1960s' generation "hashish-befuddled tour of Turkey, Afghanistan and the Northwest Frontier Province," Stephen, still in his twenties, returns home. Settling in London, he prepares to make his contribution to "the European cultural tradition, the grown-up one," by becoming a writer. Instead of writing about his travels and calling his work *Hashish,* as originally intended, he winds up writing about his "eleventh year with two girl cousins" on a summer holiday (27–29).

The manuscript of Stephen's novel, *Lemonade,* lands by mistake on the desk of Gott's children's books editor. After reading it, both the editor and her boss, Darke, are wildly enthusiastic about the book, which they insist was written for children. When Stephen attempts to correct their "terrible mistake," Darke offers an eloquent argument to the contrary, telling him: "You've spoken directly to children. Whether you wanted to or not, you've communicated with them across the abyss that separates the child from the adult and you've given them a first, ghostly intimation of their mortality" (28, 33). Darke's enthusiastic response to Stephen's novel derives from his deep-seated nostalgia for childhood, at which he can only gaze from "across the abyss." As Thelma explains to Stephen some twenty years later, after Charles's suicide, "*Lemonade* was very important to him. He said it was one part of himself addressing the other." Still, as Thelma points out, "conventional ambition is hard to break with"; Darke never heals the rift in his psyche, the abyss that separates him from the creative wellsprings of life (238–39).

Perhaps because Stephen's first novel speaks so profoundly to Darke's sense of lost childhood, Darke insists that Stephen "package it for kids." Insulted by the characterization of his novel as a children's book, Stephen haughtily declares, "I won't permit it. I'll never permit it." As the narrative ironically reveals in the following paragraph, however, *Lemonade* is duly packaged for kids. Validating Darke's intuition, the novel sells "a quarter of a million copies in hardback, and eventually several million around the world." Stephen buys a fast car and a large apartment, generating "a tax bill that two years later made it a virtual necessity to publish his second novel as a children's book too" (34). Nothing about his passive behavior is particularly unusual— except, of course, the extraordinary success with which it meets. Conventional success, one might say, is as hard to break with as conventional ambition. That Stephen cannot imagine being anything *but* a children's author at this point in his life suggests, nonetheless, that his creative and professional identity has been determined by external forces. Like Darke, he has sacrificed his original goals for worldly success. That many other adults have done the same only points to the "general problem" delineated in the text.

Stephen's urgent need to wake up from his passive, halfhearted existence is evinced from the novel's opening. While the novel's design is too subtle to suggest any facile cause-and-effect relationship between Stephen's adult passivity and the loss of his child, the faint hint of a connection does emerge. The moment Kate disappears is characterized by that same inattention, that same tendency toward automatic behavior, for which he is later chided by his tennis coach. Far from being peculiar to Stephen, such inattention strikes McEwan's readers as all too familiar; it is the same mechanical consciousness in which many of us drift through our daily lives: "He was intent on ordinary tasks, keen to finish them. He was barely conscious of being at all" (13). In this state of semiconsciousness the child is literally and figuratively lost. Kate disappears, in other words, at the very moment Stephen's adult consciousness is closed off from awareness. Cut off from "the child in time," he has ceased to participate in the present.

In contrast to this state of distraction, the child's curiosity and wonder offer the adult concrete "lessons in celebrating the specific," demonstrating "how to fill the present and be filled by it." Recalling Kate's gift for living in the present, Stephen thinks to himself that "if he could do everything with such intensity and abandonment," he "would be a happy man of extraordinary powers." He goes on to reflect, "wasn't that Nietzsche's idea of true maturity, to attain the seriousness of a child at play?" (121–22). Far from regressing from adult life, Stephen would reclaim "for the man," or grown-up, the child's intensity of perception and participation in life. The goal is not, as poor Darke would have it, to escape from time and adult responsibility by retreating into "fake boyhood" (216).

Stephen's journey toward true maturity, the process by which he wakes up to existence and discovers how to participate more fully in it, begins with the loss of his child. Kate's disappearance shatters the complacent routine of his life as it shatters his marriage. As many similarly discover when catastrophe strikes, the conventional wisdom by which we tend to live, automatically and half consciously, proves inadequate or useless in times of crisis. Hurled into stark confrontation with themselves, each other, and their environment, Stephen and Julie must summon more courage, insight, and awareness than were ever demanded of them before. In an analogous if less forgiving way, Harriet Lovatt's domestic idyll is shattered by the birth of her fifth child. Ben's presence, not his loss, compels her to confront what others, in their conventional wisdom and authority, insist on not seeing.

In *The Child in Time* the stages of Stephen's interior journey are marked by a series of literal journeys, each of which ends in a telling insight or epiphany. In nearly every case the revelation involves an experience of time that radically diverges from the conventional version. Represented in the novel by the clocks of quotidian life (Stephen's parents meet in a department store over a broken clock) is the linear, mechanical version of time measured in minutes and hours. Within that framework, signaled by the sudden expansion or "slowing of time," Stephen discovers a dimension of "meaningful time" intimately linked with the child's image (106, 251). When, for example, he makes his initial visit to Thelma and Charles at their cottage in Suffolk, he humors his friend by climbing to the tree house Charles has constructed high up in a beech tree. Though appalled by the "absurdity" of his middle-aged friend's appearance and behavior, Stephen has a sudden insight when faced with making his way up the dangerous, seemingly "endless, vertiginous branching" of the tall tree. Aware that he is "risking his life," he has to summon all his powers of concentration to keep from crashing to the ground. At this crucial moment he realizes that he cannot afford to be half conscious, half in the moment and half outside it: "It occurred to him fleetingly that he was engrossed, fully in the moment. Quite simply, if he allowed another thought to distract him, he would fall out of the tree" (127).

Here a life-or-death situation thrusts Stephen into that mode of existing *in* time—of "fill[ing] the present and be[ing] filled by it"—that he has earlier identified with the child, for whom "the moment [is] everything" (121). Earlier that day, on his way to the Darkes' cottage, Stephen has had another near brush with death. Speeding along the highway, he barely manages to avoid crashing into a huge pink truck that has jackknifed in front of him. By fully concentrating on the moment, Stephen saves himself from disaster. Instead of becoming distracted by fear or trying to analyze the situation, he exercises a form of "magical thinking." Relaxing *into* the moment, he "imagine[s] himself into the [six-foot] gap" between a "road sign and the front bumper" of "the upended lorry"—and miraculously drives through it. As though expanded by Stephen's vital participation in the moment, time appears to slow down; and "in this slowing of time, there was a sense of a fresh beginning" (106–7). Afterward, Stephen's sense of rebirth is validated by his rescue of the truck driver stuck in the overturned cab, his head "protrud[ing] from a vertical gash in the steel" (109–10). As Stephen pulls the man's body from the "dark chamber" of the crushed cab, his rescue graphically simulates the delivery of a newborn child into the world (111–12). Here and throughout, the novel signals the principal stages of Stephen's recovery, his renewed participation in existence, with images of birth and rebirth. The image of the child, particularly the newborn, serves once again as a sign of hope: the embodiment of humankind at its most potent, poised on the threshold of a fresh beginning.

Such intense participation in the moment, or the fullness of time, is utterly lacking in Darke's studied and static reconstruction of boyhood, with its regulation-style short pants, slingshot, and sticky sweets. Graphically hinting at the sterility of Charles's regression is the image that concludes Stephen's visit to his friend's tree house. Summoned to dinner by Thelma at the end of the day, Charles exits the tree house through a hole he has cut in its platform. As Stephen waits for his friend to descend below him, he observes Darke's middle-aged "head show[ing] above the level of the platform" just before it disappears, in a kind of reverse birth, through "the hole" (131). This image suggests the most extreme and unnatural form of regression: an attempt to return to the womb. In a sense, that is exactly what Darke does. In his desire to regress, he forces his wife to serve as his mother and nurse. The image of Darke's head disappearing down the hole offers a dramatic contrast to the truck driver Joe's head emerging from the gash in the truck cab from which Stephen delivers him. The awakening that attends Joe's brush with death prompts him, moreover, to stop running away from his adult responsibilities. Realizing how much he loves his wife and children, he promptly composes a good-bye letter to his girlfriend (114–15).

One of the most significant stages of Stephen's journey toward awakening and the recovery of the lost child occurs early in the novel, when he visits Julie in Kent several months after their separation. After disembarking the train, Stephen walks the three miles to Julie's cottage through the lush countryside, taking "childish—or boyish—pleasure" in his surroundings (54). Recalling how, as a child "waiting for a train" with his father, he had "marveled" at "the intricate relation of things, the knowingness of the inanimate," Stephen enters a similar state of wonder during which "all sense of progress, and therefore all sense of [linear or conventional] time, disappeared" (55). What happens to Stephen shortly after he crosses this "prairie" and reaches "the pines on the other side" is even more mysterious (60). His earlier apprehension of the knowingness of the inanimate, of nature as a conscious presence reciprocating one's awareness of it, is now infused with intense déjà vu: "He had never been here before, not as a child, not as an adult." Yet he "knew this spot intimately, as if over a long period of time," and he experiences "a kind of ache, of familiarity, of coming to a place that knew him too, and seemed . . . to expect him" (60–61). In short, he recognizes "the call of the place, its knowingness, the longing it evinced" (62).

Arriving at a pub called The Bell, Stephen looks in the window and is startled to see his parents, albeit four decades younger, seated at a table, engrossed in conversation. For a breathless moment his mother looks in his direction, but Stephen has the impression that "she could not see him." He is a "phantom beyond the spotted glass," a "spirit suspended between existence and nothingness." Suspended out of time, he believes he is observing his parents before he entered existence

(64). Stephen arrives at Julie's cottage in a state of shock and near collapse. Later, when he describes his vision to his mother, who calls it a "hallucination," she confirms that she and his father were at The Bell forty-four years earlier and that they had ridden there on bicycles closely resembling the ones Stephen sees parked outside the pub. More importantly, she recalls glancing across the saloon bar "to the window by the door" and seeing "the face of a child" gazing at her. "It was staring into the pub. It had a kind of pleading look. . . . Thinking about it over the years, I realize it was probably the landlord's boy," she adds, "or some kid off one of the local farms. But as far as I was concerned then, I was convinced, I just *knew* that I was looking at my own child. If you like, I was looking at you" (207).

The revelation that Stephen's mother now matter-of-factly dismisses as a case of subjective, distorted vision has proved crucial not only to her life but to Stephen's. Indeed, he would not *have* a life if this vision had not occurred. It is Stephen's unborn life that the young, as yet unmarried couple are discussing in The Bell. Before this crucial moment Stephen's pregnant mother, convinced that her fiancé does not want her to have the baby, has privately resolved to have an abortion. Suddenly, however, with the appearance of the child's face at the window, the unborn fetus is no longer "an abstraction": "The baby, her baby, was suddenly flesh. It was holding her in its gaze, claiming her. . . . It was at the window now, a complete self, begging for its existence, and it was inside her, unfolding intricately, living off the pulse of her own blood. It wasn't a pregnancy they should be discussing; it was a person." Knowing "herself to be in love with" this child, her child, Stephen's mother breaks free from the "passive spirit" that has held her in thrall. Recognizing that "this [is] her responsibility and . . . her time," she decides, then and there, that she is "having the baby" and "having this husband" (207–8).

Just as Stephen simultaneously experiences, within an expanded present, two discrete moments of linear or sequential time, his mother recognizes in a single instant that her child is both the unborn fetus in her womb and the child peering in at the window. All that prevents such experiences of temporal fullness from being regarded as reasonable, or sane, is the conventional notion of time. But as Thelma's discussions with Stephen on the subject of time eloquently suggest, such conventional wisdom is being challenged everyday by "a whole supermarket of theories" proposed by contemporary physicists, philosophers, and

astronomers. In discussing these theories, Thelma even cites an actual
scientist, the physicist and philosopher David Bohm, whom she identifies as her "colleague" at Birkbeck College and whose work has
had an obvious influence on McEwan. (Bohm's ideas are reflected not
only in Thelma's theoretical speculations on time but in Stephen's immediate and unorthodox experiences of it, most notably in the scene
at The Bell.)[6] "Whatever time is," Thelma observes, "the commonsense, everyday version of it as linear, regular, absolute, marching from
. . . the past through the present to the future, is either nonsense or a
tiny fraction of the truth. . . . In relativity theory, time is dependent on
the speed of the observer. What are simultaneous events to one person
can appear in sequence to another. There's no absolute, generally recognized 'now'" (135–36).

More important than any theoretical argument is the immediate
effect that the experience of expanded, "meaningful time" has on both
Stephen and his mother at The Bell (251). Not only does this moment
of insight save Stephen's unborn life; it significantly contributes to his
sense of rebirth, of gradual reawakening to existence during the
course of the novel. In his case as in his mother's, an epiphany shatters
the "passive spirit" holding him in thrall. As he stands outside The Bell
gazing at his young parents through the window, Stephen discovers
the cold weight of nonexistence. His misery at being excluded from
the human world is described in terms that might well be claimed by
Sethe's slaughtered child, Beloved: "A cold, infant despondency sank
through him, a bitter sense of exclusion and longing" (64). As Stephen
turns away from the window, estranged from the moment his future
parents are sharing, he is engulfed by despair—the despair of being
nothing and nowhere:

> He was light, made of nothing. He did not see himself walk back
> along the road. He fell back down, dropped helplessly through a void,
> was swept dumbly through invisible curves, and rose above the trees,
> saw the horizon below him even as he was hurled through sinuous
> tunnels of undergrowth. . . . His eyes grew large and round and lidless
> with desperate, protesting innocence, his knees rose under him and
> touched his chin, his fingers were scaly flippers, gills beat time, urgent,
> hopeless strokes through the salty ocean that engulfed the treetops
> and surged between their roots; and for all the crying, calling sounds
> he thought were his own, he formed a single thought: he had nowhere
> to go, no moment that could embody him, he was not expected, no

destination or time could be named. . . . And this thought unwrapped
a sadness that was not his own. It was centuries, millennia old. It swept
through him and countless others like the wind through a field of
grass. (65–66)

Like a fetus recapitulating in reverse the species' phylogenetic stages,
Stephen feels himself borne back through countless millennia to the
primordial salty ocean. Here, in these infinite stretches—this void
without consciousness or history, destination or time—he experiences
the ancient sadness of a universe before the dawn of humankind.
Rising above the trees like a lost bird crying and calling out from
nowhere, he is literally aeons away from that joyous sense of freedom
the Romantics identified with the flight of birds. Thus the poet of
The Prelude exults in his flight from "the vast city," in being "Free as a
bird to settle where I will" (book 1, ll. 7, 9).

By contrast, Stephen's birdlike self discovers a horrifying wilderness where human memory offers no resistance to the wind of imper-
manence sweeping through it. This sad oblivion recalls the primordial
void into which Beloved vanishes at the end of Morrison's novel:
"By and by all trace is gone, and what is forgotten is not only the footprints but the water too. . . . The rest is weather. Not the breath of the
disremembered and unaccounted for, but wind in the eaves, or spring
ice thawing too quickly. Just weather" (*Beloved* 275). In this primordial
wilderness Stephen discovers the utter desolation of nonbeing. In the
final, paradoxical sentence that closes the long passage describing his
sad epiphany, he, like Beloved, can call nothing his own: "Nothing was
his own, not his strokes or his movement, not the calling sounds, not
even the sadness, nothing was nothing's own" (66). Stephen has not even
a self to claim in the act of disclaiming his right to claim anything.

As indebted as *The Child in Time* is to the Romantic image of childhood, passages like this demonstrate the changes McEwan (along with
other contemporary writers, from Nabokov to DeLillo) rings on the
traditional theme while honoring its legacy. Just as the novelist undermines the Romantics' celebration of flight in Stephen's anguished
vision—in which the fetus wanders homeless, like a lost bird soaring
through infinite wastes—he radically undercuts their nostalgia for a
lost paradise. "Our birth is but a sleep and a forgetting," Wordsworth
writes in the immortality ode, a poem that postulates a perfect first
world lost to us in this one (l. 58). In his vision at The Bell, on the other
hand, Stephen cries out for mortal existence. Contrary to Wordsworth,

he discovers that "our birth" is a splendid awakening, that the human being's true home is not some platonic realm transcending time but existence in the here and now. All the joy and radiance that Wordsworth attributes to "a glory" that "hath passed away," Stephen discovers on earth, in the universe inhabited by human beings (l. 18). If, as has been suggested, the image of the lost child operates on virtually every plane of this novel, so does its counterimage: the child not lost but found, not absent but present, not outside time but in it. It is this hopeful image of childhood, announced in the novel's title, that McEwan ultimately constructs for his readers.

After his vision at The Bell, Stephen somehow makes his way to Julie's doorstep, where he apparently collapses. Sometime later, he wakes up in the bed, a "wedding gift from friends," that they have shared for years as a married couple. Silently acknowledging "that this was where he belonged," he and Julie temporarily rediscover their old intimacy and make love in their "marriage bed" (66–67, 72). In the darkening room Stephen feels profoundly at "home" not only with Julie but in time and space. As time "assume[s] purpose all over again," he discovers himself at the farthest possible reach from the oblivious void of nonbeing. No longer excluded from the world, he belongs intimately to it. Rejoicing at the way that "biology, existence, matter itself had dreamed this [lovemaking] up for its own pleasure and perpetuity," Stephen once again senses the reciprocity or "knowingness of the inanimate." This universe must be "benevolent," he affirms; "it likes us, it wants us to like it, it likes itself" (71–72). Soon, however, this joyful moment passes. Stephen and Julie recognize once again that "the daughter they did not have was waiting for them." The "lost child was between them again," and both must deal with her loss in their own way (72).

By what the narrator calls "a perverse collusion in unhappiness," nine months pass before Stephen and Julie come together again (74). At this time, and as if to confirm the benevolence of this "place" or universe, Julie is on the verge of giving birth to their second child— conceived on that fateful afternoon (72). After waiting nine months in silence, she summons Stephen to her side; having come to terms with Kate's loss, she is again ready to face being a mother and a wife. Meanwhile, Stephen, though unaware that Julie is pregnant, gradually senses that he is "in training for an undisclosed event; he expected change" (186). As he grapples with his loss and inertia during the ensuing months, he comes to accept the fact "that Kate was no longer a living presence, she was not an invisible girl at his side"; and this recognition paves the way for a fresh beginning (179). Although he knows "he [is] still in the shadows," he is able to think more and more of "tides turning, fresh winds, shadows lifting" (186). Among the many images of Julie that he calls to mind during this period of gestation, there is one in which, for no ostensible reason, "she look[s] pregnant" (160). As though inspired by this subliminal premonition of fertile "increase," Stephen is able to "remove the dustcover from his typewriter" and resume his writing (179).

Making his way to Julie's cottage for a second time, Stephen feels "the imperative of his summons" as "a cold thrill," even though he is still unaware, consciously at least, of its significance. When, however, he arrives once more at The Bell, he suddenly grasps the meaning of Julie's summons. In a flash of "recognition" he sees that "all the sorrow, all the empty waiting, had been enclosed within meaningful time, within the richest unfolding conceivable" (251). Now he knows that his earlier experience at The Bell had "been a continuation, a kind of repetition" of a crucial moment in his parents' lives. His mother's discovery of her love for her unborn child is now informed and expanded by Stephen's revelation that he and Julie are blessed with a second child.

Arriving at Julie's cottage, Stephen's joyful "premonition" is fulfilled (251). Swelling the "dignified and potent" body of his wife is the announcement of their new baby: "What had grown in her was not confined to the womb but was coiled in every cell" (254). As Julie recounts to Stephen the stages of her reaction to this second pregnancy —which went from "thinking seriously about an abortion" to realizing what a "gift" had been given them—she also describes the painful process of coming to terms with Kate's loss: "I came out here to face up to losing Kate. . . . If I didn't face it, I thought I could go under. There were some bad, bad days when I wanted to die. . . . I had to stop running after her in my mind. I had to go on loving her, but I had to stop desiring her" (254). After Stephen listens to his wife's painful account of her ordeal, which in many ways parallels his own, they begin, "three years late," to "cry together at last for the lost, irreplaceable child who would not grow older for them." While he and Julie "could never redeem the loss of their daughter, they would love her through their new child" (256).

Able to mourn the loss of their child—the child lost to time, the child who will never grow old with them—Stephen and Julie can begin to create a new life together, as they have already conceived a new life in Julie's womb. At the end of the novel they are ready to face the "harsh world" and "take their love," embodied in their newborn child, with them into it. Such acts of renewal, participation in life's increase and direction, have proved beyond the scope of Charles Darke's longing. Unable to stop desiring the lost child of his own lost youth, Darke remains literally and figuratively sterile. Even the mode of his suicide—after undressing and "put[ting] himself out in the cold," he freezes to death—signifies his estrangement from life. Unable to integrate the child he was with the adult he becomes, Darke makes suicide his final act of regression. "As suicides go," Thelma tells Stephen, "it was petulant and childish" (242). If time robs us of our first world, it also affords the possibility of growth and development. As the novel's title indicates, the child exists in time and is destined to grow up. In adulthood the child's promise is fulfilled, not denied.

At the end of *The Child in Time* Julie's contractions begin in earnest. After running to call the midwife, Stephen returns to find that she will arrive too late. As he watches the "protruding head" emerging from Julie's womb—an image prefigured by Stephen's delivery of Joe, the truck driver, from his cab—he has another "revelation" of what it means to come into this world. Unlike his initial vision at The Bell, however, mortality is now seen from the happy perspective of the living, not from the void of nonexistence. Announcing in no uncertain terms that *"I am here,"* the fledgling emerging from Julie's body is "both inert and intent." Inert because not yet born, it is nonetheless intent on arrival. (Hence the vital distinction between the fledgling's inert body and Darke's frozen corpse, which Stephen could barely carry back to the cottage from the woods where he found his dead friend [236].) With "clarity and precision of purpose," this fetus, Stephen perceives, is *demanding* to be born: "It was not alive, it was a head on the block, and yet [its] demand was clear and pressing. *This was my move. Now what is yours?*" (261). Here, as in the moment Stephen's mother experiences at The Bell, the unborn child appears "begging" for "its existence" (207).

The child demanding life is at the same time a gift *from* life. "This is really all we have got," Stephen thinks to himself, "this increase, this matter of life loving itself; everything we have has to come from this"

(261). As Julie gives birth, Stephen sees "in an instant how active and generous the verb"—to *give* birth—"really is." Rejoicing in the generosity of life, the wonderful "home" their child has safely entered, Stephen and Julie lie together on their bed, keeping the infant warm between them. Through the window above they watch the white moon, followed by Mars, descend "through a sky that was turning blue" (262–63). On the threshold of a new morning and a new life together, they gaze at their "beautiful child."

Beyond the window, however, an angry planet trails the peaceful moon, reminding the couple of the discordant world that, with the dawn, awaits them. Far from being the "feminist romance" that critics such as Ryan Kiernan have labeled it, *The Child in Time* does not depict the intimate circle of family life, Lessing's domestic "fortress," as a refuge from the strife-torn world. In the family's constellation, so to speak, the angry planet Mars is always in the ascendant. Inhabiting a genre that, according to Margaret Doody, "best describes and interprets the dynamics of family life," McEwan's protagonists honor their origins. Like countless other novelistic characters, they return "to be reunited with the original constellation" of the family. But, as Doody adds, "that is never a simple homecoming": if the novel stays truthful to its subject, "what once existed is not restored."[7]

While the ending of *The Child in Time* has been called unduly optimistic, or even sentimental, it hardly suggests that the past can be restored.[8] Kate will continue to be the "lost, irreplaceable child" who can be neither retrieved nor forgotten. Stephen and Julie must do their best to integrate her memory with the new life on which they are embarked. Thus, "while they can never redeem the loss of their daughter," they resolve to "love her through their new child" (256). The embattled world, under the planet Mars, will continue to exact losses on the living and grind against the fragile structure of the family. Still, at the heart of existence—this "place" that "likes us" and "likes itself"—is the "idea of home" that Stephen and Julie discover in each other and their new child (72, 253).

Unlike Harriet and David Lovatt in *The Fifth Child,* the Lewises do not assume that they can find safety in retreat. Nor do they expect, or want, to escape from time into an idyllic past. Stephen and Julie are ready "to take their love" with them into the "harsh world." Armed with the idea of home, as the turtle is protected by its shell, the soldier by his armor, Stephen and Julie will carry that shelter and that shield with them into the fray. Whether home means one's family, friends, nation, planet, or universe, it is an idea that must be actively lived and fought for. For the moment, however, they can bask in the "triumph and wonder" of their newborn, this tiny creature "pulsing" with life. Here, in this radiant image of childhood, all their hope and joy lie miraculously coiled, ready to unfold with the child in time.

CHAPTER

11

The Child as Mysterious Agent
DeLillo's *White Noise*

Like McEwan's *The Child in Time,* Don DeLillo's eighth novel, *White Noise* (1985), takes family life as its setting and focus, exploring the relationship between adult and child. An early scene in this quintessentially American novel bears particular comparison with McEwan's British one: here the youngest member of the Gladney clan, two-year-old Wilder, disappears in a supermarket in the suburban community of Blacksmith, which the author locates somewhere in middle America. To everyone's relief (including the reader's) Wilder is soon found; but the dread of loss, the pervasive sense of danger threatening the contemporary child's (and adult's) well-being, haunts the atmosphere like the mysterious toxic cloud that eventually darkens the sky.

Children appear in several of DeLillo's works, but *White Noise* is his lone foray into the domestic novel. As Frank Lentricchia points out, however, DeLillo "deploys that popular literary form" in ways that undermine the genre's more complacent effects. Here, as in his other fiction, DeLillo performs a kind of cultural anatomy—exposing, in Lentricchia's words, "the large and nearly invisible things [that] invade our kitchens, the various coercive environments within which the so-called private life is led."[1] From the airborne toxic event that forces the Gladney family and hordes of others to evacuate their homes; to the insidious waves, particles, and radiation invisibly at work in the environment; to the "dull and unlocatable roar," or "white noise," humming through the atmosphere and in the human brain, DeLillo catalogs the invasive elements of postindustrial culture as they steadily erode the borders between public and private life (36).

At the center of every American household drones the television, and in front of every set the nation's children sit transfixed by electronic images and sounds. "Kids," says Murray Jay Siskind, one of Jack Gladney's colleagues at the College-on-the-Hill, "are a true universal": they have not yet lost their "group identity," do not yet "feel estranged from the products" they consume. Employing the language of Rousseau and Wordsworth to parodic effect, Murray calls attention to the bizarre transformation of the romantic child by consumer culture. It is no longer the poet's faith in natural innocence or the philosopher's ideal conception of human nature that sustains the child's privileged image; rather, it is the crucial position that children occupy "in the marketing scheme." The culture of late capitalism, DeLillo satirically implies, has little use for any concept of self or identity that is not "targetable by advertisers and mass-producers of culture" (50).

A caricature of the postmodern family set adrift in consumer culture, the Gladney clan is a mélange of half siblings and stepsiblings. Existing at the far end of that powerful social phenomenon, no-fault divorce—whose stupendous impact James already noted at the turn of the century in *What Maisie Knew*—the Gladney children take their convoluted family histories for granted. Their parents (or stepparents), Jack and Babette, have been married a total of eight times: Jack five times (twice to the same woman), Babette three. The "family trees of the children living in the Gladney household," notes Thomas Ferraro, parody "the state of domestic art in contemporary middle America." As Ferraro's list of the Gladney offspring indicates, the children's genealogies also reflect the bizarre configurations of a culture whose constant flow of consumer goods and novel lifestyles depends on global security, political intrigue, and technological advancement at any cost:

> Heinrich, fourteen, from the marriage of Jack to Janet Savory (who as Mother Devi runs a profitable ashram in Tubb, Montana); Denise, eleven, from the marriage of Babette to Bob Pardee (who raises money for the legal defense fund of the nuclear industry); Steffie, a couple or so years younger than Denise, from the marriage of Jack and Dana Breedlove (who is a CIA courier in the third world); and Wilder, two, from the marriage of Babette to an unnamed "researcher" in the outback of Australia. Heinrich has a sister living with their mother; Wilder has a brother living with their father; Jack has at least one more daughter (Bee) from his middle wife (Tweedy Browner).

Summing up the "fearful symmetry" of the Gladney household, Ferraro notes that everyone in it "lives with five other people, *each of whom* is related on average by no more than . . . 20 percent to *everyone else* in the house." Not one child "is living with both parents or even a full brother or sister. Above all, the current assemblage has not been together longer than Wilder's two years of age, and in all probability less than that."[2]

The shifting sands on which the Gladney household is founded may appear to defy definition, but such vagaries attest to the contingent nature of domestic life in contemporary America. In the Gladneys' continual realignment of relationships, only the faintest outlines of the traditional family—that once stable institution held together by strong bonds of kinship, hallowed bloodlines, and a sacred covenant—can be detected. In the postmodern universe of *White Noise* the family looks like one more simulacrum—a copy, à la Jean Baudrillard, for which there is no discernible original—in a world of endless simulation.[3] Here no one can even remember what "the most photographed barn in America" looked like before it was photographed (12–13). Reality has become "virtual," nature thoroughly reified: "CABLE HEALTH, CABLE WEATHER, CABLE NEWS, CABLE NATURE" (231). All the more remarkable, therefore, is the sense of wonder permeating the Gladney household; its contingent and haphazard structure notwithstanding, the family operates as a source of mystery and awe within the novel. In the bosom of the postmodern family (and even here the maternal image of warmth and closeness is relevant), DeLillo's readers discover what Lentricchia calls the "poetry" of commitment: "a commitment to the possibility, however laid waste by contemporary forces, of domesticity as the life support we cannot do without."[4]

As head of the household, the novel's narrator, Jack Gladney, is acutely aware of his dependence on both wife and children, from whom he draws psychic as well as physical sustenance. Yet the sense of wonder and awe, indeed of sacred reverence, inspired in him by his children (whether his or Babette's) stems from something greater than practical or emotional need. Even in the midst of a routine family dinner, observing the Gladney children as they trade "looks and glances" and engage in all the "teeming interactions" that constitute domestic life, Jack marvels at the wondrous nature of the ordinary. As he says at one point, "family life [is] the one medium of sense knowledge in which an astonishment of heart is routinely contained" (117). With that adverb, "routinely," Jack underscores the extraordinary power and impact of the seemingly ordinary. This "sense of the importance of daily life and of ordinary moments," DeLillo said in an interview, is what he tries to convey in his fiction. "In *White Noise,* in particular," he added, "I tried to find a kind of radiance in dailiness," "a sense of something extraordinary hovering just beyond our touch and just beyond our vision."[5]

Even in the spectral universe of *Libra* (1988), in which DeLillo depicts Lee Harvey Oswald as a puppet created and destroyed by the shadowy agents of political intrigue, the unlikely figure of a child beams signals from that transcendent plane of reality the author locates "beyond our vision." In a scene reminiscent of *White Noise* Win Everett, a retired Central Intelligence Agency man trapped, like everyone else in the novel, in a maze of plots and counterplots, experiences his own version of Gladney's "astonishment of heart" when, sitting in his daughter's room, he listens to the child read aloud from a book: "It was uncanny how these tales affected him, gave him a sense of what it was like to be a child again. He found he could lose himself in the sound of her voice. He searched her face, believing he could see what she saw, line by line, in the grave and fateful progress of a tale. His eyes went bright. He felt a joy so strong it might be measured in the language of angelic orders, of powers and dominations. They were alone in a room that was itself alone, a room that hung above the world" (*Libra* 220–21). Soon the transcendent moment is over, and Everett finds himself back downstairs, caught up once again in a labyrinth of endless lies and plots, unable to find "a way out of fear and premonition" (221). No matter how short-lived, however, these unexpected moments of transcendence cast a mysterious light, a kind of metaphysical glow, on the postmodern character of DeLillo's fiction, puzzling many of his readers and critics.

According to Michael Valdez Moses, the "increasingly nonreferential character of postmodern culture" is what DeLillo's novels brilliantly expose: "Since the technological media . . . ultimately create their own reality, they appear to . . . possess the seemingly limitless power to transform and reconstitute the very being of the contemporary individual."[6] In *White Noise* the Gladney family, most particularly the children, are caught in the force field of that media culture, subjected to an onslaught of advertisements and images that vibrate like white noise in their brains. Yet these children possess special powers of discernment

and knowledge—as though they, like Wordsworth's child, had entered
the world "trailing clouds of glory" from some prior realm of being.
Hinting at the secret store of knowledge that children acquire from
some primal or preconscious condition, Jack declares, "I take these
children seriously. It is not possible to see too much in them. . . . It is
all there, in full force, charged waves of identity and being. There are
no amateurs in the world of children" (103). Viewed in this light, the
most unexpected, indeed radical feature of *White Noise* is not its clever
take on consumer culture or the humor it wrests from horrific events;
rather, it is the way that such late-twentieth-century material yields,
under the author's deft hand, a provocative new version of the Romantics' myth of childhood.

True, DeLillo's fiction ceaselessly undermines modernist and pre-
modernist notions of transcendence. Yet his novels evince both a faith
in and a "fascination with children" that not only recalls his Romantic
predecessors but complicates his postmodernist label. "I think we feel,"
DeLillo told an interviewer, "that children have a direct route to, have
direct contact to the kind of natural truth that eludes us as adults. . . .
There is something they know but can't tell us. Or there is something
they remember which we've forgotten." DeLillo said that his fiction
"has always been informed by mystery," which "weaves in and out of
[his] work" and leaves the novels "open-ended." He added, "I can't tell
you where it came from or what it leads to. Possibly it is the natural
product of a Catholic upbringing." Raised a Roman Catholic and
educated at Fordham University—where, he says, "the Jesuits taught
me to be a failed ascetic"—DeLillo admits to exploring in his work
the "important subjects, eternal subjects" treated by religious thinkers.[7] This is not to suggest that his works are religious in the customary
sense. The visionary moments recorded in *White Noise* are, as Jack
admits, distinctly secular in context and effect. Clearly, however, the
sense of mystery permeating DeLillo's fiction implies something more
than the scientist's or the positivist's definition of the unknown—
more, that is, than a problem awaiting solution.

The mystery that surrounds DeLillo's characters, the persistent
sense of a source operating just beyond our apprehension and understanding, comes closer to the force or power defined by the French
Catholic philosopher and writer Gabriel Marcel. Mystery, Marcel
points out, is not a problem human beings are capable of solving but a
condition in which they exist: "a genuine problem is subject to an

appropriate technique by the exercise of which it is defined; whereas a mystery, by definition, transcends every conceivable technique." In his *Metaphysical Journal* Marcel draws the distinction in another way: "What is unknown and does not know is merely ignored. What knows and does not wish to be known, and proceeds in such a way as not to be known, is mysterious."[8]

In *White Noise* Jack's intimations of a transcendent realm of being are informed by this potent sense of the unknown. Serving as agent or emissary of this mystery is the child, who appears vitally in contact with what DeLillo calls "natural truth." Thus, as Jack gazes into the eyes of his twelve-year-old daughter, Bee, he discovers a living message, like a "secondary sea-life moving deep" in the "optic fluids" of her eye and containing both "the subject matter and its hidden implications" (95). In a language that adults appear to have forgotten—one that transcends conventional speech and is indecipherable by them—the child signals her profound connection to the unfathomable source of being.[9]

Jack's deepest contact with his children comes not in conversation but through those "extrasensory flashes and floating nuances of being" wordlessly transmitted from child to parent. Cherishing these "pockets of rapport," Jack thinks of family life as a "magic act, adults and children together, sharing unaccountable things" (34). It is when they are asleep, however, when consciousness yields to the dreaming or preconscious self, that Jack's children—specifically the younger ones, Steffie and Wilder—strike him as emissaries from some other, profounder realm of being (154). As he tells the reader, "Watching children sleep makes me feel devout, part of a spiritual system. It is the closest I can come to God. If there is a secular equivalent of standing in a great spired cathedral with marble pillars and streams of mystical light slanting through two-tier Gothic windows, it would be watching children in their little bedrooms fast asleep" (147).

In this passage the subjective nature of Jack's revelation is clear. Like any experience of faith, of making contact with some higher power in the universe, Jack's visionary moment is subjectively convincing, not objectively verifiable. He recognizes, moreover, that his is a secular form of illumination—intermittently grasped, unsupported by any stable belief in religious dogma and its affirmations of absolute truth. Far from taking refuge in ancient truths, Jack evinces—even in his keenest visions—the formative or coercive power that the invasive

postmodern environment exerts on the individual's innermost feelings and perceptions. In a later passage, for example, he is again stirred
by "cosmic" feelings of "piety" when he observes the "trust so absolute
and pure" that radiates from the faces of his sleeping children. Yet
when he reaches for a metaphor to express his profound "intimations,"
the effect is more comic than cosmic: "These sleeping children were
like figures in an ad for the Rosicrucians, drawing a powerful beam of
light from somewhere off the page" (154). The simile is blatantly derivative, another copy or simulacrum stamped out for public consumption
by the advertising industry's dream factory.

Still, in DeLillo's universe the comic and the cosmic prove as closely
aligned as their alphabetic configurations. In the simplest names or
crudest hieroglyphs, the author hints, occult mysteries reside. As Paul
Maltby observes, these names or words "are often invested with a
significance that exceeds their immediate, practical function."[10] In
a passage that closely resembles the scene from *Libra* in which Win
Everett is enthralled by his daughter's reading aloud, Jack listens with
awe to his nine-year-old daughter, Steffie, muttering in her sleep.
What he hears is a kind of "ecstatic chant," transmitted in "a language
not quite of this world." To Jack, Steffie's mysterious utterance sounds
like an invocation, an appeal to "the name of an ancient power in the
sky, tablet-carved in cuneiform." As it turns out, however, this charged
and magical language originates not in the remote past but in the
futuristic present. In a flash Jack realizes where he has heard those
"beautiful and mysterious" words before: "She uttered two clearly
audible words, familiar and elusive at the same time, words that
seemed to have a ritual meaning, part of a verbal spell or ecstatic chant.
Toyota Celica." As the cosmic and the comic collide, Jack deciphers the
"simple brand name, an ordinary car. How could these near-nonsense
words, murmured in a child's restless sleep, make me sense a meaning,
a presence?" he wonders. "She was only repeating some TV voice. . . .
Supranational names, computer-generated. . . . Part of every child's
brain noise, the substatic regions too deep to probe" (154–55).

Despite the comical disjunction between Steffie's incantatory language and its seeming referent, her utterance retains its magical effect
on Jack—one that overtakes and subverts what Raymond Williams
defines as the advertiser's *false* magic: "a highly organized and professional system of magical inducements" that attempt to associate the
consumption of an object or product "with human desires to which it

has no real reference." This "unsuccessful attempt to provide meanings and values," Williams adds, is meant to obscure "the real sources of [human] satisfaction."[11] The magical effect of Steffie's utterance on her father radically reverses this process. After identifying the near-nonsense words his daughter is babbling, Jack finds that they "only amazed me more. The utterance was beautiful and mysterious, gold-shot with looming wonder. . . . Whatever its source, the utterance struck me with the impact of a splendid transcendence" (155). The magic of the brand name Toyota Celica does not send Jack running to the local car dealer or mall. Instead, it puts him in touch with a realm of "meaning and values" that have nothing to do with the product, its purchase, or its consumption. Without blinking an eye, the sleeping child has subverted the massive system of commercial advertising, shored up by multinational corporations and economic markets, which only appears to hold her in thrall.

"One hardly knows what to make of" such "epiphanic moments," says Arnold Weinstein, when DeLillo transmutes "dross to gold, makes out of the pollution of advertising a beautiful postmodern lyricism and tenderness."[12] Crucial to the meaning of Jack's fleeting contact with transcendence, I would suggest, is not its objective validity but the subjective force and authority of feeling: both the affect and effect of revelation. As many of the casual conversations among the novel's characters suggest, no stable truths underpin the Gladneys' elusive, fluctuating universe. Jack's son Heinrich, for example, repeatedly points out to his father that human sense perception, and the empirical evidence on which it relies, is often misleading: "Our senses are wrong a lot more often than they're right. . . . Even sound can trick the mind. Just because you don't hear a sound doesn't mean it's not out there. . . . Coming from somewhere" (23). As Heinrich later says, "the major events in the universe can't be seen by the eye of man" (148).

To prove his point, Heinrich insists on questioning the very existence of the rain pelting down on his father's car as he and Jack are seated inside. Gazing at the wet windshield, Jack tells his son that, after all, he can "*see* it's raining." The precocious fourteen-year-old replies, "You see the sun moving across the sky. But is the sun moving across the sky or is the earth turning?" He adds, "Can you prove, here and now, that this stuff is rain? How do I know that what you call rain is really rain? What *is* rain anyway?" When his father sarcastically replies, "It's the stuff that falls from the sky and gets you what is called wet,"

Heinrich retorts: "I'm not wet. Are you wet?" Acknowledging that
Heinrich has won this round, Jack congratulates him on scoring a "victory for uncertainty, randomness and chaos. Science's finest hour" (24).

From another vantage, however, Heinrich's victory suggests that
daily existence is itself a matter of vision or faith. If "the evidence of
our senses" is not always trustworthy, neither is the scientific (or any
other) model of reality (23). Seen in this light, problematic uncertainty
looks a lot like a new version of ancient mystery. Even Heinrich,
enamored as he is with scientific indeterminacy, betrays this possibility
when, in another querulous conversation, he calls the structure of
the eye "a mystery" (158). That "Heinrich's hairline is beginning to
recede," although he is only fourteen, further hints at the adolescent's
tenuous relationship to childhood and its immanent contact with
mystery. (On a more literal plane, Jack worries that Heinrich's reced-
ing hairline is a symptom of early exposure to some lethal chemical or
"industrial waste" [22].)

What proves crucial to Jack is not the possible validation of an insight
by some outside observer but his own capacity to experience a revelation as true. Just as he finds meaning in the supermarket tabloids, which
keep "inventing hope" in the face of "large-scale ruin," Jack honors his
subjective "yearnings and reachings" for belief (146, 154). That someone might accuse him of mere wish fulfillment, of constructing his
own meaning out of desire and longing, carries little weight in a world
already revealed as a synthesis of constructs and copies, or simulacra. It
may be the human being's capacity to invent, to dream up expressions
of faith and hope, that deserves our greatest wonder. As Murray tells
Jack, "Think of the great poetry, the music and dance and ritual that
spring forth from our aspiring to a life beyond death. Maybe these
things are justification enough for our hopes and dreams" (286). Humanity's ability to conjure, dream, and hope is, in a sense, its own reward,
affirming the adult's connection to that world of wonder and radiance
signaled by the child. As Murray, in another nod to Wordsworth, tells
his students, we "have to learn to look as children again" (50).

When, in the second section of the novel, an enormous and (as it
turns out) highly toxic cloud appears in the sky, numerous conflicting
rumors about its origin immediately circulate. What strikes Jack about
the proliferation of this "unverified information" is not its dubious
status as fact but the "spirit of imagination" it evinces. "We were no
closer to believing or disbelieving a given story," he comments. "But

there was a greater appreciation now. We began to marvel at our own ability to manufacture awe" (153). At first glance Jack's statement is satiric. Assuming a binary opposition between spontaneous and invented wonder, readers will perceive in the verb "manufacture" a decidedly negative connotation. To manufacture awe is to invent or produce an artificial version of the real thing—another simulacrum. Manufactured wonder lacks, in other words, that principle of moral and aesthetic viability or truth identified, at least since the Romantic period, as natural or authentic. On the other hand, we might ask, is not wonder or awe a response produced or manufactured by imagination and consciousness, whatever its object? And is not this human capacity to experience awe—to perceive in reality a source of wonder—what Jack discovers, or recovers, through his children?

Patently manufactured or devised, as well, is the religion practiced by the nuns who rescue Jack at the end of the novel. To their clinic, in the old German section of nearby Iron City, Jack brings Willie Mink, the man he shoots in a jealous rage and then, in sudden desperation, rushes to save. Dressed in black habits, "rosaries swinging from their belts," the nuns initially strike Jack as the embodiment of religious devotion (316). As one of them, Sister Hermann Marie, cleans Jack's wound (Mink manages to turn Jack's third bullet on his attacker), Jack gazes at a picture on the wall absurdly depicting "Jack Kennedy holding hands with Pope John XXIII in heaven." When he asks the sister whether the church still believes in "the old heaven," she glances at the picture and then sputters in her heavily accented English, "Do you think we are stupid? . . . We are here to take care of sick and injured. Only this." Disabusing Jack of the notion that the nuns cleave to church dogma, the old woman adds, "The nonbelievers need the believers. They are desperate to have someone believe. . . . It is our task in the world to believe things no one else takes seriously. To abandon such beliefs completely, the human race would die. This is why we are here" (316–18).

Dismayed by this pronouncement, Jack asks if she means that the nuns' "dedication is a pretense." She fires back, "Our pretense is a dedication. . . . Our lives are no less serious than if we professed real faith, real belief. . . . We surrender our lives to make your nonbelief possible" (319). Commenting on this scene, Paul Cantor says, "DeLillo gives us another perfect postmodern moment: a nun who is a simulacrum of religious faith."[13] Viewed from another perspective, however, the nuns' devotion is freighted with mystery. From what source, readers may ask, do the nuns derive their courage to serve others and, as Sister Hermann Marie says, to pray "for the world" (319)? Are these devout nonbelievers even more wondrous to behold than those whose absolute faith sustains their sacrifice, hard work, and devotion? That the nuns at the clinic are willing to dedicate themselves to humanity with little hope of heavenly reward borders on the miraculous. Knowing firsthand what it is to suffer disbelief, they carry on the rituals of belief for the sake of others. Here is devotion wholly inspired by the needs of others. What could be more Christlike? In the face of doubt the nuns carry out their role as God's holy fools, even though God may not exist: "We are your fools, your madwomen, rising at dawn to pray, lighting candles, asking statues for good health, long life" (319).

A sense of sacred wonder radiates from this undeniably "postmodern moment," as Cantor calls it: wonder and awe for humanity itself. How amazing that human beings are willing to sacrifice themselves for others. It is a mystery as potent as the awe Jack experiences when gazing on his sleeping children. In this, our "materialist age," as Arnold Weinstein describes it, "belief and passion" have been "displaced, renamed, . . . and commodified" out of all recognition. Yet DeLillo, the chronicler of consumer culture, plumbs the unsuspected "spiritual impulses" at work beneath its surface.[14] Through the alchemy of language, DeLillo evokes a postmodern universe touched by the transcendent, shot through with wonder at the "radiance of dailiness."

In the world of *White Noise* radiance is everywhere. But nostalgia for lost beliefs or a lost paradise is not the key to its discovery. "Nostalgia," Murray tells Jack, expresses the "dissatisfaction and rage" of those who have a "grievance" with the present (258). For Jack, on the other hand, the present is filled with awe, the most ordinary moments alive with the extraordinary. Even when he opens the freezer compartment of his refrigerator, "a cold dry sizzle" emits metaphysical implications: "An eerie static, insistent but near subliminal," makes Jack "think of wintering souls, some form of dormant life approaching the threshold of perception" (258).

Jack's revelations, his reverence for the child in particular, may recall the Romantics and their metaphysics; but his insights do not come wrapped in the same assurances. Contrary to Maltby's charge that DeLillo endeavors "to validate the visionary moment as the sign of a redemptive order of meaning," *White Noise* only hints at the possibility of transcendence, just as it hints at the possibility that transcendence is a delusion. The question that vexes so many of DeLillo's critics—whether or not these visionary moments are validated by the text and thus undermine its postmodern indeterminacy—cannot be objectively answered.[15] Gnostic in nature, ambivalent in effect, the text shimmers with possibilities that can only be resolved by the reader. Like James's readers, faced with the multiple ambiguities of *The Turn of the Screw,* DeLillo's must bring their own perceptions and experience to bear on the text. *White Noise,* in Lentricchia's words, refuses "to let its readers off the hook of self-reliance by giving them an omniscient perspective." The "final answer, if there is one at all," says DeLillo, lies "outside the book" with the reader. "My books," he adds, are "open-ended."[16]

Jack's contact with the "fullness of being," which descends on him like grace, is intense but intermittent. Such moments evoke awe and wonder, but no stable faith or religious belief issues from these epiphanies, only hints of "splendid transcendence" (155). The mystery with which Jack makes contact is, to subvert an old adage, mystery with a human face. Although Jack feels "closest to God" when he gazes on his sleeping children, it is always a child's face, not a deity's, that he beholds. At the same time his apprehension of mystery—and its medium, the child—is never far from his terror of death. In another departure from his Romantic precursors DeLillo exposes the vital relationship of mystery to terror, of intimations of immortality to existential dread. Jack's intense fear of death does not dampen but fuels his sense of wonder. These dual aspects of consciousness, seemingly at odds, are inextricably bound up in each other. As DeLillo explained in an interview, "our sense of fear" is "something we almost never talk about. . . . I tried to relate it in *White Noise* to this other sense of transcendence that lies just beyond our touch. This extraordinary wonder of things is somehow related to the extraordinary dread, to the death fear we try to keep beneath the surface of our perceptions."[17]

The relationship between Jack's fear of death, which he struggles but fails to repress, and his extraordinary wonder is dramatized throughout the novel, even in the most mundane scenes of domestic life. In one such passage Jack and Heinrich have just concluded another of their father-son debates in the kitchen. Heinrich has criticized Jack for the inefficient way he makes coffee, needlessly wasting "time and energy." The notion of saving time leads Jack to think of death, both his own and Babette's. Thoughts of death bring on the inevitable terror, and suddenly he wants to cry out in the wilderness, "Don't let us die." But to whom should he cry? "Who decides these things?" he wonders. "What is out there? Who are you?" Then in a flash his doubt and uncertainty undergo a striking transformation, as dread turns into awe. Watching the coffee bubbling up in the "pale globe" of the pot, he is deeply moved by the "roundabout, ingenious, human" nature of this mundane contrivance: "It was like a philosophical argument rendered in terms of the things of the world—water, metal, brown beans. I had never looked at coffee before" (103).

Here is the extraordinary wonder of things writ large—and small. All the poignancy of humanity's plight is suddenly revealed in the familiar rite of making coffee. As Jack wonders at this "marvelous and sad invention," the homely coffeepot, the narrative draws attention to the touching ingenuity by which human beings convert earth's elements (water, metal, beans) into cultural artifacts. The result is a pleasing but superfluous concoction that, like so many others, has come to seem an essential part of daily life—and a guarantee that it will continue. In practicing this rite, we assure ourselves that each day will follow the next without end, that life will never cease. The daily ritual of making coffee, DeLillo's readers begin to glean, is itself a form of devotion, a kind of secular prayer.

When "the black billowing cloud, the airborne toxic event," appears in the sky over Blacksmith, the combined experience of awe and dread only intensifies. "It was a terrible thing to see," Jack comments, "so close, so low, packed with chlorides, benzines, phenols, hydrocarbons, or whatever the precise toxic content." At the same time, Jack adds, "Our fear was accompanied by a sense of awe that bordered on the religious. It is surely possible to be awed by the thing that threatens your life, to see it as a cosmic force, so much larger than yourself, more powerful, created by elemental and willful rhythms" (127). Fear of death reminds us at once of our finitude and of the existence of a cosmic mystery so much larger and more powerful than ourselves that we feel oddly liberated. To know that "death is in the air," Murray later tells Jack, "is liberating"; it releases "suppressed material" in the human psyche. "It is getting us closer to things we haven't learned about ourselves" (151). Even after the toxic cloud disappears, death remains permanently "in the air." Jack's exposure to the cloud—the toxic chemical it carries is identified as Nyodene D.—appears to have been lethal, although only time will tell. "Death has entered," he avows to himself; it now dwells "inside" him (140–41).

In a larger sense, of course, death inheres in all things. The "underlying" condition of mortal life, as Babette remarks to Jack, is death; that is the "terrible secret," in Murray's words, "of our decaying bodies" (197, 285). But exposure to Nyodene D. brings Jack more intimate awareness of death, which both terrifies and in another sense liberates him. No better cure exists, after all, for habit and complacency—"the death that exists in routine things"—than recognition of life's finitude (248). Awareness of death can, paradoxically, free one from its iron grip. As Jack's colleague, the elusive and eccentric neurochemist Winnie Richards, tells him, "I think it's a mistake to lose one's sense of death, even one's fear of death. Isn't death the boundary we need? . . . You have to ask yourself whether anything you do in this life would have beauty and meaning without the knowledge you carry of a final line, a border or limit." Fear of death, she adds, "gives you a renewed sense of yourself, a fresh awareness" of both "the self" and "familiar surroundings" (228–29).

Subject to his gnawing fear of death, Jack refuses to grant Winnie her point. To the reader, however, his dread seems to bring heightened self-awareness. In what he calls his "current state, bearing the death impression of the Nyodene cloud," Jack admits he is "ready to search anywhere for signs and hints, intimations of odd comfort" and of life's "cosmic" mystery. His search, more often than not, leads back to the "soft warm faces" of his sleeping children, which emit a "shining reliance [on] and implicit belief" in existence (154). Part of the comfort Jack derives from the younger children may lie in the adult's assumption, supported by contemporary experts in child care and psychology, that young children do not know about death. At one point Jack confesses to Murray, "I feel so good when I'm with Wilder," adding, "It's not like being with the other kids." That is because, Murray says, Jack senses the child's "freedom": He "doesn't know he's going to die. He doesn't know death at all" (290). Perhaps for the same reason Babette begins to crave the company of her two-year-old son. As Jack later discovers, much to his surprise, his confident and capable wife also lives in fear of death. Taking solace in Wilder's apparent obliviousness, Babette later confesses to Jack, "Wilder helps me get by" (263). Ultimately, however, it is what the child appears to *know* rather than not know that has the most telling effect on his stepfather.

That children know far more than they can say holds particularly true of two-year-old Wilder, who has scarcely begun to talk. Early in the novel Wilder goes on a seven-hour crying jag, the cause of which no one, including the family doctor, can make out. Midway through the ordeal, Jack takes the little boy for a ride in the car: "The huge lament continued, wave on wave. It was a sound so large and pure I could almost listen to it, try consciously to apprehend it. . . . He was not sniveling or blubbering. He was crying out, saying nameless things in a way that touched me with its depth and richness. This was an ancient dirge. . . . Ululation." Jack adds, "I let it wash over me, like rain in sheets" (78).

Wilder's lament is not, Jack indicates, the self-preoccupied wail of a toddler having a fit. In this "ancient dirge," Jack thinks he hears a far more profound message, that of the prophet or holy man giving voice to the sadness and beauty of life and to the human failure to understand what we are given. In the child's "soul-struck" wailing Jack also discovers a medium for expressing his own sorrow, for releasing his pent-up fear. As the sound of Wilder's "uniform lament" washes over him, the adult feels magically cleansed, purified, renewed. After "nearly seven straight hours of serious crying," Wilder stops as abruptly as he began—having fulfilled, it would seem, some profound ritual signified by the mystical number seven. Quietly circling the child, fearful of "disturbing the grave and dramatic air he had brought with him into the house," the Gladney clan "watch him with something like awe." Eliciting their "mingled reverence and wonder," Wilder has delivered his wordless message. "It was as though," Jack concludes, "he'd just returned from a period of wandering in some remote and holy place" (78–79).

Later, Wilder again performs the role of messenger, in a way that further suggests his unspoken resources of knowledge and under-standing. Now the message is silently transmitted, as the child leads Jack to confront the figure of death that both terrifies and liberates the adult. In the third, and final, section of the novel Jack awakens to find Wilder "standing two feet from the bed, gazing into [his] face." With his "great round head" set on a "small-limbed body," the toddler looks like some minor deity or "household idol." With wordless authority Wilder, a tiny Mercury in "quilted booties," leads his stepfather into the hall, to a window overlooking the Gladneys' backyard. In the yard Jack spies a mysterious stranger seated in a wicker chair, "a figure of eerie stillness and composure." As fear clutches his heart, he looks around to find that Wilder is no longer at his side. (Having fulfilled his mission, the child goes back to bed, where Jack finds him already fast asleep.) Convinced that "Death, or Death's errand-runner," is waiting for him below, Jack is "scared to the marrow." At the same time the sensation of seeing "Death in the flesh" charges his perceptions, lights the world in wonder (242–43). The discovery to which the child, in New Testament fashion, leads him is the miracle of creation itself.

Drenched in sweat and fear, Jack finds himself, as he says, "looking into my hands. So much remained. Every word and thing a beadwork of bright creation. My own plain hand, crosshatched and whorled in a mesh of expressive lines, a life terrain, might itself be the object of a person's study and wonder for years. A cosmology against the void" (243). Couched in the language of spiritual revelation and sacred wonder, Jack's epiphany bears a remarkable resemblance to that of Sim Goodchild in *Darkness Visible*. Under Matty's prophetic influence, we recall, Sim has a similar Blakean vision when he stares into his own hand; his gaze, like Jack's, seems to penetrate the source of mystery, as though the palm were "made of light." Staring "into the gigantic world of his own palm," Sim sees "that it [is] holy." When Matty releases Sim's hand, the revelation is over: Sim's hands are "nothing more than just hands again" (231–33). Jack's epiphany ends just as abruptly when, approaching the "numinous" figure, he sees that it is not "Death in the flesh" but his father-in-law, Vernon Dickey (244).

DeLillo's and Golding's novels are worlds apart; yet the foregoing passages are so similar that they bear remarking. Both characters' epiphanies are charged with ambivalence and uncertainty; both are subjective and ephemeral. When vision fades, both characters find themselves back in the world of the ordinary, where things are nothing more than what they seem. The most marked contrast between the dramatizations, I would suggest, is the extreme self-consciousness of DeLillo's protagonist. Not only does Jack have an epiphany, he is highly aware that he is having one. In describing his immediate experience, he entertains the metaphysical possibilities to which it gives rise: the promise it holds out of a "cosmology against the void." Should Jack's epiphany be read as a dramatized version of authentic revelation or its simulacrum? The distinction is far from clear. Here, in miniature, we encounter that same blurring of borders, that same erosion of categories, that occurred with the German nuns. Is their devotion authentic or a mere copy of true spiritual dedication?

In the world of *White Noise,* where sweaters come marked "virgin acrylic," even the glossy fruit in the local supermarket has "a self-conscious quality about it. It look[s] carefully observed, like four-color fruit in a guide to photography" (49, 170). Here the historical mirror stage of Western culture, to which James alerted his readers at the turn of the century, is writ (or, more precisely, reproduced) large in an endless series of replications that have lost all trace of an original. Even so-called natural phenomena have been so carefully observed and replicated that they prove indistinguishable from their simulacra. Even the most photographed barn in America can no longer be seen as real. Nothing, it would seem, not even the narrator's innermost thoughts and feelings, escapes the self-conscious nature of this endlessly replicated, derivative universe: nothing, that is, but the child.

It is the child's contact with "natural truth," as DeLillo calls it, that proves uniquely inaccessible and inviolate—at least until the child acquires the power, or habit, of speech. Looking for signs of that contact, Jack is drawn to his children sleeping. In their profound slumber these otherwise talkative, precocious creatures appear silently engaged in articulating another code of meaning. More subliminally, Jack's wife, Babette, appears to make a similar distinction. Unlike most fond parents, ambitious for their children's success and thus eager to teach them to talk, she is reluctant to have Wilder speak. When Jack asks whether she has noticed that Wilder is "talking less than ever," she replies, "There's enough talk. What is talk? I don't want him to talk. The less he talks, the better" (264).

By the time this scene takes place Jack has discovered the drastic steps Babette has taken to cope with her fear of death. It is Denise, Babette's eleven-year-old daughter, who informs him that her mother is secretly taking a drug that appears to induce loss of memory. After he confronts Babette with this information, she confesses that she has been taking a "top secret drug, code-name Dylar," believed by researchers to eliminate fear of death by blocking certain receptors in the brain. Dangerous and potentially fatal, the drug is far from being approved for human consumption. Significantly, Babette is willing to risk death to eliminate her dread of it. Her desperation for a cure also leads to her "capitalist transaction" with one of the drug's developers, Willie Mink; in return for her sexual favors, he provides her with an illegal supply of Dylar. In the end, however, the drug fails to work (193–94, 200–201).

Just as Babette risks death to overcome her fear of it, Jack attempts to overcome his dread by killing Mink. After Babette confesses her trysts with Mink in a seedy motel, her husband becomes increasingly jealous and angry. Eventually he devises an "elegant" plan to kill the man who has cuckolded him. By this time the source of Jack's personal and professional fascination with Hitler and German fascism—he is the chair of the Department of Hitler Studies at his college—has become clear. Like countless other "helpless and fearful people," Jack perceives in this "mythic" or "epic" figure a powerful representation of invincibility: "Hitler," as Murray puts it, "is larger than death" (287). Now, propelled by murderous zeal, Jack suddenly feels that he has gained "control" over death. Exulting in his new role as "killer," he thinks he has escaped his identity as "dier" (304, 297, 290).

In a farcical scene whose grotesque comedy and surreal atmosphere recall Humbert's slaying of Quilty in *Lolita,* Jack abruptly discovers that he is not in control—and that murder (or in this case, attempted murder) is messy. Far from effecting his escape from mortality, Jack's attempt to kill Mink only mires him further in the "old human muddles and quirks." As he gazes at his would-be victim, whose lap has become "a puddle of blood," Jack's plan abruptly collapses under the weight of his "compassion" and "remorse." For the first time he sees his enemy "as a person" and resolves to "help Mink" (313). For the human being there is no elegant solution to the terror of death—except, perhaps, death itself. Like the capacity for language, dread of death is an aspect of human consciousness, one that distinguishes us from other animals. In this novel "saturated with awareness of mortality," as Tom LeClair puts it, "fear of death" serves as "the mainspring of human motivation."[18]

While the secret research conducted to develop Dylar suggests how widespread is Jack and Babette's fear of dying, its failure to work implies that the only way to eradicate this fear is to eradicate the human. "The greatest threat of technology" to human culture, says Michael Valdez Moses, "is its promise of immortality; its most Faustian form in *White Noise* is Dylar." By promising "to eliminate the individual's fear of death," he adds, Dylar would annihilate that "innate characteristic of *Dasein,*" or being, to which Martin Heidegger devoted so much philosophical analysis. Persuasively arguing the influence of Heidegger's thought on DeLillo, Moses helps to account for the intimate relationship between dread and awe that permeates the novel. According to

"Heidegger's existential analysis, particularly as represented by *Being and Time*," says Moses, the "acute perception of one's own mortality supplies the necessary preliminary step to an openness to Being." This recognition of "personal finitude" opens the individual "to other possible ways of understanding himself and his relation to the world. *Angst,* or dread, which initially strikes man with such powerfully negative force, provides the potentially liberating experience par excellence. It is *Angst,*" according to Heidegger, "that sets man on the way to a fundamental philosophic reassessment," opening "him up to the possibility that Being will reveal itself to him."[19]

The intimate relationship between dread and awe, between terror of death and human creativity is a paradox that both implicates and culminates in DeLillo's image of childhood. In a crucial scene near the end of the novel Wilder once again serves as the agent of revelation. As Jack's narration draws to a close, he inserts into the text an "awe-struck account" related to him by "two elderly women." Their story describes how, "from the second-story back porch of a tall house," they find themselves helplessly watching Wilder cross the crowded highway on his plastic tricycle. No one in Wilder's family is present to witness his astonishing confrontation with death; faced with recounting a miracle, Jack, like some biblical narrator, must rely on the testimony of strangers.

As the "mystically charged" little boy pedals his three-wheeler onto the busy expressway, he is impervious to the shouts and gesticulations that issue from the second-story perch of the two distraught women. Confronted with the "little rotary blur" that suddenly appears in "the broad-ribboned modernist stream" of speeding cars, the drivers on the expressway are mystified. To them, it seems, "some force in the world had gone awry." Here in concrete form is the disaster everyone dreads, the death by machine that virtually every form of contemporary life seems to announce: environmental pollution, chemical poisons, airplane crashes, nuclear accidents, terrorist bombs, industrial explosions, assembly-line breakdowns, or the mere steady emission of "waves and radiation" by the kitchen microwave and color television. But as the drivers brake wildly and sound their horns, Wilder does not "even look at them" (323). Pedaling straight ahead, "deliberate in his movements," he appears to be "following some numbered scheme," intent on his mystifying goal. Meanwhile the cars keep coming, "whipping into the straightaway" and then dodging, swerving, climbing the curbstone to avoid the all too obvious target. Amid the shriek of horns and the screams of the motorists, Wilder finally reaches the other side of the expressway.

Far from offering "an image of the child's immersion into the flow" of ordinary life, as Arnold Weinstein contends, Wilder's safe crossing not only disrupts the circulation of traffic but shatters the surface of mundane reality. Far from demonstrating, as Weinstein says, "that life moves everything and everyone into its gravitational pull," the child's amazing venture, from which he emerges unscathed, counters all our notions of probability.[20] What are readers to make of this miracle? How does the two-year-old manage to escape destruction? Does the secret lie in the child's blind trust? In his blissful ignorance of death? What Wilder knows or does not know remains a mystery.

What is clear, on the other hand, is the monumental effort of those hundreds of strangers hurtling by—an effort that is truly awesome. The source of wonder, as with the nuns, is human rather than divine; and it is inextricably linked to our dread of death. Speeding along the busy highway in their noisy machines, preoccupied with work and worry, the anonymous drivers demonstrate a preternatural concern for the child's safety and welfare. What has happened to the mechanical indifference that individuals routinely display toward one another in a society overrun by technology? Where is the preference for machines over humans that we are so accustomed to observe? Against all the familiar formulas and exhausted clichés DeLillo pits a child, who wins without even trying.

Making no effort to explain this miracle, or to explain it away, DeLillo leaves his readers with a mental image of hundreds of anonymous motorists who, at top speed and on the verge of "uncontrollable terror," engage in a communal effort to save an unknown child. Underscoring the impression of some mysterious communication flowing among these isolated individuals is a "passing motorist" who closes the scene. Once Wilder reaches the other side of the expressway and is out of danger, he suddenly loses his balance; he and his tricycle tumble down the grassy embankment and land in a creek at the bottom. The motorist sees him, "alertly pull[s] over," and jumps out of his car. Skidding down the embankment, he plucks the boy from "the murky shallows" and holds him "aloft for the clamoring elders to see" (323–24). No commentary by the narrator follows this account; we note, however, the significant omission of any qualifying phrase (a handy "as if") to undermine our impression that the motorist is in mysterious communication with the elderly women as he lifts the child into the air "for the clamoring elders to see." Do the two women (having linguistically acquired the status of biblical elders) believe that the stranger *knows* he is being watched from a house on the other side of the expressway? Does Jack? The mystery is left unresolved; the account, open-ended.

Wilder's appearance on the crowded expressway is no more explicable to the drivers who save him than his seven-hour lament was to his family. The mystifying nature of his behavior disrupts the surface order of appearances and exposes its mystery. Trailing his own "clouds of glory" into the postmodern universe of "split-second lives" and gleaming supermarkets, DeLillo's child reveals the "radiance of dailiness" (322–23). Through this tiny figure readers glimpse the extraordinary wonder of things at the heart of the ordinary.

The radiance emitted in *White Noise* is singularly lacking in nostalgia. Like the citizens of Blacksmith dazzled and bewildered by the sublime sunsets that light up the skies, readers cannot plumb the source of the novel's brilliant effects. Like these "postmodern sunset[s]," DeLillo's fiction elicits from its readers a new kind of "awe," one that originates in "uncertainty" and is implicated in "dread" (227, 324). Not even the child's image is free of ambiguity and, as Wilder's seven-hour crying jag suggests, of a pervasive sense of dread. At the same time, however, this tiny creature signals a mystery at the heart of being, one that transcends culture and our most prized formulations about it. As Wilder's name suggests, the child's relatively wild state of cultural undress proves crucial to our sense of his immanent powers.[21] Emissary from the adult's forgotten origins, DeLillo's literary child—still trailing "clouds of glory," still gleaming in his (linguistic) nakedness—dazzles readers with hints of their own connection to some unfathomable source of being. Through the mysterious agency of the child *White Noise,* this quintessential postmodern novel, unwraps the muffled wonder of the world.

Conclusion

Far from evoking nostalgia for old certainties, DeLillo's literary children grow out of a present that is hurtling toward the future. Like the novels its author has singled out for praise (*Pale Fire* and *Ulysses* are at the top of the list), *White Noise* evinces no "homesickness for lost values or for the way fiction used to be written."[1] Yet if James can be credited with filling in the child's blank image at the turn of the century—adding nuance, sexual suggestion, and ambiguity to the figure flattened out by late-Victorian morality—DeLillo has revived the Romantic child at the century's end. In an era whose shifting cultural ground and disjunctive relationship to the past are indicated by a vague prefix— *post-,* as in postmodern, postindustrial, posthistorical—DeLillo's innovative fiction, like Nabokov's and McEwan's, honors the tradition of original innocence in fresh and surprising ways.

In celebrating that tradition, the novelist, as Nabokov reveals in *Lolita,* need not invoke nostalgic return or the sexless simplicity of the Victorian image of childhood. As James Kincaid argues in *Erotic Innocence,* whose argument takes up where his earlier *Child-Loving* left off, the Victorian image of blankly "adorable" children is an anemic rather than healthy descendant of the "Romantic heritage of the child." To a culture like ours, still enthralled by that blank image, "Wordsworth's child" serves as a "potent call to action." By "reimagining our Romantic roots, and the Romantic investment in the child," we may find a way out of the labyrinth in which passive images of the child have ensnared us. Torn between our desire to protect children and our covert attraction *to* them—to their "sexuality, sensuousness, and the appeal it has for adults"—we stifle our guilt in protestations of outrage. But the constant media attention, the barrage of stories of sexual child abuse, keeps "the subject hot," says Kincaid, "so we can disown it while welcoming it in the back door."[2] Keeping the image of the passive, helpless child constantly before us, we zealously feed the dragon we insist we want to slay.

Kincaid calls, therefore, for the reinvigoration of the child's image —a renewed emphasis on the individual's nascent creativity, resourcefulness, resilience. "It's not," he says, "that we've been trapped by Romantic images of the child. We haven't been nearly Romantic enough." It is up to our "best creative talent to devise and make stick a cultural story about children and sexuality that is out in the open and does not bolt at the first sign of complexity."[3] The intensity of our culture's resistance to that complexity, I might add, was confirmed by the outcries against Adrian Lyne's film adaptation of *Lolita,* despite its unrelenting emphasis on Humbert's guilt for ruining a child's life.

By "cultural story," Kincaid implies not only fiction but the countless forms of narrative—news, social commentaries, speeches, television shows, movies, essays, reviews—that constitute society's ongoing account of itself. Still, for reasons outlined by Patricia Meyer Spacks, Margaret Doody, and others, the novelist's creative talent offers the most vital and compelling versions of that collective story. Kincaid says as much when he lauds Dickens's achievement in the nineteenth century, adding, "We need new stories because they will create a way of imagining new actions and new beings. . . . With these stories will come the opportunity to conceive the child and its welfare, its body and its feelings" in more dynamic, "productive" ways.[4] Kincaid's assumption that new stories offering more complex and vital images of the child will have an *immediate* effect on the lives of children may not be shared by many people, for whom the relationship between literature and life is tenuous at best. But if, as I have been arguing, the novels or stories produced by some of the best contemporary writers articulate the ambivalence and complexity of our current attitudes toward children, such stories may help to lay the groundwork from which more productive cultural images arise.

As noted earlier, at least three of the novels I have discussed— *Lolita, The Child in Time,* and *White Noise*—reinvigorate the child's image by penetrating to the roots of the Romantic heritage and grafting new and vital offshoots. By contrast, other writers I have discussed—

Kosinksi, Golding, Lessing, Kundera, and Rushdie—are more inclined to debunk than to celebrate the Romantic legacy. Stressing the child's capacity for evil, conformity, or sheer obliviousness, their works nonetheless challenge, from a multiplicity of cultural vantage points, the blankly adorable child so dear to advertisers and politicians. Fostering the complacency intrinsic to the successful operation of mass society and consumer culture, the angelic image of children—those "diapered cherubim," as Mark Edmundson wittily notes—has become a fixture in what Edmundson deems "the culture of facile transcendence." A reductive parody of the Romantic writers' arduous idealism, the "culture of facile transcendence" has more to do with the escapist fantasies of popular romance than with Blakean vision. Based on "the belief that self-transformation is as simple as a fairy-tale wish," it fosters "formulas for easy self-remaking that now flourish in the American marketplace." As examples, Edmundson cites "the inner-child movement," "New Age panaceas," the "angel craze," "power ads," and the "mild high" produced by various self-help books, television talk shows, and feel-good movies.[5]

To this list one might add a host of other familiar formulations. Take, for example, those upbeat names—Sun City, Happy Hollow, Paradise Village—that promote fantasies of never-ending pleasure and are routinely affixed to shopping malls, subdivisions, and adult communities, where, in fact, most people go to die. In 1998, in a subdivision of Springfield, Ohio, named Shangri-la, fifteen-year-old Phillip "Kip" Kinkel, whom neighbors characterized as the "all-American kid," shot his parents, both schoolteachers, to death. Shortly thereafter he proceeded to his high school cafeteria, where he discharged fifty-one rounds of ammunition from a semiautomatic rifle and two pistols— killing two students and injuring eighteen others. Kip, who as a small child cut up cats and squirrels, "seemed," according to his classmates, "to take pleasure in killing." But for reasons left unexplained—unless, that is, we turn to the novels of Lessing and Golding for some illumination of these dark matters—Kinkel's "classmates failed to report his darker side." His "teachers," we are told, "seemed equally nonchalant."[6]

Perhaps the name of Kinkel's subdivision tells us something about those silent classmates and their teachers. If you are promised a rose garden, or a Shangri-la, why contemplate a darker side of existence? Why peer into that endless black cave, to recall Lessing's metaphor, over which Shangri-la has been carefully erected? But what happens

when the all-American kid rips the garden wide open and bares the
wilderness lurking beneath? The angel grows talons and tail; the darling
turns into a demon. Between these polarized images, as Edmundson
observes in a different context, "a reciprocal relationship" exists: one
extreme "creates the need for the other." As a culture, we are equally
obsessed with "angels" and "images of the serial killer." Beneath the
longing for "facile transcendence" lurks our fascination with the dark
underworld of "cruelty, lust, perversion, and crime." Developing a similar line of thought in *Erotic Innocence,* Kincaid observes that "idealized
angels" are "made possible by matching devils. And it's a simple economy to use the same body for both parts: the dream child becomes the
demon."[7] Here one thinks of Humbert's self-serving equation, where-
by the "demoniac" nymphet is conveniently removed from the sphere
of innocent children, who deserve the adult's protection, and delivered
into the arms of her "bewitched" admirer.

What, one might ask, does the preceding discussion, which focuses
on the tribulations of Anglo-American society, have to do with the
contrasting cultures and histories reflected in Rushdie's Anglo-Indian,
Kundera's and Kosinski's Eastern European, and Morrison's African
American fictions? *Beloved*'s demonic ghost-child, as many scholars
have noted, owes more to African folktales and the history of the Middle Passage than to the obsessions of contemporary white America.
And yet, in his negative review of Morrison's novel, Stanley Crouch
ignores these distinctly African themes to focus on *Beloved* as "a holocaust novel." Crouch points to the novel's dedication to "Sixty Million
and more," observing that Morrison deliberately multiplies by ten
the number of Jews killed in the Holocaust to underscore the number
of Africans who died during centuries of slave trade. Criticizing
Morrison for setting up an insidious competition between Africans
and Jews as the greatest sufferers or victims, he lists other features of
the holocaust novel that she borrows: "disenfranchisement, brutal
transport, sadistic guards, failed and successful escapes, murder, liberals
among the oppressors, a big war, underground cells, separation of
family members, losses of loved ones to the violence of the mad order
and characters who, like the Jew in *The Pawnbroker,* have been made
emotionally catatonic by the past."[8]

Any number of arguments can be leveled against Crouch's negative
assessment, including the simple observation that Morrison, along
with other American writers of her generation—black or white—has

a right to claim the history of World War II and the Holocaust as part of her imaginative past. Still more to the point, she is aware that her audience includes many white readers, both American and non-American, for whom the Holocaust plays a vivid role in historical, if not personal, memory. Indeed, it would be hard to find a serious reader, in the West at least, whose vision of reality has not been profoundly affected by knowledge of that catastrophe. In a novel like *Beloved*—which is, among other things, about the power of personal and collective memory—an appeal to the reader's historical memory seems not politically suspect but culturally viable.

One point should by now be obvious: contemporary acts of reading and writing (Crouch's and Morrison's included) are embedded in a global consciousness. Crouch may be African American, but the reach of his impressions and the range of his responses incorporate more than his immediate background and environment—even when he is reading a novel that focuses on the African American past. By the same token, an Anglo-American reader may have trouble grasping Rushdie's references in *Midnight's Children* to Bombay "Talkies" or to *Ramayana* and *Mahabharata,* just as his Anglo-Indian readers may miss more than a few of the novel's abundant allusions to Sterne's *Tristram Shandy,* Grass's *The Tin Drum,* and García Márquez's *One Hundred Years of Solitude.* The point is we are no more "naked" as readers than is each image of the child these novels construct. Our perceptions, like our versions of childhood, are cut from the cloth in which culture clothes us. As we read Rushdie or Kosinski, Kundera or Morrison, we inevitably proceed—as we do whenever we meet strangers or visit new places —to weave into the fabric of our perceptions, our cultural clothing, the patterns we discern in the other. The more curious or knowledgeable we are about that other, the more meaningful the patterns we appropriate. The process is ongoing, endless—even if those people and places, like the books we read, become familiar. Still, to recall Clifford Geertz's insight, "it is not necessary to know everything in order to understand something."

The literary children discussed in these pages were created in far-flung corners of the world. They speak to us in a variety of cultural languages that, in the process of reading, we translate into our own. Yet something of those disparate worlds of experience—those contrasting places, cultures, histories, those dramatically different economic and political realities—comes through. Just as Saleem Sinai in *Midnight's*

Children thumbs his big nose at the (Western) notion of locating a fixed origin, or a single set of progenitors, for himself, his family, his nation, Rushdie's readers are invited to ponder the ambiguous nature of their own origins. The more we gaze as if in a mirror at the image of childhood, the more opaque that seeming transparency becomes. Where if not here, we ask ourselves, can we hope to discover the naked truth of human nature? But the more we try, the more elusive the object appears. To recall the fable with which this inquiry began, the little boy who cries out that the emperor is naked cannot himself be unclothed; he cannot be seen in his original condition. Perhaps that is what makes his image so tantalizing: it draws us into the depths of our own fathomless being, from where the secret life of the child endlessly beckons.

Notes

Introduction

1. Suransky, *Erosion of Childhood,* 188; Williams, *Culture and Society,* 335.
2. Kuhn, *Corruption in Paradise,* 230.
3. Trilling, *Sincerity and Authenticity,* 139.
4. Derrida, "Structure, Sign, and Play," 93.
5. Suransky, *Erosion of Childhood,* 28; Spacks, *Adolescent Idea,* 13–14.
6. Spacks, *Adolescent Idea,* 17; Doody, *True Story of the Novel,* 483.
7. Geertz, *Interpretation of Cultures,* 43, 20.
8. Kuhn, *Corruption in Paradise,* 3–5; see also 67.
9. Blum, *Hide and Seek,* 90; Bradbury, *Modern American Novel,* x.

1. The Image of Childhood, Present and Past

1. "My Child, My Fear," CNN, 15 Sept. 1996. On 5 March 1994 National Public Radio (NPR) reported that the U.S. attorney general, in a speech sponsored by the Children's Defense Fund, stated that youth crime is "the No. 1 social problem in the U.S.A. today." On *All Things Considered* of 4 January 1994 NPR reported a 1993 California study showing that 20 percent of the murders in the state were committed by juveniles. Summarizing, in a news program on 3 December 1993, a front-page story published by the *Chicago Tribune* in 1992, NPR reported that in Chicago in 1992 sixty children under the age of fifteen were murdered—forty-four of them were black, four out of five victims knew their murderers, and only ten of them lived with both biological parents. On 13 July 1996 NPR aired a news story about a six-year-old boy accused of beating a baby almost to death after breaking into a neighbor's house to steal a tricycle; the judge ruled that he was not competent to stand trial. On 21 March 1996 NPR featured a program on the death

of five-year-old Eric Morse, who was thrown out the window of a Chicago
housing project by two boys, aged ten and eleven, because he refused to steal
candy for them. On 19 December 1996 NPR reported that two second-
grade boys attempted to suffocate another second-grader on the school playground during recess when she "broke up with" the leader of the children's
gang; only when her struggles became violent did they release her and run
away.

2. *Prime Time,* ABC, 18 Nov. 1993; "The Monsters among Us," *Frontline,*
PBS (WHYY, Wilmington-Philadelphia), 9 Nov. 1993; "When Children
Accuse, Who to Believe?" *Turning Point,* ABC, 14 Nov. 1996; the statement
about Nazi youth was made by Alfons Heck, the narrator of a 1991 Home
Box Office production, "Heil Hitler! Confessions of a Hitler Youth," PBS
(WHYY, Wilmington-Philadelphia), 6 Apr. 1994. Featured in "When Children Accuse, Who to Believe?" were Scott and Brenda Knipper, parents
imprisoned for nearly a decade after their two young sons were apparently
coerced into testifying against them. The Knippers were released on appeal
after their now grown-up sons testified in court that they were coerced by
social workers and psychologists into saying what the latter wanted them to
say; in support of their adult testimony, tapes of the sons' earlier interviews
were played in court.

3. Blake Morrison reports on the murder trial of the two ten-year-olds,
Robert Thompson and Jon Venables, for killing James Bulger, not quite three
years old, in Liverpool, England. On 12 February 1993 the two boys, truant
from school, lured a toddler they did not know away from a shopping center
and led him several miles away to a railway embankment. There they kicked
and beat him, dashed paint in his face, threw more than twenty bricks at his
body, and hurled a two-pound fishplate at his head. After sustaining "forty-
two injuries, including extensive shattering of the skull," as well as "torture
and mutilation," the toddler was lain facedown on the railroad tracks. After
piling a large number of bricks on the little boy's head and upper torso, the
ten-year-olds left him there to die. Around the time that Thompson and
Venables were watching cartoons at a local video-rental store, a train arrived
on the tracks to finish the job. When the body was discovered forty-eight
hours later, "it had been cut in half by a freight train" ("Children of Circumstance," 48–49, 54–55).

4. Franklin E. Zimring challenges the alarming prediction by John J.
DiIulio, a Princeton professor, of a massive number of "juvenile superpredators" ("Spurious Predictions of a Coming Horde of Teenage Superpredators,"
Philadelphia Inquirer, 13 Sept. 1996, sec. A, p. 27); Ariès, *Centuries of Childhood,*
411.

5. Marcus, *Childhood and Cultural Despair,* 246; Postman, *Disappearance of
Childhood,* 139, 5. Postman maintains that some of the most obvious champi-

ons of children's rights—including Ivan Illich (*Deschooling Society* [1971]) and John Holt (*Escape from Childhood* [1976])—are among its worst enemies. Arguing against the restrictions of "the social category 'children,'" they further the process by which children are deprived of hard-won protections against neglect and abuse.

6. Hiner and Hawes, *Growing Up in America,* xvii; Shattuck, "Papa Gets the Blame," 24; Ariès, *Centuries of Childhood,* 43–47, 128–33, and passim.

7. Ariès, *Centuries of Childhood,* 173–77, 284–85, 412–15, and passim. Stone challenges details of Ariès's argument, but Stone's study *Family, Sex, and Marriage in England, 1500–1800* lends support to the concept of childhood as a historical phenomenon ("Massacre of the Innocents," 27–28). Grylls contends that Ariès "overestimates the rapidity with which ideas about the special nature of childhood achieved recognition" (*Guardians and Angels,* 15, 17–18). Pollock maintains that "contrary to the belief of such authors as Ariès, there was a concept of childhood in the 16th century" and that "there have been very few changes in parental care and child life from the 16th to the 19th century in the home" (*Forgotten Children,* 267–68). Shahar similarly argues that the concept of childhood was rooted in medieval life (*Childhood in the Middle Ages,* 102). Other scholars who refute Ariès's time scheme or premise are cited in DeMause, *History of Childhood,* see esp. his "Evolution of Childhood." Zelizer, *Pricing the Priceless Child,* 4, 208.

8. Blum, *Hide and Seek,* 9, 14 n. 3, 12, 192.

9. Krauthammer deems child abuse the "1990s version of original sin." Pointing to "an epidemic of over-reporting" of child-abuse cases, he sums up a telling passage from a popular self-help book on sexual abuse: "If you are unable to remember any specific instances [of childhood sexual abuse] . . . but still have a feeling that something abusive happened to you, it probably did" ("Defining Deviancy Up," 22). In subsequent issues of the *New Republic,* in which Krauthammer's article was published, strong critical as well as supportive responses from readers were printed; see *New Republic,* 20 Dec. 1993, 4–5, and 27 Dec. 1993, 4–5.

10. Winn, *Children without Childhood,* 17.

11. Ibid., 16–17. Oates also traces the popular image of monster children to William March's 1954 novel, *The Bad Seed,* and its subsequent film adaptation. March's novel, Oates points out, inspired "a flood of novels and films about psychopathic, demonically possessed, and/or simply murderous children." Among the titles she lists are those mentioned by Winn plus numerous others: *The Omen, The Other, The Changeling, Children of the Corn, Kill Baby Kill, Child's Play, The Midwich Cuckoo* (from which the film *Village of the Damned* was made), *The Good Son, Mikey, Bloody Birthday, The Reflecting Skin, Unman, Wettering, Zygo,* and, more recently, Stephen King's *Carrie* and David Cronenberg's *The Brood* ("Killer Kids," 19–20).

12. Sokoloff, *Imagining the Child,* 3.

13. Postman, *Disappearance of Childhood,* 141–42, 134. Pinpointing the paradoxical nature of child worship in the "remarkably dichotomized society" of Victorian England, Carter notes that "the more little girls were idealized, the more child-prostitution flourished" ("Sexuality and the Victorian Artist," 150); on the flourishing state of prostitution and pornography in Victorian England, see Chesney, *Anti-Society,* 307–64. Discussing another aspect of this social dichotomy, the "domestic split between sex and affection," Spilka notes the "double message" conveyed by the Victorian parent's "combination of pious affection and grim correction" ("Enrichment of Poor Monkeys," 167, 169).

14. Cited in Louv, *Childhood's Future,* 4.

15. Postman, *Disappearance of Childhood,* 144; Douglas, *"Structures de culinaire,"* cited in Vincent, "A History of Secrets?" 238.

16. Davenport, *Balthus Notebook,* 16.

17. Foucault, "Body of the Condemned," 177.

18. Foucault, "Subject and Power," 208; Foucault, "Body of the Condemned," 177–78; Foucault, "Politics of Health," 279–80.

19. Geertz, *Interpretation of Cultures,* 48–49, 14, 82–83.

20. Ibid., 52–53.

21. Ibid., 20.

22. Doody, *True Story of the Novel,* 5; Pattison, *Child Figure in English Literature,* 45; Marcus, *Childhood and Cultural Despair,* 243–44.

23. Spilka, "Enrichment of Poor Monkeys," 163–65. Boas identifies the Romantic idealization of the child with the development of "cultural primitivism" in Western culture; like the "Noble Savage" or "the Folk," the child was valued by the "cultural primitivist" for being "innocent of all the arts and sciences, unspoiled by the artifices of civilization" (*Cult of Childhood,* 8, 11).

24. Miller, *For Your Own Good,* xvii, xiii.

25. Coveney, *Image of Childhood,* 192, 80; Cohen, "Lewis Carroll and Victorian Morality," 12; Spilka, "Enrichment of Poor Monkeys," 165; Williams, *Culture and Society,* 96.

26. Carter, "Sexuality and the Victorian Artist," 150; Hugo cited in Martin-Fugier, "Bourgeois Rituals," 337; Spacks, *Adolescent Idea,* 72, 226.

27. Kincaid, *Child-Loving,* 71; Freud, *Theory of Sexuality,* 232.

28. Spilka, "Enrichment of Poor Monkeys," 177; Coveney, *Image of Childhood,* 300–302. Crews cites, among others, Adolf Grünbaum's *Foundations of Psychoanalysis* (Berkeley: Univ. of California Press, 1984), which demonstrates "that 'clinical validation' of Freudian hypotheses is an epistemic sieve; as a means of gaining knowledge, psychoanalysis is fatally contaminated by the inclusion, among its working assumptions and in its dialogue with patients, of the very ideas that supposedly get corroborated by clinical experience"

("Unknown Freud," 55). Other major studies that debunk Freud's allegedly scientific methods and approach include Malcolm Macmillan, *Freud Evaluated: The Completed Arc* (Amsterdam: North-Holland, 1991); Allen Esterson, *Seductive Mirage: An Exploration of the Work of Sigmund Freud* (Chicago: Open Court, 1993); and John Kerr, *A Most Dangerous Method: The Story of Jung, Freud, and Sabina Spielrein* (New York: Knopf, 1993). Erich Fromm, in *Greatness and Limitations of Freud's Thought* (New York: Harper and Row, 1980), offers a more politely revisionist account of Freud's thought and work.

29. Coveney, *Image of Childhood*, 240.

30. Bradbury, *Modern American Novel*, 38.

31. See Strachey's "Editor's Note," in Freud, *Theory of Sexuality*, 127–29. The "first mention of erotogenic zones . . . liable to stimulation in childhood," Strachey also points out, occurs in a letter Freud wrote to his colleague Wilhelm Fliess at the end of 1896. By 1895 he "had a complete explanation of hysteria based on the traumatic effects of sexual seduction in early childhood." Then, in "the summer of 1897," Freud abandoned "his seduction theory. . . . He announced the event in a letter to Fliess of September 21," along with "his almost simultaneous discovery of the Oedipus complex in his self-analysis," which he described in his letters of 3 and 15 October 1897.

32. Freud, *Theory of Sexuality*, 176; in his reference to the year 1896 Freud is alluding to the last paragraph of section 1 of his paper on the etiology of hysteria, listed as 1896c in Strachey's bibliography in *Theory of Sexuality*.

33. Edel, *Life of Henry James*, 14–15, 175, 261–64; Bradbury, *Modern American Novel*, 21, 41. Edel also notes that simultaneously with James in London and Freud in Vienna, Marcel Proust was at work in Paris, "examining that part of reflective experience which relates to association and memory." Independent of one another, "these three different men" embarked on similar journeys "at this singular moment of the history of mind and psyche" (15).

34. Fiedler, *Love and Death*, 578, 555.

35. Coveney, *Image of Childhood*, 339, 337.

36. Ibid., 312.

37. Ibid., 291, 210.

38. Grylls, *Guardians and Angels*, 16.

2. Innocence on the Brink

1. Shine, *Fictional Children*, vii.

2. Winn, *Children without Childhood*, 124, 130–31.

3. Fiedler, *Love and Death*, 586–88.

4. Shine, *Fictional Children*, 172.

5. Kincaid, *Child-Loving*, 12–13. "As emptiness," Kincaid says of Copperfield, "the child David can be variously eroticized by those around him:

his kissing mother, his hugging nurse, his beating stepfather and schoolmaster, the adult narrator, and, arguably, the reader."

6. Philip Weinstein, *Henry James*, 82.

7. Carter, "Sexuality and the Victorian Artist," 148–49.

8. Shine, *Fictional Children*, 76; Geismar, *James and the Jacobites*, 208.

9. Freud, *Theory of Sexuality*, 173.

10. Ibid., 228.

3. The Child at a Turning Point

1. Kincaid, *Child-Loving*, 81, 77.

2. Kuhn, *Corruption in Paradise*, 130.

3. Coveney, *Image of Childhood*, 192–93.

4. Vincent points out that before the twentieth century "mirrors were still rare and expensive items. Full-length mirrors were found only in the homes of the wealthy. Working-class and rural homes generally contained one at most, a small shaving mirror fastened above the sink" ("History of Secrets?" 231).

5. Heilman, "'Turn of the Screw' as Poem," 219.

6. Heller, *Thomas Mann*, 16. In his textual notes to the Norton edition of *The Turn of the Screw*, Kimbrough points out that James made "major revisions" for the "1908 New York version" that added to the tale's original ambiguities. "Here," says Kimbrough, "James seemed intent on shifting the center of attention away from the details of action observed by the governess to the reactions felt by the governess." The author's revisions include his removing commas in order to approximate more closely "the stream of her consciousness," "increasing the use of the possessive pronoun 'my,'" and "replacing verbs of perception and thought with those of feeling and intuition" (91).

7. Spilka, "Turning the Freudian Screw," 248.

8. Wilson attributes the sexual significance of Flora's gestures to the governess's repressed or morbid sexual interest, which stems from "her inability to admit to herself her natural sexual impulses" ("Ambiguity of Henry James," 90, 95). Felman deconstructs the self-styled Freudian analysis mounted by Wilson, censuring his attempt to overrule, silence, and repress the story's inherent ambiguities. Such ambiguities, she maintains, evince "literature's subversion of the very possibility of psychoanalytic mastery" ("Turning the Screw of Interpretation," 199). Felman's emphasis on ambiguity does not prevent her from weaving her own forceful (and occasionally forced) interpretation of the text; see, for example, 171, 193.

9. Wilson labels the governess "a neurotic case of sex repression" and the ghosts "not real ghosts but [her] hallucinations" ("Ambiguity of Henry James," 88). Edel also detects "deep hysteria" in the governess, for whom the

ghosts are "private phantoms," creations of a "too-vivid imagination." Emphasizing the young woman's fear of evil rather than her alleged sexual phobia, Edel is convinced that Flora's "beautiful eight-year-old innocence" remains unambiguous. Miles's death at the end of the story is brought on by a woman who has literally killed "innocence" (*Life of Henry James,* 204–6, 213). Goddard defends Miles and Flora's stainless innocence in an overt plea for the survival of romantic faith: "Otherwise, in what but infamy would the younger generation ever end?" To sustain this faith in the children's "armor" of "innocence," Goddard charges the governess with "insanity" ("Pre-Freudian Reading," 206–7).

10. Edel reports that James discussed the tendency of "psychical research" to "wash ghosts clean of all mystery and horror" with the archbishop of Canterbury Edward White Benson, whom he visited in January 1895 (*Life of Henry James,* 89–90).

11. Woolf, "James's Ghost Stories," 179–80; Bell, *Meaning in Henry James,* 228.

12. Spilka, "Turning the Freudian Screw," 248.

13. Coveney, *Image of Childhood,* 209–10.

14. Ibid., 210, 193.

15. Spilka, "Turning the Freudian Screw," 252–53.

16. Foucault, "Repressive Hypothesis," 312, 314.

17. Ibid., 318–20.

18. Felman, "Turning the Screw of Interpretation," 199.

19. Bell, extending the analogy, observes that in "crafting her story," the governess is "like the writer" as well as the reader (*Meaning in Henry James,* 228).

4. Nabokov's Novel Offspring

1. Winn, *Children without Childhood,* 3.

2. For a comparison of Kubrick's film with the novel and with Nabokov's published screenplay, see Pifer, "Incomplete Metamorphosis of *Lolita.*"

3. Tapping the resources of English, French, and Russian Romanticism, Humbert's evocation of the nymphet combines the *rusalka,* the water nymph or sprite of Russian folklore, with the *neznakomka,* the incognita or alluring stranger, in the neoromantic poems of the Russian symbolist Aleksandr Blok; for a discussion of the *rusalka* as well as of the incognita in Blok and other writers who may have influenced Nabokov, see Johnson, "L'inconnue de la Seine."

4. Alexandrov observes that Nabokov's later Russian translation of *Lolita* "makes the point even more bluntly"; instead of the sentence "Lolita had been safely solipsized," the Russian version reads: "Real'nost' Lolity byla

blagopoluchno otmenena" (Lolita's reality was successfully canceled) (49) (*Nabokov's Otherworld,* 170–71). Humbert's description of the solipsized, will-less child echoes the language of Victorian child-rearing manuals that fostered, as Kincaid says in *Child-Loving,* "wax and clay" images of passive children waiting to be molded by the adult's will; as one manual bluntly puts it, children "have no will of their own" (90).

5. Rougemont incorrectly argues that by "disenchanting" romantic "Myth," irony ensures *Lolita's* failure to "move" us (*Love Declared,* 52–54). Appel more accurately employs the definition of *parody* Nabokov provides in one of his novels—"as a kind of springboard for leaping into the highest region of serious emotion"—to characterize *Lolita's* ultimate effects (*Sebastian Knight,* 91; cited in Appel, *Annotated Lolita,* liii). Like Rougemont, Blum argues that *Lolita's* parodic structure prohibits the reader from taking the characters seriously. The plight of the abused child, in particular, is robbed of poignancy by "a text that parodies all literary conventions" and manifests a "brand of narcissism" that is "pathological" (*Hide and Seek,* 214). For a critical overview of a half century of similar charges, see chap. 1 of Pifer, *Nabokov and the Novel.*

6. Fiedler, cited by Phyllis Roth in her introduction to *Critical Essays on Vladimir Nabokov,* 13; Fiedler, *Love and Death,* 326–27.

7. Watt, *Rise of the Novel,* 156–57.

8. Kincaid states, "The idea that children might be invested with a low-level, junior-grade sexuality—something between nothing whatever and full-fledged carnality—is seldom advanced and less often welcome" (*Child-Loving,* 183).

9. Appel, *Annotated Lolita,* l n. 2; Appel, "Nabokov's Puppet Show," 26.

10. See Boyd, *American Years,* 166–98.

11. For a discussion of the connections Nabokov privately drew in his teaching copy of *Bleak House* between Dickens's "gentle little nymphs" and his own unfortunate "nymphet," see Pifer, "Innocence and Experience Replayed," 20–21.

12. The quote from Leavis is in his introduction to Coveney, *Image of Childhood,* 23.

13. Nabokov, cited in Boyd, *Russian Years,* 187–88.

14. Cowart notes that the middle-aged, eponymous hero of Nabokov's *Pnin* is sympathetically rendered as a *childlike* adult: "With his bald head and 'infantile absence of eyebrows' . . . , Pnin seems hairless as a baby, and in fact the author consistently characterizes him as a child: he speaks English with difficulty; he has tiny feet; and he occupies, on more than one occasion, rooms furnished for children" ("Art and Exile," 199).

15. Nabokov, cited in Toker, *Nabokov,* 177–78.

16. For a discussion of *Lolita's* political implications, see Pifer, "Nabokov's Discovery of America."

17. Postman, *Disappearance of Childhood,* 108.

18. Spilka ventures on shaky ground when he equates Humbert's desire to escape to "an idyllic realm" with Nabokov's own "regressive" longing and "nostalgia" ("Enrichment of Poor Monkeys," 174–76). Blurring the distinction between *Lolita's* author and narrator, Spilka overlooks the ways the novel's style and structure undermine the narrator's self-serving claims.

19. Although Humbert's narrative never directly refers to *Frankenstein,* Nabokov, from childhood a voracious reader in three languages, undoubtedly read Shelley's popular classic in his youth. It is quite likely, moreover, that he would have reacquainted himself with the novel in the course of his research for the thousand-page scholarly commentary that accompanies his translation of Aleksandr Pushkin's *Eugene Onegin.* Here Nabokov's prodigious knowledge of the English Romantics—Byron, Wordsworth, and Percy Bysshe Shelley, as well as their European precursors, contemporaries, and epigones—is both obvious and well documented. Nabokov, in his commentary on the translation of *Eugene Onegin,* refers to Shelley's "widow" when glossing a line (chap. 3, stanza 9, l. 8) of Pushkin's novel in verse: "according to his widow," Nabokov comments, "one summer evening [the poet] heard the skylark and saw the 'glow-worm golden in a dell of dew' mentioned in his famous ode" (2:344).

20. Knoepflmacher, "Aggression of Daughters," 100–101.

21. Stevick discusses the "problematic comedy" of Shelley's novel, which belongs to "a class of works" that "generate simultaneously mythic seriousness and uncomfortable laughter" ("*Frankenstein* and Comedy," 222).

22. Oates detects in Humbert's reference to the nymphet as "some immortal daemon disguised as a female child" a "cultural relationship" between *Lolita,* the manuscript of which Nabokov evidently finished in the spring of 1954, and William March's *The Bad Seed,* published in that same "watershed" year. She implies that "[al]though Nabokov the aesthete would have distanced himself from March," he shares something of the latter's demonic vision of childhood ("Killer Kids," 20). To the contrary: not only Nabokov's aesthetics but his ethical and epistemological understanding of reality—in which the child embodies human creativity and freedom—places him in diametric opposition to March's deterministic vision of the "bad seed," the child's genetic predisposition to evil.

23. For an extended comparison of Quilty and the creature in their function as doubles, see Pifer, "Her Monster, His Nymphet."

24. Brooks, "Godlike Science/Unhallowed Arts," 220, 217.

25. Alexandrov observes that Nabokov regarded human evil not as the manifestation of some vital force or *presence* but as the outcome or effect of *absence*—the absence of good (*Nabokov's Otherworld,* 53–55). His discussion draws on the essay in which Nabokov declares his "irrational belief in the

goodness of man," adding: "Now 'badness' is a stranger to our inner world; it
eludes our grasp; 'badness' is in fact the lack of something rather than a nox-
ious presence; and thus being abstract and bodiless it occupies no real space
in our inner world" ("Art of Literature," 373, 375–76).

26. Wood, *Magician's Doubts*, 7, 115; on this point Nabokov says, "I do think
that Humbert Humbert in his last stage is a moral man because he realizes
that he loves *Lolita* [*sic*]," but "it is too late, he has destroyed her childhood"
(cited in Rampton, *Critical Study of the Novels*, 202 n. 34). For a discussion of
the liberating power of love in Nabokov's universe, see Pifer, "Shades of
Love."

27. Grylls, *Guardians and Angels*, 140.

5. Ambiguous Constructs

1. The 1976 edition of *The Painted Bird*, to which all references here are
made, incorporates material that did not appear in the first edition. Park
recounts that on 22 June 1982 a controversy over Kosinski's authorship of his
works was launched by a cover story in the *Village Voice* titled "Jerzy Kosinski's
Tainted Words" (*Jerzy Kosinski*, 388). Although the original exposé has since
proved to contain inaccuracies and false claims of its own, that Kosinski privately employed editors and translators (from Polish into English) to help
him revise and polish *The Painted Bird*, as well as other works published under
his name, has been established. For details, see Park's carefully documented
biography, *Jerzy Kosinski*, 5–6, 174, 197–202, 205–7, 385–93, and passim.

2. Sokoloff, *Imagining the Child*, 223 n. 11; Couturier, "Nabokov in Postmodernist Land," 255.

3. The parallels between Kosinski's childhood in Nazi-occupied Poland
and that of his protagonist are, we now know, far from exact—despite the
autobiographical claims he made in interviews. Nevertheless, many documented experiences in his early life serve as the genesis for events depicted in
the novel, often in nightmarish and surreal form. For a detailed account of
the parallels as well as transmogrifications, see Park, *Jerzy Kosinski*, on the
novelist's childhood (7–58); his fictitious accounts of that childhood (107–9,
171–72); and the writing and publication of *The Painted Bird* (189–95, 214–18).

4. In Teicholz, Kosinski describes his prose style as the "opposite" of
"what Nabokov does." Nabokov's "language is made visible . . . like a veil or
transparent curtain with a beautiful design. You cannot help seeing the curtain as you peek into the intimate room behind. My aim," he says, "is to
remove the veil" (*Conversations with Jerzy Kosinski*, 29, ellipses in original).

5. Sokoloff, *Imagining the Child*, 112–13.

6. Lilly, *Words in Search of Victims*, 37; Kosinski, cited in Lavers, *Jerzy
Kosinski*, 56.

7. In marked contrast to Dolores Haze, the girls whom Kosinski's boy meets in the orphanage after the war are, like him, thoroughly conditioned by their sordid experiences: "They stripped and asked boys to touch them. They discussed blatantly the sexual demands which scores of men had made on them during the war. There were some who said they could not go to sleep without having had a man. They ran out into the parks at night and picked up drunken soldiers" (228–29).

8. Baudrillard, *Simulacres et simulation,* 16; cited in Couturier, "Nabokov in Postmodernist Land," 256. Gelfant observes that "while critics may differ in their definitions of *postmodern,* they generally agree that the term implies a fundamental questioning, if not outright dismissal, of the grounds upon which belief in truth has traditionally been established. This dismissal would invalidate claims, however circumstanced, for the absoluteness or universality of human values, for essentialism, and for the possibility of transcendence" (*Cross-Cultural Reckonings,* 48 n. 3). According to this definition, Nabokov— whose image of childhood is based on just such values, essentialism, and the possibility of transcendence—is decidedly *not* a postmodernist.

9. According to Kosinski's deterministic vision, all "the children, the painted birds themselves," who survived the war are destined to pay the "blood debt of revenge" with a hatred to which "no death is granted" (*Passing By,* 219–22).

6. The Child of Apocalypse

1. Golding, cited in Ginden, *William Golding,* 14; Golding, cited in Crompton, *View from the Spire,* 14.

2. L. L. Dickson notes that Matty's name translates as gift of God; he also discusses the relevance of Matthew 7 to the novel (*Modern Allegories,* 112). Crompton notes that Matty's surname undergoes successive distortions in the mouths of the other characters—who call him everything from Wandgrave to Wildwort to Windgraff—and is only identified as Windrove in the last pages of the novel (e.g., 247, 264) (*View from the Spire,* 97).

3. Crompton, *View from the Spire,* 100–101. Assigning Matty the role of "true innocent," Crompton confuses this character's otherworldliness and intense spirituality with "primal innocence"; earlier in *View from the Spire* he more accurately notes that for Golding loss of innocence is "the universal experience of mankind"; both adult and child share in that universal "loss of innocence . . . embodied in the myth of the fall" (14).

4. Cantor, "Adolf, We Hardly Knew You," 39.

5. When Goodchild makes this comment to Edwin about Pedigree's use of bait to attract young boys, he is referring to the children's books Pedigree once tried to steal from his shop. What Goodchild does not tell Edwin is that

he has also used children's books as bait to attract the Stanhope twins to his store (195).

6. Golding, in a letter cited in Crompton, *View from the Spire,* 11; Redpath, *William Golding,* 52–55.

7. Kuhn, *Corruption in Paradise,* 156; Crompton, *View from the Spire,* 10.

7. New Versions of the Idyll

1. Empson demonstrates the constancy of the theme of nature's benignity in the different forms and periods of pastoral writing; informing the Romantic idyll of childhood, for example, is the idea of the child as being "in the right relation to Nature" (*Some Versions of Pastoral,* 128–29, 261). Bakhtin notes the idyll's characteristic "association of *food* and *children*": "This matrix is shot through with the beginnings of growth and the renewing of life. In the idyll, children often function as a sublimation of the sexual act and of conception" (*Dialogic Imagination,* 227).

2. Mellor, *Mary Shelley,* 50.

3. The Lovatts' suggestive-sounding name may be another allusion to Shelley's novel, life, and work. Mellor points out that Mary's stepmother, Mary Jane Clairmont, gave the nickname Love-will to her youngest son, William—whom her husband and Shelley's father, William Godwin, named after himself and who was "the favored child in the Godwin-Clairmont household" (ibid., 47). Mary, whose mother died shortly after her birth, was not well loved by her stepmother. As Butler says in her introduction to *Frankenstein,* Shelley's stepmother "had uneven relationships with her step-daughters" and was "jealous of the clever Mary, her rival for Godwin's attention" (ix).

4. Brooks, "Godlike Science/Unhallowed Arts," 216–18; Moers, "Female Gothic," 77.

5. Mellor, *Mary Shelley,* 122.

6. Ibid., 124.

7. Spacks, *Adolescent Idea,* 260.

8. May, "Myths and Realities," 540.

9. Singleton points out that in Lessing's novels "the characters are never separate from their society; their individual ills are always reflections of larger social ills" (*City and the Veld,* 164). Sprague similarly notes that "the private and the public, the individual and the collective, make a permanent dialectic in Lessing's work" (*Rereading Doris Lessing,* 8).

10. Incorporating elements of the fantastic, *The Fifth Child* nonetheless continues the enterprise begun in Lessing's earlier series of realist novels, *Children of Violence:* to "study," as the novelist says in "Small Personal Voice," "the individual conscience in its relations with the collective" (22). Lessing's

five-novel series comprises the following works: *Martha Quest* (1952); *A Proper Marriage* (1954); *A Ripple from the Storm* (1958); *Landlocked* (1965); and *The Four-Gated City* (1969).

11. Coveney, *Image of Childhood,* 124.

12. Spilka, "Enrichment of Poor Monkeys," 166–67; Houghton, *Victorian Frame of Mind,* 344–46.

13. Ariès, *Centuries of Childhood,* 406–7.

14. The financial toll exacted by the Lovatts' dream house calls to mind Zelizer's statement, cited in chapter 1, about the mounting cost of the economically useless child in today's society. Like the outsize house, the Lovatts' domestic dream is a luxury or indulgence they can ill afford.

15. In Rodenberg, Lessing discusses the institution to which Ben is taken: "I once saw such a place, by chance, and then you suddenly realize that [our civilization] may not *murder* these damaged creatures that are born, the ones that are totally deformed or [have] no brains or something. They don't get *murdered,* they just get stuck in institutions, and . . . people turn the other eye" (*"Fifth Child,"* 4).

16. Mellor, *Mary Shelley,* 131, 128.

17. Suransky, *Erosion of Childhood,* 8, 32, 189.

18. Barnouw indicates Lessing's affinity with Robert Musil, whose *Man without Qualities* is cited in a lengthy epigraph to the second part of *The Four-Gated City* and whose hostility to modern-day specialization Lessing shares: "The split between experience and knowledge has [in Musil's view] become too wide; the caricature of knowledge, scientific specialization, carries a great potential of destruction. The evil is by no means science *per se* . . . but its openness to exploitation by the stupidity of power" ("Disorderly Company," 94).

19. Mellor, *Mary Shelley,* 134.

20. Derrida, "Structure, Sign, and Play," 93–94.

21. Kundera, cited in Philip Roth, "Afterword," 234.

22. Ibid., 233.

8. History's Offspring

1. Parameswaran notes that Rushdie got the idea of placing his narrator-protagonist at the center of "so many political events" from observing the way that "a child usually sees himself centre-stage" ("Handcuffed to History," 40).

2. White, "Historical Text as Literary Artifact," 407.

3. Chaudhuri, "Writing the Raj Away," 29.

4. Philip Weinstein, *What Else but Love?* 74.

5. Booker, "Beauty and the Beast," 983.

6. Hutcheon, "Politics of Postmodernism," 65.

7. Doody, *True Story of the Novel,* 480–81, 485.

8. Parameswaran, "Handcuffed to History," 41; Srivastava, "Empire Writes Back," 63. Malak identifies the open-ended or indeterminate structure embraced by the narrator with Rushdie's postmodernist vision: "Like all postmodern writers, [Rushdie] sees reality . . . as an unfinished project, a flux of phenomena that resists containment or closure and remains open to multiple renditions and projections" ("Reading the Crisis," 182).

9. For a detailed discussion of the nose theme and its historical implications in *Tristram Shandy* and *Midnight's Children,* see Hawes, "Leading History by the Nose."

10. Batty compares Padma's role in the novel with that of King Shahryar in *The Arabian Nights:* "Padma becomes an index for reader-response to the framed narrative," an effect "further reinforced by Saleem's explicit dependence on Padma as a conduit for his narrative." As the novel progresses, "Padma not only serves as an index for Saleem's successes and failures as an autobiographer but also plays an important role in the creation of his story" ("Art of Suspense," 53).

11. Booker, "Beauty and the Beast," 987, 995.

12. On the affinities of *Midnight's Children* with *The Tin Drum,* as well as with Gabriel García Márquez's *One Hundred Years of Solitude,* see Merivale, "Saleem Fathered by Oskar."

13. Srivastava draws an analogy between the way "Saleem suffers history through his body" and Foucault's account, in "Nietzsche, Genealogy, History," of the way a human body, "imprinted by history," traces "the process of history's destruction of the body" ("Empire Writes Back," 69; "Nietzsche, Genealogy, History," 148).

9. Memory's Child

1. Clemons cites Morrison as saying that sixty million signifies "the best educated guess at the number of black Africans who never made it into slavery—those who died either as captives in Africa or on the slave ships" ("Ghosts of 'Sixty Million More,'" 75). In Taylor-Guthrie, Morrison explains that sixty million was the smallest number or estimate she came across in her research (*Conversations with Toni Morrison,* 257).

2. Spillers notes that the "cultural text" of institutionalized slavery is inscribed on Sethe's body in a "hieroglyphics of the flesh" ("Mama's Baby, Papa's Maybe," 67). Philip Weinstein observes that "Sethe's history is a history of her body"—the "slave body" being "wholly exposed, invaded and operated by others, the locus of an entire people's humiliating nonownership" (*What Else but Love?* 176–77).

3. Philip Weinstein, *What Else but Love?* 74.

4. Taylor-Guthrie, *Conversations with Toni Morrison,* 247.

5. Carmean, *World of Toni Morrison,* 87.

6. In Taylor-Guthrie, Morrison says that she based her novel on a historical incident reported in a newspaper clipping about a runaway slave named Margaret Garner, who in 1851 "succeeded in killing one [of her children]; she tried to kill two others." Morrison points out that the ending of her "story, [her] invention, is much happier than what really happened" to Garner, who was "returned to slavery" and "sold down river" by her owner (*Conversations with Toni Morrison,* 206–7, 250–51).

7. Wyatt says that "Sethe extends her rights over her own body . . . to the 'parts of her' that are her children, folding them back into the maternal body in order to enter death as a single unit" ("Giving Body to the Word," 476); see also Rigney, "A Story to Pass On," 231.

8. Bradley et al. point out that no one knows why Twain changed his "stated plan to send Jim up the Ohio toward freedom"; it is a "problem" that "seems to have perplexed [Twain] himself" (Adventures of Huckleberry Finn, 77 n. 5). Morrison offers her own explanation for Twain's decision. To allow Jim "to enter the mouth of the Ohio River and pass into free territory" would be to grant the black man absolute freedom. Such freedom would have proved fatal to the novel's "premise": without Jim, Huck could not "mature into a moral human being" (*Playing in the Dark,* 56).

9. Trilling, *Liberal Imagination,* 107; Toni Morrison, *Playing in the Dark,* 56–57.

10. Trilling, *Liberal Imagination,* 108; Carmean, *World of Toni Morrison,* 88. Otten notes Beloved's "remarkably ambiguous force" but employs religious paradox to explain it: "she is on the one hand 'an evil thing,' on the other a Christ figure come to save" (*Crime of Innocence,* 84).

11. Arnold Weinstein notes that "the coupling of Paul D and Beloved . . . is presented as a dark, elemental current that cannot be resisted, a force that *moves* Paul D and betokens . . . union of the sundered self, of name and body, of blocked past and present state"; Beloved's "pivotal structural role" is "to *move* others, to be the fluid principle of linkage and connection" (*Nobody's Home,* 273). Barnett characterizes Beloved's seduction of Paul D as rape ("Figurations of Rape," 423); she disagrees with critics, myself included, who hold with Valerie Smith that "the act of intercourse with Beloved restores Paul D to himself" ("Circling the Subject," 348).

12. Arnold Weinstein, *Nobody's Home,* 271.

13. Barnett identifies Beloved as both "succubus and incubus" and interprets her craving for life as a deliberate attempt to get pregnant—a reading for which there is little textual evidence: Beloved "collects sperm from Paul D to impregnate herself, then uses the life force of her mother's body to sustain her spawn" ("Figurations of Rape," 422).

14. Holloway and Demetrakopoulos, *New Dimensions of Spirituality,* 161.

15. Rodrigues,"Telling of *Beloved,*" 162.

16. Taylor-Guthrie, *Conversations with Toni Morrison,* 247.

17. Phelan enumerates a number of sometimes contradictory readings to which the repeated phrase "not a story to pass on" gives rise. Like Beloved's multiple identities, these multiple meanings end by thwarting the would-be interpreter's "desire for mastery and possession" of the text and of Beloved's definitive identity ("Rhetorical Reader-Response Criticism," 720–23). Pérez-Torres develops a different line of argument:"by ambiguously suggesting that Beloved's story should neither be forgotten nor repeated," the phrase "to pass on" encapsulates the novel's thematic "interplay of absence and presence"; *Beloved,* he adds, evokes an African American "presence" based "upon a historical, cultural and political absence" ("Knitting and Knotting the Narrative Thread," 691, 707). Both critics recognize what Morrison calls the "oral quality" of her language—the way that stress, rhythm, "intonation, volume," and "gesture" determine the meaning of what is said and heard (Taylor-Guthrie, *Conversations with Toni Morrison,* 166).

18. Doody, *True Story of the Novel,* 379–80, 383.

10. Reclaiming the Lost Child

1. In his acknowledgments McEwan lists three works of nonfiction that influenced the writing of *The Child in Time:* Hardyment's *Dream Babies,* Pearce's *Magical Child,* and Bohm's *Wholeness and the Implicate Order.* The first two books deal with children and child rearing; the third, written by a theoretical physicist and philosopher, offers a new theory of time and reality. Bohm, like Pearce, holds that the traditional, Cartesian dichotomy of mind and matter is false, closing us off from the child's initial, intuitively correct apprehension of the universe as a whole or continuum.

2. Slay, *Ian McEwan,* 38–39.

3. Blake Morrison reports the precise timing of these taped events:"The security videotape shows James [Bulger] alone outside the butcher's shop at 15:38:55 and his mother searching for him at 15:40:24. At 15:43:08, some four minutes after he left the butcher's, there is that last shot of him leaving the shopping center, his hand placed trustingly in the hand of Jon Venables" ("Children of Circumstance," 49).

4. Kiernan, *Ian McEwan,* 49. McEwan, citing Hardyment's *Dream Babies,* says:"What comes out of [Hardyment's] book quite wonderfully is how any age distills itself into its childcare books.... You get late 18th century books that are very much influenced by Rousseau, then mid-Victorian harshness, then Edwardian sentimentality....The postwar era was dominated by Spock and again, libertarian, optimistic ideas of human nature." For *The Child in*

Time McEwan imagined "that the next childcare book could be authoritarian and that the state would write it" (Amanda Smith, "PW Interviews," 69).

5. Pearce suggests that "magical thinking," a term first employed by Jean Piaget to describe the child's wishful thinking or fantasizing, has a basis in reality: that, in other words, "some connection exists between thought and reality, that thinking enters into and can influence the actual world" (*Magical Child,* xiii–xiv). McEwan's professor Brody similarly states, "We are both alienated and stunted by abstraction, removed from the profound and immediate apprehension—which is the hallmark of a whole person—of the dancing interpenetration of the physical and the psychic, their ultimate inseparability" (85).

6. Bohm advances a view of reality that attempts to bridge the gap between quantum mechanics and relativity theory and, like Pearce, the conventional divide between mind and matter. To Bohm "the nature of reality in general and consciousness in particular [is] a coherent whole, which is never static or complete, but which is in an unending process of unfoldment." Beneath the more apparent "explicate order" of discrete elements and events, each occupying its "own particular region of space" and time, he postulates a multidimensional "implicate order." Using the example of a hologram, which records and stores an entire image in each part of its pattern, Bohm says that the implicate order consists of "everything . . . enfolded into everything." Through an intricate process of reasoning, he suggests an order of time radically different from conventional notions. In this temporal structure "sequences of moments that 'skip' intervening spaces are just as allowable forms of time as those which seem continuous." At The Bell, Stephen appears to apprehend the implicate order, whose elements he experiences not as isolated moments separated by decades of continuous unfoldment but simultaneously, as part of what Bohm calls the "totality of existence" (*Wholeness and the Implicate Order,* ix, 177, 211, 172).

7. Kiernan, *Ian McEwan,* 53; Doody, *True Story of the Novel,* 473.

8. See Slay, *Ian McEwan,* 133; and Kiernan, *Ian McEwan,* 54.

11. The Child as Mysterious Agent

1. Lentricchia, introduction to *New Essays on* White Noise, 7.

2. Ferraro, "Whole Families Shopping at Night!" 16–17. Jack also has two daughters by Dana Breedlove, to whom he was married twice; separated from Steffie, her full sister, by "ten years and two marriages," as Jack puts it, nineteen-year-old Mary Alice does not live with the Gladneys (*White Noise* 236).

3. Baudrillard coined the term *simulacrum* in *Simulacres et simulation* in an effort to distinguish between simulation and representation in literary texts.

He goes further in *America,* where he describes the American environment as "the perfect simulacrum"—a world cut off from the real: "Everything is destined to reappear as simulation. Landscapes as photography, . . . terrorism as fashion and the media, and events as television" (28, 32).

4. Lentricchia, introduction to *New Essays on* White Noise, 7.

5. DeCurtis, "Outsider in This Society," 63.

6. Moses, "Lust Removed from Nature," 72.

7. DeCurtis, "Outsider in This Society," 64, 55; DeLillo's latter statement cited in Keesey, *Don DeLillo,* 2.

8. Marcel, *Mystery of Being,* 1:211–12; Marcel, *Metaphysical Journal,* 160–61.

9. According to DeLillo, the creative power of language is a power through which the writer can "make or remake himself" and "restructure reality." But the novelist is also aware of the limits of language: what proves "untellable" to the writer "points to the limitations of language" as we know it; what intrigues him is the possibility that "another, clearer language" lurks "somewhere in the brain" but is not transmitted through conventional speech. "Will we speak it and hear it when we die?" DeLillo rhetorically asks. "Did we know it before we were born?" He adds, "Maybe this is why there's so much babbling in my books. Babbling can be frustrated speech, or it can be a purer form, an alternate speech. I wrote a short story that ends with two babies babbling at each other in a car. This was something I'd seen and heard, and it was a dazzling and unforgettable scene. I felt these babies *knew* something" (LeClair, "Interview with Don DeLillo," 81–84).

10. Maltby says the "idea that language has 'fallen' or grown remote from some pure and semantically rich primal state is" characteristically "Romantic, and most reminiscent of views held by, among others, Rousseau and Wordsworth" ("Romantic Metaphysics," 262, 263–64).

11. Williams, *Problems in Materialism and Culture,* 185, 189.

12. Arnold Weinstein, *Nobody's Home,* 306.

13. Cantor, "Adolf, We Hardly Knew You," 60.

14. Arnold Weinstein, *Nobody's Home,* 291, 299.

15. Maltby, "Romantic Metaphysics," 274–75. Assuming that the "order of meaning" DeLillo's characters discover carries objective rather than subjective significance, Maltby finds that the novelist's "fiction betrays a conservative tendency," one that radically undermines DeLillo's status "as an exemplary postmodern writer." Cantor finds that "DeLillo wavers between criticizing postmodernism and practicing it"; he "seems unable to break out of the postmodern circle and offer a convincing alternative to its diminished reality. In short, he can give us a vision of the inauthentic but not, it seems, of the authentic" ("Adolf, We Hardly Knew You," 60–61).

16. Lentricchia, "Tales of the Electronic Tribe," 106; DeCurtis, "Outsider in This Society," 55.

17. DeCurtis, "Outsider in This Society," 63.

18. LeClair, *In the Loop,* 213. LeClair maintains that *White Noise* "can be read as a dialogue with Ernest Becker's *The Denial of Death,* which is one of the few 'influences' DeLillo will confirm"; the novelist "seems to accept Becker's Existential and Rankian positions that the fear of death is the main-spring of human motivation and that man needs to belong to a system of ideas in which mystery exists."

19. Moses, "Lust Removed from Nature," 75, 79–80.

20. Arnold Weinstein, *Nobody's Home,* 311.

21. DeLillo has alluded to the child's state of linguistic undress: "It's as though language is something we wear," and the "more we know someone, the easier it is to undress, to become childlike" (LeClair, "Interview with Don DeLillo," 84).

Conclusion

1. LeClair, "Interview with Don DeLillo," 85.

2. Kincaid, *Erotic Innocence,* 281, 284, 6.

3. Ibid., 284, 289.

4. Ibid., 290.

5. Edmundson, *Nightmare on Main Street,* 33, xv.

6. Margot Hornblower, "The Boy Who Loved Bombs," *Time,* 1 June 1998, 42–43.

7. Edmundson, *Nightmare on Main Street,* 4, xv; Kincaid, *Erotic Innocence,* 140.

8. Crouch, *Notes of a Hanging Judge,* 205.

Bibliography

Primary Sources

DeLillo, Don. *Libra.* New York:Viking, 1988.

———. *White Noise.* 1985. New York: Penguin, 1986.

Dickens, Charles. *Bleak House.* 1852–53. New York: Dell, 1965.

———. *Dombey and Son.* 1846–48. New York: Fawcett, 1963.

———. *Great Expectations.* 1860–61. New York: New American Library, 1963.

Golding,William. *Darkness Visible.* New York: Harcourt Brace, 1979.

———. *The Hot Gates and Other Occasional Pieces.* New York: Harcourt Brace, 1966.

———. *Lord of the Flies.* London: Faber and Faber, 1954.

James, Henry. *The Art of the Novel: Critical Prefaces.* Ed. R. P. Blackmur. New York: Scribner's, 1934.

———."The Pupil." 1891. In *The Great Short Novels of Henry James,* ed. Philip Rahv, 565–619. New York: Carroll and Graf, 1986.

———. *The Turn of the Screw.* 1898. In *Henry James,* The Turn of the Screw: *An Authoritative Text, Backgrounds, and Sources, Essays in Criticism,* ed. Robert Kimbrough, 1–88. New York: Norton, 1966.

———. *What Maisie Knew.* 1897. Garden City, N.Y.: Doubleday, 1954.

Kosinski, Jerzy. *The Painted Bird.* 1965. Rev. ed. New York: Bantam, 1976.

———. *Passing By: Selected Essays, 1962–1991.* New York: Random House, 1992.

Kundera, Milan. *The Book of Laughter and Forgetting.* 1978. Trans. Michael Henry Heim. New York: Penguin, 1984.

Lagerkvist, Pär. *The Dwarf.* 1945. Trans. Alexandra Dick. New York: Hill and Wang, 1945.

Lessing, Doris. *The Fifth Child.* 1988. New York: Vintage, 1989.
————. "The Small Personal Voice." In *Declaration,* ed. Tom Maschler, 12–27. London: MacGibbon and Kee, 1957.
McEwan, Ian. *The Child in Time.* Boston: Houghton Mifflin, 1987.
Morrison, Toni. *Beloved.* New York: New American Library, 1987.
————. *Playing in the Dark: Whiteness and the American Imagination.* Cambridge, Mass.: Harvard Univ. Press, 1992.
Nabokov, Vladimir. "The Art of Literature and Commonsense." In *Lectures on Literature,* 371–80.
————. *Bend Sinister.* 1947. New York: McGraw-Hill, 1974.
————. *Invitation to a Beheading.* 1938. Trans. Dmitri Nabokov in collaboration with the author. New York: Putnam, 1959.
————. *Lectures on Literature.* Ed. Fredson Bowers. New York: Harcourt Brace, 1980.
————. *Lolita.* 1955. New York: Putnam, 1958.
————. *Lolita.* Russian trans. Vladimir Nabokov. New York: Phaedra, 1967.
————. *The Real Life of Sebastian Knight.* Norfolk, Conn.: New Directions, 1941.
————. *Speak, Memory: An Autobiography Revisited.* Rev. ed. New York: Putnam, 1966.
————. *Strong Opinions.* New York: McGraw-Hill, 1973.
Pushkin, Aleksandr. *Eugene Onegin: A Novel in Verse.* Trans. with commentary by Vladimir Nabokov. Bollingen Series 72. 1964. Rev. ed. 2 vols. Princeton, N.J.: Princeton Univ. Press, 1975.
Rushdie, Salman. *Imaginary Homelands: Essays and Criticism, 1981–1991.* London: Granta in association with Penguin, 1991.
————. *Midnight's Children.* 1980. New York: Penguin, 1991.
Shelley, Mary. *Frankenstein, or the Modern Prometheus.* 1818. Ed. Marilyn Butler. New York: Oxford Univ. Press, 1994.
Twain, Mark. *The Adventures of Huckleberry Finn.* 1884. New York: Bantam, 1981.

Secondary Sources

Alexandrov, Vladimir E. *Nabokov's Otherworld.* Princeton, N.J.: Princeton Univ. Press, 1991.
Appel, Alfred, Jr. "Nabokov's Puppet Show, Pt. II." *New Republic,* 21 Jan. 1967, 25–32.
————, ed. *The Annotated Lolita.* New York: McGraw-Hill, 1970.
Ariès, Philippe. *Centuries of Childhood: A Social History of Family Life.* Trans. Robert Baldick. New York: Knopf, 1962.
Ariès, Philippe, and Georges Duby, eds. *A History of Private Life.* Trans. Arthur

Goldhammer. 5 vols. Cambridge, Mass.: Belknap Press of Harvard Univ. Press, 1987–91.

Bakhtin, Mikhail. *The Dialogic Imagination: Four Essays.* Trans. Caryl Emerson and Michael Holquist. Austin: Univ. of Texas Press, 1981.

Barnett, Pamela E. "Figurations of Rape and the Supernatural in *Beloved.*" *PMLA* 112, no. 3 (May 1997): 418–27.

Barnouw, Dagmar. "Disorderly Company: From *The Golden Notebook* to *The Four-Gated City.*" In *Doris Lessing: Critical Studies,* ed. Annis Pratt and L. S. Dembo, 74–97. Madison: Univ. of Wisconsin Press, 1974.

Batty, Nancy E. "The Art of Suspense: Rushdie's 1001 (Mid-)Nights." *Ariel* 18, no. 3 (July 1987): 49–65.

Baudrillard, Jean. *America.* Trans. Chris Turner. London: Verso, 1988.

————. *Simulacres et simulation.* Paris: Galilée, 1981.

Becker, Ernest. *The Denial of Death.* New York: Free Press, 1973.

Bell, Millicent. *Meaning in Henry James.* Cambridge, Mass.: Harvard Univ. Press, 1991.

Blum, Virginia L. *Hide and Seek: The Child between Psychoanalysis and Fiction.* Urbana: Univ. of Illinois Press, 1995.

Boas, George. *The Cult of Childhood.* London: Warburg Institute, 1966.

Bohm, David. *Wholeness and the Implicate Order.* London: Routledge, 1980.

Booker, M. Keith. "Beauty and the Beast: Dualism as Despotism in the Fiction of Salman Rushdie." *ELH* 57 (1990): 977–97.

Boyd, Brian. *Vladimir Nabokov: The American Years.* Princeton, N.J.: Princeton Univ. Press, 1991.

————. *Vladimir Nabokov: The Russian Years.* Princeton, N.J.: Princeton Univ. Press, 1990.

Bradbury, Malcolm. *The Modern American Novel.* Rev. ed. New York: Viking, 1992.

Bradley, Sculley, et al., eds. The Adventures of Huckleberry Finn: *An Authoritative Text, Backgrounds and Sources, Criticism.* 2d ed. New York: Norton, 1977.

Brooks, Peter. "'Godlike Science/Unhallowed Arts': Language, Nature, and Monstrosity." In *The Endurance of* Frankenstein: *Essays on Mary Shelley's Novel,* ed. George Levine and U. C. Knoepflmacher, 205–20. Berkeley: Univ. of California Press, 1979.

Cantor, Paul A. "Adolf, We Hardly Knew You." In Lentricchia, *New Essays on* White Noise, 39–62.

Carmean, Karen. *The World of Toni Morrison.* Troy, N.Y.: Whitston, 1993.

Carter, Geoffrey. "Sexuality and the Victorian Artist: Dickens and Swinburne." In *Sexuality and Victorian Literature,* ed. Don Richard Cox, 141–55. Knoxville: Univ. of Tennessee Press, 1984.

Chaudhuri, Una. "Writing the Raj Away." *Turnstile* 2, no. 1 (1990): 26–35.

Chesney, Kellow. *The Anti-Society: An Account of the Victorian Underworld*. Boston: Gambit, 1970.

Clemons, Walter. "The Ghosts of 'Sixty Million More.'" *Newsweek*, 28 Nov. 1987, 74–75.

Cohen, Morton. "Lewis Carroll and Victorian Morality." In *Sexuality and Victorian Literature*, ed. Don Richard Cox, 3–19. Knoxville: Univ. of Tennessee Press, 1984.

Couturier, Maurice. "Nabokov in Postmodernist Land." *Critique* 34, no. 4 (summer 1993): 247–61.

Coveney, Peter. *The Image of Childhood: The Individual and Society, a Study of the Theme in English Literature*. Rev. ed. Baltimore, Md.: Penguin, 1967.

Cowart, David. "Art and Exile: Nabokov's *Pnin*." *Studies in American Fiction* 10, no. 2 (1982): 197–207.

Crews, Frederick. "The Unknown Freud." *New York Review of Books*, 18 Nov. 1993, 55–65.

Crompton, Don. *A View from the Spire: William Golding's Later Novels*. Ed. and completed by Julia Briggs. Oxford: Basil Blackwell, 1985.

Crouch, Stanley. *Notes of a Hanging Judge: Essays and Reviews, 1979–1989*. New York: Oxford Univ. Press, 1990.

Davenport, Guy. *A Balthus Notebook*. New York: Ecco Press, 1989.

DeCurtis, Anthony. "'An Outsider in This Society': An Interview with Don DeLillo." In *Introducing Don DeLillo*, ed. Frank Lentricchia, 43–81. Durham, N.C.: Duke Univ. Press, 1991.

DeMause, Lloyd, ed. *The History of Childhood*. New York: Psychohistory Press, 1974.

Derrida, Jacques. "Structure, Sign, and Play in the Discourse of the Human Sciences." In *Writing and Difference*, trans. Alan Bass. Chicago: Univ. of Chicago Press, 1978. Rpt. in *Critical Theory since 1965*, ed. Hazard Adams and Leroy Searle, 83–94. Tallahassee: Univ. Press of Florida, 1986.

Dickson, L. L. *The Modern Allegories of William Golding*. Tampa: Univ. of South Florida, 1990.

Doody, Margaret Anne. *The True Story of the Novel*. New Brunswick, N.J.: Rutgers Univ. Press, 1996.

Douglas, Mary. *"Les structures de culinaire."* *Communications* 31 (1979): 145–70.

Edel, Leon. *The Life of Henry James: The Treacherous Years (1895–1901)*. Vol. 4. Philadelphia: Lippincott, 1969.

Edmundson, Mark. *Nightmare on Main Street: Angels, Sadomasochism, and the Culture of the Gothic*. Cambridge, Mass.: Harvard Univ. Press, 1997.

Empson, William. *Some Versions of Pastoral*. 1935. Rpt. Norfolk, Conn.: New Directions, 1950.

Felman, Shoshana. "Turning the Screw of Interpretation." *Yale French Studies* 55/56 (1977): 94–207.

Ferraro, Thomas J. "Whole Families Shopping at Night!" In Lentricchia, *New Essays on* White Noise, 15–38.

Fiedler, Leslie. *Love and Death in the American Novel.* New York: Criterion, 1960.

Foucault, Michel. "The Body of the Condemned." In *Discipline and Punish: The Birth of the Prison,* trans. Alan Sheridan. New York: Pantheon, 1977. Rpt. in *The Foucault Reader,* ed. Paul Rabinow, 170–78. New York: Pantheon, 1984.

————. "Nietzsche, Genealogy, History." In *Language, Counter-Memory, Practice.* Ithaca, N.Y.: Cornell Univ. Press, 1977.

————. "The Politics of Health in the Eighteenth Century." In *Power/ Knowledge: Selected Interviews and Other Writings, 1972–1977,* ed. Colin Gordon. New York: Pantheon, 1980. Rpt. in *The Foucault Reader,* ed. Paul Rabinow, 273–89. New York: Pantheon, 1984.

————. "The Repressive Hypothesis." In *The History of Sexuality.* Vol. 1: *An Introduction,* trans. Robert Hurley. New York: Random House, 1978. Rpt. in *The Foucault Reader,* ed. Paul Rabinow, 301–29. New York: Pantheon, 1984.

————. "The Subject and Power." In *Beyond Structuralism and Hermeneutics,* ed. Hubert L. Dreyfus and Paul Rabinow, 208–26. 2d ed. Chicago: Univ. of Chicago Press, 1983.

Freud, Sigmund. *Three Essays on the Theory of Sexuality,* ed. James Strachey. Vol. 7 of *The Standard Edition of the Complete Psychological Works of Sigmund Freud.* London: Hogarth Press, 1953.

Geertz, Clifford. *The Interpretation of Cultures.* New York: Basic Books, 1973.

Geismar, Maxwell. *Henry James and the Jacobites.* Boston: Houghton Mifflin, 1963.

Gelfant, Blanche H. *Cross-Cultural Reckonings: A Triptych of Russian, American, and Canadian Texts.* New York: Cambridge Univ. Press, 1995.

Ginden, James. *William Golding.* Basingstoke, U.K.: Macmillan, 1988.

Goddard, Harold C. "A Pre-Freudian Reading of *The Turn of the Screw.*" *Nineteenth-Century Fiction* 12 (June 1957): 1–36. Rpt. in Kimbrough, *Henry James,* The Turn of the Screw, 181–211.

Grylls, David. *Guardians and Angels: Parents and Children in Nineteenth-Century Literature.* London: Faber and Faber, 1978.

Hardyment, Christina. *Dream Babies: Three Centuries of Good Advice on Child Care.* New York: Harper and Row, 1983.

Hawes, Clement. "Leading History by the Nose: The Turn to the Eighteenth Century in *Midnight's Children.*" *Modern Fiction Studies* 39, no. 1 (1993): 147–68.

Heilman, Robert. "'The Turn of the Screw' as Poem." *University of Kansas City Review* 14 (summer 1948): 277–89. Rpt. in Kimbrough, *Henry James,* The Turn of the Screw, 215–28.

Heller, Erich. *Thomas Mann: The Ironic German*. Cleveland, Ohio: World Publishing, 1958.

Hiner, N. Ray, and Joseph M. Hawes, eds. *Growing Up in America: Children in Historical Perspective*. Urbana: Univ. of Illinois Press, 1985.

Holloway, Karla F. C., and Stephanie A. Demetrakopoulos. *New Dimensions of Spirituality: A Biracial and Bicultural Reading of the Novels of Toni Morrison*. New York: Greenwood, 1987.

Houghton, Walter E. *The Victorian Frame of Mind, 1830–1870*. New Haven, Conn.: Yale Univ. Press, 1957.

Hutcheon, Linda. *The Politics of Postmodernism*. New York: Routledge, 1989.

Johnson, D. Barton. "'L'inconnue de la Seine' and Nabokov's Naiads." *Comparative Literature* 44, no. 3 (1992): 225–48.

Keesey, Douglas. *Don DeLillo*. New York: Twayne, 1993.

Kiernan, Ryan. *Ian McEwan*. Plymouth, U.K.: Northcote, 1994.

Kimbrough, Robert, ed. *Henry James,* The Turn of the Screw: *An Authoritative Text, Backgrounds and Sources, Essays in Criticism*. New York: Norton, 1966.

Kincaid, James R. *Child-Loving: The Erotic Child and Victorian Culture*. New York: Routledge, 1992.

———. *Erotic Innocence: The Culture of Child Molesting*. Durham, N.C.: Duke Univ. Press, 1998.

Knoepflmacher, U. C. "Thoughts on the Aggression of Daughters." In *The Endurance of* Frankenstein: *Essays on Mary Shelley's Novel,* ed. George Levine and U. C. Knoepflmacher, 88–122. Berkeley: Univ. of California Press, 1979.

Krauthammer, Charles. "Defining Deviancy Up." *New Republic,* 22 Nov. 1993, 20–25.

Kuhn, Reinhard. *Corruption in Paradise: The Child in Western Literature*. Hanover, N.H.: Univ. Press of New England, 1982.

Lavers, Norman. *Jerzy Kosinski*. Boston: Twayne, 1982.

LeClair, Tom. *In the Loop: Don DeLillo and the Systems Novel*. Urbana: Univ. of Illinois Press, 1987.

———. "An Interview with Don DeLillo." In *Anything Can Happen: Interviews with Contemporary American Novelists,* ed. Tom LeClair and Larry McCaffery, 79–90. Urbana: Univ. of Illinois Press, 1983.

Lentricchia, Frank. "Tales of the Electronic Tribe." In Lentricchia, *New Essays on* White Noise, 87–113.

———, ed. *New Essays on* White Noise. Cambridge, U.K.: Cambridge Univ. Press, 1991.

Lilly, Paul R., Jr. *Words in Search of Victims: The Achievement of Jerzy Kosinski*. Kent, Ohio: Kent State Univ. Press, 1988.

Louv, Richard. *Childhood's Future*. Boston: Houghton Mifflin, 1990.

Malak, Amin. "Reading the Crisis: The Polemics of Salman Rushdie's *The Satanic Verses.*" *Ariel* 20, no. 4 (1989): 176–86.

Maltby, Paul. "The Romantic Metaphysics of Don DeLillo." *Contemporary Literature* 37, no. 2 (1996): 259–77.

Marcel, Gabriel. *Metaphysical Journal.* Trans. Bernard Wall. Chicago: Henry Regnery, 1952.

———. *The Mystery of Being.* Vol. 1. Trans. G. S. Fraser. Chicago: Henry Regnery, 1950.

Marcus, Leah S. *Childhood and Cultural Despair: A Theme and Variations in Seventeenth-Century Literature.* Pittsburgh, Pa.: Univ. of Pittsburgh Press, 1978.

Martin-Fugier, Anne. "Bourgeois Rituals." In Perrot, *From the Fires of Revolution,* 261–337.

May, Elaine Tyler. "Myths and Realities of the American Family." In Prost and Vincent, *Riddles of Identity in Modern Times,* 539–91.

Mellor, Anne K. *Mary Shelley: Her Life, Her Fiction, Her Monsters.* New York: Routledge, 1988.

Merivale, Patricia. "Saleem Fathered by Oskar: *Midnight's Children,* Magic Realism, and *The Tin Drum.*" In *Magical Realism: Theory, History, Community,* ed. Lois Parkinson Zamora and Wendy B. Faris, 329–45. Durham, N.C.: Duke Univ. Press, 1995.

Miller, Alice. *For Your Own Good: Hidden Cruelty in Child-Rearing and the Roots of Violence.* Trans. Hildegarde Hannum and Hunter Hannum. New York: Farrar Straus Giroux, 1990.

Moers, Ellen. "Female Gothic." In *The Endurance of* Frankenstein: *Essays on Mary Shelley's Novel,* ed. George Levine and U. C. Knoepflmacher, 77–87. Berkeley: Univ. of California Press, 1979.

Morrison, Blake. "Children of Circumstance." *New Yorker,* 14 Feb. 1994, 48–60.

Moses, Michael Valdez. "Lust Removed from Nature." In Lentricchia, *New Essays on* White Noise, 63–86.

Oates, Joyce Carol. "Killer Kids." *New York Review of Books,* 6 Nov. 1997, 16–20.

Otten, Terry. *The Crime of Innocence in the Fiction of Toni Morrison.* Columbia: Univ. of Missouri Press, 1989.

Parameswaran, Uma. "Handcuffed to History: Salman Rushdie's Art." *Ariel* 14, no. 4 (1983): 34–45.

Park, James Sloan. *Jerzy Kosinski: A Biography.* New York: Dutton, 1996.

Pattison, Robert. *The Child Figure in English Literature.* Athens: Univ. of Georgia Press, 1978.

Pearce, Joseph Chilton. *Magical Child: Rediscovering Nature's Plan for Children.* New York: Dutton, 1977.

Pérez-Torres, Rafael. "Knitting and Knotting the Narrative Thread—*Beloved* as Postmodern Novel." *Modern Fiction Studies* 39, nos. 3–4 (1993): 689–707.

Perrot, Michelle, ed. *From the Fires of Revolution to the Great War.* Trans. Arthur Goldhammer. Cambridge, Mass.: Belknap Press of Harvard Univ. Press, 1990. Vol. 4 of Ariès and Duby, *A History of Private Life.*

Phelan, James. "Toward a Rhetorical Reader-Response Criticism: The Difficult, the Stubborn, and the Ending of *Beloved.*" *Modern Fiction Studies* 39, nos. 3–4 (1993): 709–28.

Pifer, Ellen. "Her Monster, His Nymphet: Nabokov and Mary Shelley." In *Nabokov and His Fiction: New Perspectives,* ed. Julian W. Connolly, 158–76. Cambridge, U.K.: Cambridge Univ. Press, 1999.

———. "The Incomplete Metamorphosis of *Lolita:* From Novel to Screenplay and Film." In *La littérature Anglo-Américaine à l'écran,* ed. Daniel Royot and Gérard Hugues, 125–34. Paris: Didier, 1993.

———. "Innocence and Experience Replayed: From *Speak, Memory* to *Ada.*" *Cycnos* 10, no. 1 (1993): 19–25.

———. *Nabokov and the Novel.* Cambridge, Mass.: Harvard Univ. Press, 1980.

———. "Nabokov's Discovery of America: From Russia to *Lolita.*" In *The American Columbiad: "Discovering" America, Inventing the United States,* ed. Mario Materassi and Maria T. Ramalho de Sousa Santos, 407–14. Amsterdam, Netherlands: VU Univ. Press, 1996.

———. "Shades of Love: Nabokov's Intimations of Immortality." *Kenyon Review* 11, no. 2 (1989): 75–86.

Pollock, Linda A. *Forgotten Children: Parent-Child Relations from 1500–1900.* Cambridge, U.K.: Cambridge Univ. Press, 1983.

Postman, Neil. *The Disappearance of Childhood.* New York: Delacorte, 1982.

Prost, Antoine, and Gérard Vincent, eds. *Riddles of Identity in Modern Times.* Trans. Arthur Goldhammer. Cambridge, Mass.: Belknap Press of Harvard Univ. Press, 1991. Vol. 5 of Ariès and Duby, *A History of Private Life.*

Rampton, David. *Vladimir Nabokov: A Critical Study of the Novels.* Cambridge, U.K.: Cambridge Univ. Press, 1984.

Redpath, Philip. *William Golding: A Structural Reading of His Fiction.* London: Barnes and Noble, 1986.

Rigney, Barbara Hill. "'A Story to Pass On': Ghosts and the Significance of History in Toni Morrison's *Beloved.*" In *Haunting the House of Fiction: Feminist Perspectives on Ghost Stories by American Women,* ed. Lynette Carpenter and Wendy K. Kolmar, 229–35. Knoxville: Univ. of Tennessee Press, 1991.

Rodenberg, Hans-Peter, and Henryk Kellerman. "*The Fifth Child:* An Interview with Doris Lessing." *Doris Lessing Newsletter* 3, no. 1 (1989): 3–7.

Rodrigues, Eusebio L. "The Telling of *Beloved.*" *Journal of Narrative Technique* 21 (1991): 153–69.

Roth, Philip. "Afterword: A Talk with the Author." In Kundera, *The Book of Laughter and Forgetting,* 229–37.

Roth, Phyllis A., ed. *Critical Essays on Vladimir Nabokov.* Boston: G. K. Hall, 1984.

Rougemont, Denis de. *Love Declared: Essays on the Myths of Love.* Trans. Richard Howard. New York: Random House, 1963.

Shahar, Shulamith. *Childhood in the Middle Ages.* London: Routledge, 1990.

Shattuck, Roger. "Papa Gets the Blame." Review of Perrot, *From the Fires of Revolution to the Great War. New York Times Book Review,* 1 Apr. 1990, 24.

Shine, Muriel. *The Fictional Children of Henry James.* Chapel Hill: Univ. of North Carolina Press, 1968.

Singleton, Mary Ann. *The City and the Veld: The Fiction of Doris Lessing.* Lewisburg, Pa.: Bucknell Univ. Press, 1977.

Slay, Jack, Jr. *Ian McEwan.* New York: Twayne, 1996.

Smith, Amanda. "PW Interviews: Ian McEwan." *Publishers Weekly,* 11 Sept. 1987, 68–69.

Smith, Valerie. "'Circling the Subject': History and Narrative in *Beloved.*" In *Toni Morrison: Critical Perspectives Past and Present,* ed. Anthony K. Appiah and Henry Louis Gates Jr., 340–54. New York: Amistad, 1993.

Sokoloff, Naomi B. *Imagining the Child in Modern Jewish Fiction.* Baltimore, Md.: Johns Hopkins Univ. Press, 1992.

Spacks, Patricia Meyer. *The Adolescent Idea: Myths of Youth and the Adult Imagination.* New York: Basic Books, 1981.

Spilka, Mark. "On the Enrichment of Poor Monkeys by Myth and Dream; or, How Dickens Rousseauisticized and Pre-Freudianized Victorian Views of Childhood." In *Sexuality and Victorian Literature,* ed. Don Richard Cox, 161–79. Knoxville: Univ. of Tennessee Press, 1984.

———. "Turning the Freudian Screw: How Not to Do It." *Literature and Psychology* 13 (fall 1963): 105–11. Rpt. in Kimbrough, *Henry James, The Turn of the Screw,* 245–53.

Spillers, Hortense. "Mama's Baby, Papa's Maybe: An American Grammar Book." *Diacritics* 17 (1987): 65–81.

Sprague, Claire. *Rereading Doris Lessing: Narrative Patterns of Doubling and Repetition.* Chapel Hill: Univ. of North Carolina Press, 1987.

Srivastava, Aruna. "'The Empire Writes Back': Language and History in *Shame* and *Midnight's Children.*" *Ariel* 20, no. 4 (1989): 62–78.

Stevick, Philip. "*Frankenstein* and Comedy." In *The Endurance of Frankenstein: Essays on Mary Shelley's Novel,* ed. George Levine and U. C. Knoepflmacher, 221–42. Berkeley: Univ. of California Press, 1979.

Stone, Lawrence. *The Family, Sex, and Marriage in England, 1500–1800.* New York: Harper and Row, 1977.

———. "Massacre of the Innocents." *New York Review of Books,* 14 Nov. 1974, 25–31.

Suransky, Valerie Polakow. *The Erosion of Childhood.* Chicago: Univ. of Chicago Press, 1982.

Taylor-Guthrie, Danille, ed. *Conversations with Toni Morrison.* Jackson: Univ. Press of Mississippi, 1994.

Teicholz, Tom, ed. *Conversations with Jerzy Kosinski.* Jackson: Univ. Press of Mississippi, 1993.

Toker, Leona. *Nabokov: The Mystery of Literary Structures.* Ithaca, N.Y.: Cornell Univ. Press, 1989.

Trilling, Lionel. *The Liberal Imagination: Essays on Literature and Society.* New York: Viking, 1951.

———. *Sincerity and Authenticity.* Cambridge, Mass.: Harvard Univ. Press, 1972.

Vincent, Gérard. "A History of Secrets?" In Prost and Vincent, *Riddles of Identity in Modern Times,* 145–281.

Wachtel, Andrew. *The Battle for Childhood: Creation of a Russian Myth.* Stanford, Calif.: Stanford Univ. Press, 1990.

Watt, Ian. *The Rise of the Novel.* Berkeley: Univ. of California Press, 1965.

Weinstein, Arnold. *Nobody's Home: Speech, Self, and Place in American Fiction from Hawthorne to DeLillo.* New York: Oxford Univ. Press, 1993.

Weinstein, Philip M. *Henry James and the Requirements of the Imagination.* Cambridge, Mass.: Harvard Univ. Press, 1971.

———. *What Else but Love? The Ordeal of Race in Faulkner and Morrison.* New York: Columbia Univ. Press, 1996.

White, Hayden. "The Historical Text as Literary Artifact." In *Critical Theory since 1965,* ed. Hazard Adams and Leroy Searle, 395–407. Tallahassee: Univ. Press of Florida, 1986.

Williams, Raymond. *Culture and Society, 1780–1950.* 2d ed. New York: Columbia Univ. Press, 1983.

———. *Problems in Materialism and Culture: Selected Essays.* London: Verso Editions and NLB, 1980.

Wilson, Edmund. "The Ambiguity of Henry James." In *The Triple Thinkers.* Rev. ed. New York: Oxford Univ. Press, 1948.

Winn, Marie. *Children without Childhood.* New York: Pantheon, 1983.

Wood, Michael. *The Magician's Doubts: Nabokov and the Risks of Fiction.* London: Chatto and Windus, 1994.

Woolf, Virginia. "Henry James's Ghost Stories." In *Granite and Rainbow,* 65–72. London: Hogarth Press, 1958. Rpt. in Kimbrough, *Henry James,* The Turn of the Screw, 179–80.

Wyatt, Jean. "Giving Body to the Word: The Maternal Symbolic in Toni Morrison's *Beloved.*" *PMLA* 108, no. 3 (1993): 474–88.

Zelizer, Viviana A. *Pricing the Priceless Child: The Changing Social Value of Children.* New York: Basic Books, 1985.

Index